THE
VOICE
DIALOGUE
ANTHOLOGY

THE
VOICE
DIALOGUE
ANTHOLOGY

Explorations of the Psychology of
Selves and the Aware Ego Process

Edited by Dassie Hoffman, Ph D

THE VOICE DIALOGUE ANTHOLOGY
Explorations of the Psychology of
Selves and the Aware Ego Process
Edited by Dassie Hoffman, PhD
Copyright © 2012 by Hal Stone, PhD and Sidra Stone, PhD

PUBLISHED BY DELOS, INC.
www.delos-inc.com
delos@mcn.org
PO Box 604
Albion, CA 95410

The authors of this book do not dispense medical advice or prescribe the use of any technique as a form of treatment for physical or mental problems without the advice of a physician whether directly or indirectly. In the event that you use any of the information in this book, neither the authors nor the publisher can assume any responsibility for your actions. The intent of the authors is to offer information of a general nature to help in your quest for personal growth.

First Printing February 2012
ISBN: 978-1-56557-021-4
E-book ISBN: 978-1-56557-031-3
Printed in the United States of America

Photo on the front cover, "Morning Mists at Thera," by Sidra Stone.
Photo on the back cover by Larry Wagner.
Photo on page 347 by Douglas Hoffman.

Contents

THE
VOICE
DIALOGUE
ANTHOLOGY

INTRODUCTION

This anthology reveals the extraordinary range of innovative techniques for self-exploration based upon the pioneering work of Hal and Sidra Stone. Their exciting new paradigm has produced original ideas about how we develop and function as human beings.

Editing this collection has been a revelation to me. I have been a member of the Voice Dialogue community since the 1980s, and have watched it grow. Yet I have been continually amazed and delighted at the scope and diversity of the articles that were submitted to me, and appear here. In addition, we can observe an excellent example of the creative process. The material herein demonstrates how, given a solid theoretical framework, creativity can be triggered, supporting explorations in many directions and through various modalities.

This anthology introduces the literature of Voice Dialogue and the Psychology of the Aware Ego. The material comes from a variety of sources, spanning the globe. The authors are from Australia, France, Great Britain, and many parts of the United States, including California, Colorado, Maryland, New York, Oregon, Pennsylvania, Tennessee, Texas, and Washington.

Part I begins with the Stones' presentation of the basic elements of Voice Dialogue, Relationship, and the Psychology of the Selves. This article provides the definitive introduction to the history and basic ideas of Voice Dialogue. Whether or not you have previously read this material on their website, it is worth revisiting for new insights that come from each rereading.

Section II demonstrates how Voice Dialogue has been integrated into a variety of modalities. These include Body Work, Dream Work, Sand Play work, and performer training.

Section III offers articles of unusual diversity, ranging from the political to the profoundly personal. This section also contains the work of two psychotherapists who developed new techniques, using Voice Dialogue, to work with their eating-disordered clients.

Part II begins with a discussion of how Voice Dialogue and the Psychology of the Aware Ego differ from other theoretical systems. It continues by expanding upon the Stones' ideas. Seven teacher/practitioners demonstrate how they have integrated Voice Dialogue into their professional work, in such diverse areas as Chinese medicine, Jungian theory and Personality Types, transpersonal psychology, Imago therapy, and homeopathy.

The richness and diversity of the material here is vast, and is a credit to each of the authors. This collection is a splendid addition to the literature of Voice Dialogue and the Psychology of the Aware Ego.

As editor, I offer my personal thanks to all of the contributing authors. You have been delightful to work with, and our collaboration has been a source of joy to me. Thank you one and all.

Dassie Hoffman, PhD

PART I

Section I

What Is Voice Dialogue?

The Basic Elements of Voice Dialogue, Relationship, and the Psychology of Selves — Their Origins and Development

Hal Stone, PhD, and Sidra Stone, PhD

The story changes depending upon who tells it, and, as the journey goes on, we view our lives from different vantage points and through different eyes as we integrate more and more selves. What seemed important at one time seems less important later. What seemed less important can assume greater importance.

At this point in our lives — our seventieth and eightieth years — we have decided that it is time to look back and to tell the story of the origins and development of Voice Dialogue and the Psychology of Selves the way we see it. We wish to honor those whom we know have directly contributed to our work, to clarify some common misconceptions, and to tell — to the best of our ability — the stories of those moments when some new element was added or our thinking changed.

Let us begin with our view of the creative process. We find that outer and inner influences blend indistinguishably. We have lived rich, complex — and jointly examined — lives. From the outer world, there have been teachers and information from many disparate sources. We have had many powerful experiences with others, both professional and personal. From the world within, we have had our individual dreams, transpersonal experiences, and moments of sudden clarity that seem to be gifts from sources outside of our personal experience. All these are digested by each of us, providing us the raw material from which we create. When an idea or a concept emerges, we are never quite sure of where it comes from.

In the past, people's first reactions to Voice Dialogue were usually: "That's a Gestalt technique" or "It's psychosynthesis." Interestingly enough, Hal's actual work in Gestalt started only after Voice Dialogue was definitively established in our lives, and although Sidra had some contact with very early Gestalt work, her experience of it was extremely limited. As for psychosynthesis, we were both fascinated with its use of imagery, but neither of us had delved deeply enough into it to know about its concepts of the different selves. Nor were we particularly influenced by psychodrama or TA, having only a passing acquaintance with both through the popular press.

We have always honored these various approaches as having some relationship to Voice Dialogue since they were clearly a part of the general psychological culture in the early 1970s. At the same time, we recognized that our own creative process was based upon a very differ-ent, and unique, set of experiences. The roots of our work go far deeper than our exposure to these newer schools of thought. We came from two contrasting — one might even say conflicting — backgrounds.

The Earliest Influences – Hal's Experiences

I was trained as a Jungian analyst, eventually becoming the president of the Society for Analytical Psychology in Los Angeles in 1968. I studied at the Jung Institute for several months in 1957 and actually had the opportunity to meet with Jung himself for an individual session. These experiences went deep into my being and have, to some extent, informed my work throughout my life.

My experiences with the Jungian community and my early training gave me the gifts of a deep understanding of dreams, myths, fairytales, and depth psychology. On the other hand I knew that something was

Hal and Sidra in the early years:
treasure hunting in the Bahamas, 1978.

missing. I didn't feel like a grownup. I go into these matters in greater detail in the five-CD series I made in 2005. The outcome of all this was that I left the Jungian community — and the traditional practice of analytical psychology — in 1970. This was two years before Sidra and I met. My experience of all of this was the end of my personal and professional life as I had known it, and the beginning of a new life that was as yet totally undefined and unknown to me.

Though I found it necessary to separate from the professional organization in 1970, I realize now that I would have had to separate from anything that I was a part of. I needed to float free and not be tied to any kind of outer professional form. Only in this way could I begin to move into an entirely new kind of creative process that has led me to where I am today. I shall be eternally grateful for the remarkable opportunity I had to discover Jungian Psychology, to the colleagues I had, to the clients I worked with, and to the innovative spirit of Jung himself. From my very first analytic session my unconscious opened and with it the life of spirit and a most remarkable dream process that has always helped me maintain some kind of objective clarity. From that first session I had come home to the symbolic life of spirit, and I was able to separate from the arid desert of my rational mind.

My first encounter with Voice Dialogue, or the idea of talking to selves, came sometime in the late 1960s. The story I am about to tell you is not about Voice Dialogue directly; it concerns a clinical experience that led me to a different place professionally and that is intertwined in my mind with the early origins of the work.

In the late '60s a couple came to see me in regard to their son whom we will call Jimmie. The couple lived in Southern California and their son had spent the past year at a special residential treatment center on the East Coast for acting-out or disturbed children. In particular, Jimmie was acting out in school, and it was felt that he couldn't function in a regular academic setting.

Jimmie was eleven years of age when his parents first came to me. They were very upset, having just received a letter from the school informing them that they had done a complete psychological evaluation on the boy because of his disturbed behavior, that he was being diagnosed as schizophrenic, and that they were strongly recommending he be placed in a special setting run by a psychoanalytic group in the area. Since they felt that he was schizophrenic, they felt that he needed a special facility for this level of mental impairment.

The parents had moved out West the year before and were looking forward to his joining them in their new home. They were very disturbed by this letter, and their question was whether I could help them. I told them I would be willing to see Jimmie and do an independent evaluation if they brought him to L.A. I would need all of the medical records that were available before seeing him. I couldn't promise them more than that.

Two to three weeks later Jimmie walked into my office. He was a very curious child, interested in everything he saw. On my desk I had a pile of psychological and psychiatric reports four or five inches high containing notes, test materials, and psychiatric evaluations. All of them concurred in the diagnosis of schizophrenia. They described how what had begun as acting-out behavior had, over the past year, developed into an increasingly disturbed state. As I sat with Jimmie I was experiencing a huge conflict because my experience of him was very different. It was very positive. I liked him very much and I thought he had a wonderful spirit. On the other hand, I had these reports from a fine school and highly qualified healthcare practitioners all making the same diagnosis of schizophrenia.

Jimmie was easy to talk to, and he told me about his school and its philosophy. Basically, their management style was to never let children be alone but to always keep them busy doing things. It was felt that being alone allowed them to collapse into their own imagination and fantasy and that this would be damaging to them. It was becoming clear to me that Jimmie was a very imaginative youngster and that the school routine might not have been the best kind of experience for him.

In the course of our discussion I asked Jimmie if he ever remembered any dreams. He told me that he had one just last evening. This was the dream:

> I am sitting in a wheelchair in the lobby of my school. My parents are visiting me before they go back to California. I am crying and begging them not to go. They feel they have no choice, however, and they get up to leave, and I wake up sobbing that they are leaving me here.

The dream was totally stunning to me. He was in a wheelchair. Why was he there? Did this mean that he was indeed crippled in the way the reports on him indicated was the case? Why else would he be in the wheelchair? Yet my every instinct felt a core of health in Jimmie that was incompatible with the diagnosis.

I asked him to close his eyes and go back into the dream and be in the wheelchair. He did this easily, just as I expected, and after half a minute or so I asked him why he was in the wheelchair. What was wrong with him? Could he tell me anything about how he felt sitting there?

Jimmie then said a remarkable thing to me: "What I feel is that there is a magnet in the back of the wheelchair and that this magnet is holding me in the chair." I said before that I was stunned when I heard his dream. Hearing his response to my questions, I was stunned to the tenth power. Suddenly it was all so simple. Everything made sense. The excitement I had been feeling began to lessen, and I really felt very happy with things.

I realized then that Jimmie was a highly creative, highly gifted, highly imaginative child who had been misplaced in this school. I'm sure the theory worked for many of their children, but for a youngster like this one it was totally counterproductive. He was a magical child to whom the world of imagination was essential. It had literally driven him into schizophrenic behavior because he had nowhere else to go. It was an artificially induced state, and I felt it could be changed.

I then said to Jimmie that if he was being held in the chair by this magnet, it seemed to me that he could do something to break the power of the magnet. We did this together. First he broke the power in his imagination and then he actually got up from his chair in my office (as though it were the wheelchair) and walked around the room. All of this was done using simple methods of active imagination. After five or ten minutes we then went into my art studio where he began to work with sand play and painting. I saw him for twelve sessions. He was now ready to stop our work together, and he began public school near his home in Southern California. I saw him for two sessions when he was in high school; he just wanted to talk over some of the issues he was dealing with in school. Through other sources I can tell you that Jimmie ultimately went into the film business where he has led a successful professional life.

A month later I received a call from Dr. Hedda Bolgar from Mt. Sinai hospital in Los Angeles. Hedda was a lovely woman, a gifted therapist and analyst; she was the director of psychology at Mt. Sinai hospital. Hedda was also affiliated with the psychoanalytic group that was in charge of the school that Jimmie attended. Apparently they were very upset because Jimmie was now in public school and they couldn't imagine how this could happen. They contacted Hedda and asked her to talk with me and find out what had happened. I told her that it was a long story, that maybe it was best for us to meet in person over lunch and I would share with her what had happened.

Hedda has always been a remarkable woman, always open to new ideas and new possibilities. When we met and I gave her the whole background on what had happened with Jimmie, she really understood it at a very deep level. Shortly after our meeting, she called and invited me to become a consultant to the department of psychology at Mt. Sinai and then to become a consultant to the department of psychiatry, also at Mt. Sinai. This was the beginning of a wonderful few years working with Hedda and other staff members and students in training in this dual capacity.

About a year after I started my consulting work, Hedda told me about a clinical demonstration she had witnessed, facilitated by a professor at U.C. Santa Barbara. She had watched him working with a client using a number of chairs for the different selves of the subject. I was fascinated by her description of what had taken place in this session. I contacted the professor to ask him about the demonstration, and he told me at that time that he had no real interest in this work and wouldn't mind at all if anyone wished to explore it more deeply. Whatever he was doing had no name, though it certainly seemed like the way a Gestalt therapist would work, even though the professor had no connection to Gestalt work.

I then began to play with the idea at home, using my daughter, Judith, and my son, Joshua (now deceased), and my then wife, Thea, as subjects. We facilitated each other, and it was fun and sometimes seemed important, but it never went any further, and within a year or so it seemed to have died a natural death. The resurrection did not happen for another two years, when Sidra and I first met.

The Earliest Influences – Sidra's Experiences

My earliest psychological influences date back to the early 1950s at Barnard College. At that time I was a committed behaviorist and basically a "Skinner groupie." My friends and I were fascinated by the early operant conditioning work as an explanation of human behavior, and we would go to hear Skinner whenever he came to New York to speak. Our favorite psychology instructor arranged for a special seminar for four of us who showed particular interest in this work. There we investigated the possible interface of the (Freudian) psychoanalytical thinking of the time and operant conditioning.

I was intrigued by the idea that a psychologist could break down complex behavior into its component parts and see how everything worked in an ultimately sensible and predictable fashion. This was only one area of fascination with how things worked. Along these same lines, I had seriously considered becoming a physicist.

I still see this early Skinnerian influence in the way I look at the development of primary selves — at how they emerged, at least in part, as a result of operant conditioning. I was always looking for ways in which they were adaptive and how, as selves, they did their best to protect us and to earn us love. So, as an old-time Skinnerian, I deeply honor a primary self.

The other major influences that I brought with me from earlier times were the writers Hermann Hesse and Nikos Kazantzakis. As a woman of the 1950s, I was uncomfortable with the psychological and psychiatric establishments as they related to women. At the time, I didn't know what it was that didn't feel right, but I felt it was important — and somehow safer — to keep my teachers more impersonal and at a distance.

Hesse and Kazantzakis were men whose lives were deeply committed to the evolution of consciousness and whose writings contained — for me — a glimpse of universal truths. All of their books explored the struggle between opposing forces within each of us, what Hal and I now call "the tension of opposites." Each had his own passionate polarities: Hesse worked primarily between the mind (the intellectual) and the feelings (the romantic) while Kazantzakis' interest was the tension between the earthy and the spiritual.

Both men were influenced by Henri Bergson and based their worldviews on the existence of an *élan vital*, a creative or evolutionary impulse within us, a powerful force that moves us toward continual evolution and greater consciousness. That concept felt like a deep truth and became a part of my life view. I recognize echoes of this in what we now call "the inner intelligence" or "the intelligence of the universe."

Hesse's *Steppenwolf* was the most impactful book I had ever read. It was my introduction to the many selves and to the "Magic Theater" in which I began to view my own tumultuous inner cast of characters. Once I peeked into my own Magic Theater through the doors opened by this book, my view of life and of people was unalterably changed. I could no longer look at any of us as single entities. From that moment on, I was fascinated by the many selves that I could see in myself and in those around me. I loved it! The following quote sums it all up:

> Harry consists of a hundred or a thousand selves, not of two. His life oscillates, as everyone's does, not merely between two poles, such as the body and the spirit, the saint and the sinner, but between thousands and thousands. Every ego, so far from being a unity is in the highest degree a manifold world, a constellated heaven, a chaos of forms, of states and stages, of inheritances and potentialities. As a body everyone is single, as a soul, never.
>
> — From *Steppenwolf* by Hermann Hesse

Interestingly, Hesse was deeply influenced by Jung, and this, I feel, provided much of the crossover between Hal's Jungian background and my own thinking. Kazantzakis, on the other hand, was a Cretan by birth and Greek to the core. His thoughts, much like those of the Jungians, were never far from the ancient gods and goddesses. He knew the importance of honoring all of them — and I always felt that as an underpinning in his writings. His greatest book, *The Odyssey, A Modern Sequel*, was like a Bible to me in my own intellectual and spiritual wanderings.

My own journey was an outer one in these early years. I traveled extensively in Europe, the Middle East, the Americas, and North Africa, and was particularly interested in ancient cultures. I visited the sacred sites in Greece and honored the gods and goddesses by visiting their shrines. Hal visited Jung; I paid my respects at the grave of my teacher, Nikos Kazantzakis, in Crete.

And so it was that from these disparate backgrounds — these opposites as carried by each of us — that something new came to be born. Now let us look at the basic elements of our work and see how each evolved.

The First Element – Voice Dialogue as a Methodology

The Beginning of the Joint Adventure

Early in 1972, Sidra read an article by Assagioli on Guided Imagery. Fascinated, she decided to try it out in her practice of psychotherapy. It was amazingly successful and totally different from anything she'd ever done before. A new kind of depth and universality — the kind she had previously experienced only in her contacts with great works of art or of literature — was now available to both herself and her client. People had such wonderful experiences that she wanted to learn more about this and — most important — wanted to go on one of those "trips" herself. She asked a friend, Dr. Jean Holroyd, head of the psychology intern program at UCLA, where she might learn more about this technique.

Hal had been teaching this work, which was central to his training in Jungian Psychology. He had recently given a very powerful demonstration of the work at UCLA that Jean had attended. She recommended that Sidra contact Hal and see him for a few training sessions. So it was that in February 1972 Sidra came to see Hal, making it very clear that she was not interested in personal therapy, not interested in anything that might change her life, but just wanted a few training sessions so she could become more effective in facilitating this process.

In the first few sessions Sidra went very deeply into the realm of the creative imagination. Her initial experience was of initiation into the ancient goddess mysteries. It was in these depths, one might say, that the two of us met. It became clear almost immediately that the exploration that was happening was a joint exploration — not a mentor/student relationship — and that Hal could only continue on this basis. In the depths of this kind of work there could be only equality between us. We began to share our dream process in addition to the visualizations, and in the course of one of these sessions we started talking about how vulnerable we were both feeling and how unfamiliar this was for both of us.

During this discussion Hal suggested that Sidra move over and *become* the vulnerability instead of just talking about it. It was the moment of the resurrection of the technique of talking to the selves. The term Voice

Dialogue did not yet exist. That came later. In this moment, the game that Hal had played with before became something quite different and the birthing process of the Voice Dialogue method began. This is how Sidra remembers that very first experience:

> Hal asked me to move over and to become the vulnerability. I knew it was the right thing to do. I trusted him. I trusted him so deeply that I moved from the couch where I'd been sitting, sat down on the floor, and put my head down on the coffee table. In total silence, I allowed myself to move into my vulnerability; I literally became someone else. I became a very small child who experienced the world in a new way. There was total stillness. I had the sense that the "I" that was sitting there had been hiding in a deep cave for my entire life and that this was the first time she felt safe enough to come out. The world around me changed, my perceptions became more acute, colors and sounds were different, and I could feel Hal's energy holding a space for me (although it would be years before we were to know more about the energetics of relationship). This was totally foreign to me; I was accustomed to experiencing the world in a rational, sensible, and controlled way. I felt that I had finally entered Herman Hesse's Magic Theater!

Hal was himself stunned by this experience. He could feel that he was in the presence of a child and knew that it was best to say nothing. He was with a preverbal child — the child was real, and the selves were real. When Sidra left her place on the floor and returned to her seat on the sofa — returning to what we later called the Aware Ego — they both sat in silence, realizing that something momentous had happened.

Hal had to wait a week before Sidra facilitated his child. His own experience was most profound. It was the beginning of Little Harry, a totally unknown quantity in his life until then, and so instead of Sidra and Hal exploring together, there were now four of us at work. There were Sidra and Lisa and there were Hal and Little Harry. Everyone's stories and ideas were different.

So the work began with what we named the Inner Child. As far as we know, we were the first to use that term. It began out of a relationship in which a deep love was evolving. It had no context as far as therapy was concerned. These children of ours were real, and the continuing work we did with them gave us a way of widening and deepening our co-exploration. We were not just stunned by what was happening; we were extremely excited. If these inner children were real, who else was there? After all, there were many doors to open in the long hallway of the Magic Theater. We were off and running, meeting the myriad selves that began to emerge into consciousness.

In the next few years we did a great deal of this kind of exploration. At this early stage there was basically no theory, no Aware Ego. We were simply two explorers who were very much in love and had no idea where our lives were heading. We knew only that what was happening was rich, creative, and original, and that it deepened our connection to each other at each step along the way. We still used the visualization process and shared dreams, but in this stage the excitement of the dialogue process quite possessed us. The theory was to come later.

Our work with relationship began with a very powerful experience quite early in these explorations. One of Sidra's visualizations was that of an ancient Minoan ship sailing on mythic seas. We were both on that ship. Emblazoned upon its sail, watching over us and protecting our journey, was a golden eye — the eye of God. As part of that visualization, we were told that we were on a journey that would not end. This meant that there was to be no real security or predictability for us. We were not permitted to set up a permanent home; we were not even permitted to spend more than one night at a time on land. It was truly the beginning of our journey of relationship — a journey in which the relationship became our teacher.

This is not the place to discuss our work in detail but only the story of how it evolved and what — to our minds — are the most important elements involved. To learn more about the work itself, we suggest the classic book *Embracing Our Selves*; or, if you prefer to listen to CDs, *An Introduction to Voice Dialogue, Relationship, and the Psychology of Selves*; and finally, if you prefer to see us as well as hear us, the documentary *The Voice Dialogue Series*.

Collaboration in the Early Years, 1983.

The Second Element – The Psychology of Selves

The Beginnings of Theory

It is difficult to remember how and when our theoretical considerations began to intermix with our deeply personal work. We were both psychologists (practicing psychotherapists). Things were happening, changes were taking place with remarkable speed, and, quite naturally, we began to organize our thinking about the events that were occurring.

The first realization to come to us was that these selves inside of us behaved like real people and that they had to be treated with the greatest respect. If they sensed that they were being judged or manipulated in any way, they withdrew. It also became clear very early that for a self to remain with the facilitator, the facilitator had to remain totally present — the self required a strong energetic connection to hold it. This was long before our more sophisticated development of the energetics of Voice Dialogue. It was, however, a beginning.

Primary and Disowned Selves

Quite early in our explorations we began to see that we are made up of primary selves — a group of selves that define our personality. (We had some question as to whether we should call them primary or dominant selves and we settled on primary.) It seemed to us like a very simple idea. Why hadn't we ever been able to see this before? Who we think we are is really a group of selves that we have identified with, and these selves become the persona, or how we present ourselves to the world.

The next step seemed quite natural and obvious as we continued our work with each other. Whenever we identify with a primary self, then on the other side, equal and opposite, is its opposite. We called this "the disowned self," a term first coined by Nathaniel Branden. When he talked of the disowned self, he was referring to it, however, as the emotions that are disowned by people who identify with the mind and have a basically rational approach to life. We spoke with Nathaniel about all of this and he was comfortable with our using the term. We are grateful to him for his largesse because the terms "disowned" and "primary" selves fit together so perfectly.

Within the first few years, these ideas were getting pretty well set. In the earliest years, we used the idea of a Protector-Controller as the main primary self, the self that set up the basic rules and was the guardian of the gates of entry to our inner world. We saw the Protector/Controller as a self that gathered and organized information about the world around us so that we could understand it, a self that protected us and controlled both our behavior and our environment.

It took time before we realized that this was a generic term and that every primary self was a protector and a controller in its own way, that each had its own way of figuring out the world around us, and that each lived by its own set of rules. The Protector-Controller is still used by many teachers and is still a very good self to use at the beginning of Voice Dialogue. It provides us a picture of what clinicians often refer to as *the basic defense structure of the personality.*

We, however, don't think in terms of defenses; instead we think of the primary selves in terms of their adaptability and creativity — we honor their attempts to contribute to a person's well-being. We saw them as selves that were central to survival, accomplishment, and the ability (however limited) to relate to others, and therefore always to be regarded with the greatest respect.

Working with Opposites

After the first excitement of exploring individual selves, and after the ideas of primary and disowned selves began to emerge in our work together, we began to work more and more with opposites. This happened gradually because in the earliest phase we enjoyed concentrating on a single self. We spent a great deal of time working with the Inner Child, the Inner Critic, the Responsible Parent, the Observing Mind, and the Protector/Controller. And we had a great time talking with the disowned selves. Those selves were a lot more adventurous and rambunctious — often quite intense — and usually irreverent.

We began to see, however, that the real gift of the work was not simply talking to selves. Instead, we began to get the sense that the real point of the work was working directly with opposites. It seemed important to learn how to separate from the primary selves, to talk with the disowned selves, and then learn to stand between the opposites (of the primary and disowned selves), clearly feeling both at the same time. It was the opposites that were important.

It took time for this shift in emphasis to occur because talking to many voices, especially to the disowned selves, was so much fun. As time passed, we increasingly put our emphasis on working between the opposites. But something was missing — we needed to address the issue of a model of consciousness that could encompass all of this.

The Third Element – The Consciousness Model

A New Definition of Consciousness

The old forms didn't quite work for us. We knew that we needed something new but weren't quite sure what it was. We remember driving across a great flat valley wondering aloud about just what it could be that would be beyond the selves and take charge of life, and what we could do to bring in the spiritual dimension. We tried and tried, but nothing gave us what we were seeking.

Finally, we looked at the term "Ego." The Ego has always been seen as the directing agent of the personality, and it is an excellent term, one with a long history. It is often described as the executive function of the psyche. It is the "I" that we refer to when we talk about ourselves.

We began to realize that this all-powerful Ego is, in fact, a group of primary selves that together run our lives and rule the personality without anyone knowing it. It can be the Rational Mind, the Pusher, the Pleaser, the Responsible Parent, the Independent One, the Rebel — it is whatever we think we are — it is whichever selves are running our lives. We decided to call this group of selves — the traditional Ego — the *Operating Ego*.

Then we had to develop a new name to describe what happened in Voice Dialogue when we separated from a primary self and returned to center. That center space was no longer occupied by the Operating, or traditional, Ego. The new term we used was the "Aware Ego." We found that this Aware Ego Process evolves and gets stronger and stronger with continuing work. What became increasingly clear to us was that the Operating Ego is here forever, but it gradually surrenders power to the Aware Ego Process as we separate from more and more primaries and integrate more and more disowned selves.

Now a new way at looking at consciousness began to emerge.

We saw three levels to the process of consciousness. First there was the level of Awareness. This has been around for a very long time. It is often referred to as the *witness state* in meditation. It gives us the ability to step back and see the big picture. It does not act. It is not attached to outcome.

We began to see the second level of consciousness as the actual experience of the selves, the experience of life itself. Awareness does not experience. It witnesses. Awareness without experience isolates us from life. Experience without awareness keeps us locked into the animal kingdom. Both are essential to an ongoing consciousness process.

Then there was the new kid on the block. Someone has to live our lives; someone has to drive our (psychological) car. Someone has to use the gift of awareness and the treasure of experience and, for us, that someone or something was the Aware Ego, or more accurately, the Aware Ego Process. We realized that this was an ongoing dynamic process that was always changing, that there was no such thing as *an* Aware Ego.

As a matter of fact, over the years we have come to see that consciousness itself is a process — with each of the three levels of consciousness representing a distinct, individually evolving process.

Honoring the Primary Selves

We were learning a great deal about primary selves in those early years, and the learning has never stopped. One thing that we understood from the beginning has stood us in good stead all through the years: One must always honor the primary self. In the practice of Voice Dialogue this is one of strongest recommendations we can make. The primary self is the ally of the facilitator. Both have the interests and well-being of the client at heart, and there must be a mutual respect and deep understanding between the primary selves and the facilitator.

What we learned early in the practice of Voice Dialogue has yet deeper and more far-reaching implications for living life. We are always dealing with people, and essentially we are always dealing with their primary selves. Knowing this can save us much unhappiness.

Many years ago, very early in our work together, we were at a social gathering and a rather traditional psychologist asked us about our work. Not yet truly appreciating how important it was to honor the primary selves in the "real world," we opened up to him and shared our ideas and work. He became very judgmental as he aggressively questioned us about the empirical basis for our work and wanted to know exactly what kinds of experiments we had designed and carried out. He accused us of making up these selves and made some vague threats about malpractice. All in all, it was a most unpleasant experience.

We are fast learners and we learned from this experience to feel into people more carefully and to explore the nature of their primary selves before sharing our ideas and feelings. We have tried our best not to share our work with people who are not ready to listen. As we've often said, "We go only where the door is already open." After this experience, we were much more cautious. We began to screen invitations to speak, and before we spoke with a new group we did our best to determine the nature of the primary self system that dominated that particular group, clinic, or center. This kind of sensitivity was particularly important when we were working in other cultures. It's important to know the rules and to use language and concepts that do not polarize the primary selves. This attention to the primary selves in our surroundings has saved us untold discomfort — both professionally and personally.

The Fourth Element – The Theory of Bonding Patterns

The Selves and Relationship

We are giving a very short version of our theoretical structure. This material is available in detailed form in our books, CDs, and DVD documentary. In this article we are attempting to give you a more sweeping view of where we have come from. Someone who worked with us in the late 1970s or '80s cannot help but have a very limited idea of what we are doing today. We do not enjoy stagnation and neither does our unconscious. When some new idea emerged or methodology changed, we let it change. Sometimes we weren't even aware of a change, it evolved so naturally. It is confusing to many people to watch this happen. For us, it is very exciting to see the work evolve and to bring everyone along as a part of this process.

We met in 1972 and were married in 1977. This article is not about our personal lives. We raised five children between us, and the personal work we were doing with each other helped us enormously in understanding our parental role. These were also the years when Sidra was the executive director of Hamburger Home, a residential treatment center for adolescent girls, and Hal was the director of the Center for the Healing Arts. Our professional lives were completely separate, but our work together and the evolution of our thinking were central aspects of our lives.

Those five years of work clarified our relationship and made marriage possible. We were using Voice Dialogue in our respective practices, and Hal had started to do some teaching of the process at the Center. It was becoming increasingly clear to us that in relationships selves were constantly interacting with the selves of the other person.

With our marriage, however, some of the interactions between us were turning quite sour. Old patterns suddenly emerged, but with the new partner — a partner who was totally different from the previous one. We called one another by the names of our former spouses. We found ourselves judging each other — often for the same qualities that had attracted us to one another in the first place. We literally became other people: judgmental, closed, and humorless. Underneath it all there was a vague feeling of betrayal, helplessness, and desperation.

What was happening? Was marriage necessarily the end of love? There had to be a way of understanding these painfully divisive interactions, of bringing them under some kind of control. We wanted our relationship back. We knew that the selves we had worked with over the previous years had something to do with this. It was obvious to us that a set of selves had taken charge of our relationship. There was no more "us," no more connection, and the vulnerable children who were a part of our relationship from the very beginning were nowhere to be found.

This was the start of a remarkable three months of a new kind of exploration. We looked at the selves that had taken over our relationship and tried to figure out what was really going on. We wrote down and diagrammed every negative interaction we had. We did this over and over and over again until a pattern began to emerge. We began to see how these negative interactions followed a basically simple pattern that repeated itself.

Hal would get angry with Sidra and suddenly he was no longer Hal, he was a cold, judgmental father talking to her. She became a victim/defensive daughter and argued back. Then, in the blink of an eye, she became a judgmental mother — withdrawn, critical, and cold — and although Hal became a hurt and vulnerable son to this cruel mother, still his judgmental father attacked. There were always four selves (or sets of selves) involved. We replayed this scenario over and over again, but now we were beginning to see the pattern. We looked for all the selves involved in these interactions. Some were more apparent than others, but they were always all there.

We named this pattern a *bonding pattern* in recognition that it was basically a set of parent/child interactions. We also felt that this was a way to honor it as a normal way of relating as contrasted with a pathological one. In those years, we looked at these patterns as basically an interaction between power selves and disempowered selves. As time went on, our views of this have clarified; the parent/child nature of the interaction has become ever more apparent, and we have come to see this bonding pattern as the basic default pattern in all relationships.

We discovered other constants in these interactions. All bonding patterns grew out of the negation or disowning of vulnerability. This took many forms, but it was always present. When our interactions became negative we could always trace back to a time when we lost contact with our core vulnerability (or what we called our Inner Child). Something had happened to hurt it, to frighten it off, and we had ignored this; instead we had reacted in a more seemingly adult fashion. We had basically disowned our vulnerable child. If we could hold on to the child (or to our vulnerability) and took care of this directly, these negative patterns lost their power; they didn't need to play themselves out.

The other constant we discovered was a truism that we had recognized from our early dealings with selves: Whatever you judge is a disowned self of your own. In these negative interactions, or bonding patterns, our judgments would flare up and assume center stage. We looked carefully at this. Gradually it became clear to us that as we reacted to each other negatively we were, in fact, being given pictures of our own disowned selves. If we recognized this, we could use it as a teaching in our own relationship — and we could help others see this in theirs.

This was almost painful to realize. We had hoped we were beyond this. Besides, our judgments were so much fun. It was such a wonderful feeling to pin the other up against the wall with brilliant and self-righteous criticisms. It was so wonderful to be unquestionably right.

If, however, our judgments are reflections of our disowned selves, then where's the fun? How can you feel righteous in the middle of a "righteous dance" in full knowledge of the fact that you are basically attacking your own disowned self or selves?

We had some wild and (in retrospect) funny interchanges as we closed in on the bonding-pattern theory. One evening we were still arguing over a particular bonding pattern at 11:00 p.m. and Sidra finally said that she was exhausted and going to bed. Hal continued to work on the pattern, simmering in the heat of his judgments and furious at Sidra's comment that he wasn't in his Aware Ego. After about ten minutes Hal stormed into the bedroom and with great grace and dignity yelled at her, "I am too in an Aware Ego." We both laughed, and that was the end of that one. Such is the snake-like path of the co-exploration of consciousness.

Our excitement at this time was enormous. What was emerging was something quite new. It was something that worked for us in everyday life. It was a simple, precise, and elegant way of looking at relationships, and had a sense of a mathematical certainty and balance. Later we came to think of it as a kind of technology of relationship.

Our excitement about all this was magnified as we realized that the theory of bonding patterns gave us a very creative (and non-pathologizing) way to look at the transference. The same principles were operating. The only difference is that we refer to it as transference if we get paid, and as bonding patterns if we don't. We've come to call this *The Psychology of the Transference*.

There was immediate gratification from our discovery of bonding patterns. We felt better. Feelings of love and intimacy returned. Of course, we had to accustom ourselves to the loss of self-righteousness (that deliciously seductive feeling) but we were a lot happier with each other.

There's something wonderfully freeing about escaping from a negative bonding pattern. And it totally changed the nature of working with couples, making it a joy rather than a nightmare. Teaching people about the bonding patterns and then working with the selves created a wonderful path to change and we used it ourselves with increasing effectiveness.

It was much later that we began to attend to the positive bonding patterns and to realize how often these set the stage for the appearance of negative ones.

Teaching in Holland, 1987.

The Fifth Element – The Psychology of the Aware Ego

With the theory of bonding patterns in place and the redefining of consciousness providing us with a model that seemed effective over time, we began to think about actually changing the title of our work to the Psychology of the Aware Ego. We realized more and more that the core work was not about talking to selves. This was important, but not as much as the development of an Aware Ego Process, which was really the key to the kinds of changes we were looking for.

We saw that people could work forever with selves, but until there was a true separation and disidentification from the primary self, changes were easily lost. We saw that, without an Aware Ego Process, the primary self would automatically regain control. This Aware Ego Process evolves between any pair of opposites. Some common opposite sets of selves are power and vulnerability, pusher and beach bum, thinking and feeling, control and release.

There are many sets of opposites, and the Aware Ego Process emerges from one set at a time. Clarity in one area does not mean clarity in all. For instance, we find that someone develops an Aware Ego process capable of holding the tension of opposites between the mental and the feeling selves, but at the same time has no Aware Ego Process when it comes to spirituality. This same individual, who does such a good job of embracing both feelings and thinking, still might be totally identified with spirituality and reject selves that are ordinary or instinctual.

For a spiritually identified person to develop an Aware Ego Process in relationship to spirituality, he or she would have to do work that separates him/her from the spiritual self so that there is an Aware Ego Process that can see it and experience it but not be identified with it. This separation can be very difficult, but we have discovered a truly fascinating self we call the *spiritual pusher* that runs the life of many a spiritual seeker. After the separation from this spiritual self (or the spiritual seeker) there would be the challenge to discover and integrate the spiritual sloth, the "ordinary" self, and the instinctual.

Conversely, someone who rejects spirituality from a primary self that is rational and mental must learn to unhook from the rational mind so that the Aware Ego can begin to see the rational mind as a separate self/ energy system. This makes a space for the spiritual selves to emerge and be properly embraced. At this point, we have an Aware Ego standing between the more earthbound rules and experiences of the mind and the numinous realms and experiences of the world of the spirit.

At times it has felt to us as though we were running a divorce court.

In this framework we help people learn how to get a divorce from their primary selves. Once a person is divorced from a primary self, the Aware Ego can learn how to use the energy of that primary self in a conscious way. Nothing is lost. The primary self simply begins to operate under the aegis of an Aware Ego that has all the information and input from that primary self but, in addition, has the complementary information and input from the opposite self or selves.

We have tried to give you a feeling of the ongoing process we have been in as our work has developed. The focus on the Aware Ego dramatically changes the nature of the Voice Dialogue process. Whatever work we may be doing with selves, the primary focus is how to support the Aware Ego in its evolutionary process. It is this transformation of the work that moves the system onto the larger world stage. It now becomes more of a philosophy of life, yet at the same time it remains a system that anyone can integrate into their work, and it is not opposed to, or fighting against, any psycho-spiritual system.

The Importance of the Aware Ego Process

Our hope is that all the facilitators and teachers will have a basic understanding of the Aware Ego Process. If this understanding is there, then the applications of the Psychology of Selves and the actual use of Voice Dialogue will be much more effective. Deliberately activating a self or energy system is a very exciting use of the Psychology of Selves, but we do not see this as Voice Dialogue. For us, Voice Dialogue — in addition to the direct work with selves — includes an experience of opposites and an Aware Ego Process.

We finally decided not to officially change the name of the work to the Psychology of the Aware Ego a number of years ago. Voice Dialogue, Relationship and the Psychology of Selves has achieved such strong name recognition that we decided to let it rest there. Our sense is that there is a gradual increased use of the terms "Aware Ego Process" or "Psychology of the Aware Ego" amongst practitioners and teachers, and eventually this shift in name may well take place.

The Aware Ego and Spirituality

We are often asked: "What is the relationship of the Aware Ego to spirituality?" or "How does the Voice Dialogue process address the issue of spirituality?" We would like to address these questions.

For us, it is important to understand that spirituality has two different components, which have to be considered separately. One component has to do with the rules. The second has to do with transcendent experiences — the experience of God, of the Higher Intelligence, the Transpersonal, or whatever name best expresses an experience that goes beyond ordinary consciousness and the words that can describe it.

Generally in the development of religious institutions there is first the transcendent experience, and then a body of rules develops to support this experience and bring it to others. These rules usually become more numerous and powerful as time passes, and eventually they may well obscure the original experience.

For us, the transcendent experience is a very real and glorious gift. Who in us receives this gift and what is done with it can vary. When a self receives this gift — let us assume that it is a spiritual self — that self usually develops a series of rules and expectations about the experience; that self then judges other selves that are different, and polarizes against anything or anyone who does not fit in with its expectations and follow its rules.

We see this as the way in which many spiritual or religious institutions evolve. The original experience is taken up by a primary self (or the primary self of the group) that guards it and keeps out anything that might destroy it. Only the energy of that particular self is considered good, and it is to that self and its rules that one must surrender. We know that much can be gained by this kind of surrender; it is the basic premise of the Guru/disciple relationship. The disciple surrenders to the Guru, and in doing so can receive the gift of the transcendent experience.

In contrast, the Aware Ego surrenders to all energies or selves. This is quite different from surrendering only to the spiritual energies. It means very simply that the Aware Ego is committed to hearing, seeing, and feeling all the different selves. It excludes none. When one self starts to dominate, it is the job of the Aware Ego to find the opposites on the other side and to consider their input as well. In this sense the Aware Ego is like an orchestra conductor who welcomes all the instruments and then uses their individual contributions to sing the song of the soul.

Learning to surrender to all of the selves requires constant work with our negative judgments toward people (and things) to help the Aware Ego in its continual evolution toward clarity. Whenever we feel judgments toward someone or something, we know that we are in a primary self, because the judgments come from the selves, not from the Aware Ego.

You may well ask: "But how do you know when you are in an Aware Ego? How do you know that it is an Aware Ego that is doing the surrendering at any moment? Might you n4ot be fooled by the Mind, which loves to act as though it were God, or by any other primary self for that matter?"

The answer is that we don't. We don't know when we are in an Aware Ego except for brief moments. If your responsible self has just been facilitated and you can feel your separation from it, the most you can say is that at this moment you have an Aware Ego Process operating in relationship to responsibility; at this moment you have a certain level of understanding of this responsible self and a certain separation from it.

A second answer is that when we are convinced we are operating from an Aware Ego, we are not. We are most probably identified with a spiritual self, a rational mind, or a control self. All of these have a sense of certainty to them, and they like to masquerade as the Aware Ego.

So, as the Aware Ego bows down to the different gods and goddesses of the light and the dark, of heaven and earth, of good and bad, of body and spirit, of knowing and not knowing, it is embracing *both* of the opposites. It is the "and" rather than the "either/or." It truly represents the Middle Way.

We see the Aware Ego as surrendered to the Intelligence of the Universe. This intelligence can manifest in many different ways. It is not personal in any sense, though for some of us it may manifest through our personal relationships. Others can see it with utmost clarity in the dream process. For still others it may manifest in meditation or spiritual practice. For many scientists it manifests in the organizing principle at work in the material world and — on a grand scale — in the galaxies. Whatever the case, the Aware Ego must be surrendered to the reality of this higher intelligence and how it can be perceived operating in his or her personal universe.

For us, the Aware Ego must also be surrendered to the way that this higher intelligence operates in human relationship. It must be surrendered to the idea that everyone in our life is potentially a teacher for us. We understand that people's reactions to us must be taken seriously, and we learn to use our own negative judgments of people as a teaching device to discover our own disowned selves.

The Aware Ego is an expression of a psycho-spiritual consciousness process. The Aware Ego has the job of embracing the world of Spirit in all of its glory, and on the other side, the world of physical matter, of emotion, of passion, and of psychological and mental realities.

For us, it is important to not confuse spirituality with consciousness. A consciousness process encompasses spirituality. Spirituality does not necessarily encompass a consciousness process. Spirituality does not encompass matter or instinctual energies. That is why so many people in the spiritual tradition lose the connection to their bodies and their instincts. An Aware Ego process requires us to do the work of spirit and the work of relationship and the physical world. For ourselves, we must say what a delight it has been, and continues to be, to spend our lives in these kinds of explorations.

Moving Into Many Worlds

People use Voice Dialogue and the Aware Ego Process in many different settings and with many different kinds of clients. Management consultants have found a way to use the Voice Dialogue technique and the concepts of the Psychology of Selves and bonding patterns in a business setting with individuals who are not at all interested in consciousness issues. They have translated the language we use here to make it work within a different frame of reference and for a different set of primary selves.

Teaching in France, 1989.

Coaches or management consultants might, for example, speak of "traditional habits" or "familiar strategies" versus "unexplored creative potential" rather than speak of primary versus disowned selves. They are not likely to use a term like "Aware Ego" because this kind of language might not be acceptable in a business setting. So they improvise — some quite brilliantly — and many have experienced great success.

One of our major teachers keeps a focus on what we call *being energy* because she feels that is extremely important. Others use this being energy as a vehicle for igniting the spiritual energies.

Other teachers are specializing in working with the selves involved in addiction. In the field of Western medicine, there are researchers who are beginning to investigate the neurobiological aspects of consciousness, meditation, and the selves.

In a totally different arena, this work has proven extremely valuable for training actors. There, too, different words are used that match the requirements of the situation. There is even an internationally acclaimed Tango coach who uses the energetics of this work in his training of competitive dancers.

There are myriad ways to work with the selves, and we are delighted to see the creativity and diversity of these new developments.

Body Dialogue: The Work of J. Tamar Stone

This is a perfect place to introduce the innovations of J. Tamar Stone, Hal's daughter, who has added an entirely new dimension to this work. In her early twenties Tamar was working at Blue Cross and very much committed to a career in business. Her plans were interrupted when she developed a debilitating medical condition that was diagnosed as rheumatoid arthritis. Her symptoms were so severe that she had to abandon those professional plans and devote herself to her own healing process.

Tamar made a choice at that time to not follow the orthodox medical model generally prescribed for these kinds of arthritic conditions. She found an MD who was open to the idea of her trying different treatment modalities, and this began a remarkable journey of exploration and healing that lasted five years in its more active phase but in reality has continued to this day.

Tamar opened herself to ongoing psychotherapy, to many different forms of complementary medicine, and to certain aspects of traditional Western medicine. She took all of us along with her on her journey. Hal, in particular, has been delighted to work with many of the people Tamar discovered in her own explorations. Without the constant health-oriented input and recommendations Tamar has given to Hal through the years, it is quite possible that he would not be here today.

Very gradually, out of the profound experience that she was going through in her own healing process, Tamar began to develop a very special and different kind of connection to her body. It became much more real to her than it is to most of us who don't spend much time sensing into the body. She began to shift her overall professional identification to psychology, and she used the Voice Dialogue work as one of the central healing modalities of her healing journey. Over the years she has become one of the senior teachers of our work.

What also began to evolve was an entirely new and different aspect

In Central Australia, 2002.

of the Voice Dialogue work, which Tamar called *Body Dialogue*. What she realized, from her own experience, was that the body had a voice that could speak for it. She also discovered that many of the individual parts of the body were able to speak and to give specifically targeted information and guidance.

Even more significantly, Tamar began to tune in to the fact that the physical body carried an intelligence and that one could activate this "intelligence of the body" and receive remarkable information and guidance. The process of working with the body in this way began slowly and through the years has developed into what we consider a major contribution to Voice Dialogue and the Psychology of Selves.

The Sixth Element – The Energetics of Relationship

There have been a great many periods of excitement in our adventures together as we developed this body of work. Certainly one of the most profound and most gratifying has been the Energetics of Voice Dialogue and the Psychology of Selves. Hal was first introduced to the world of energy by the work of William Brugh Joy in 1974 when he made his first public appearance at the Center for the Healing Arts' summer conference. It was a truly seminal moment in the world of consciousness because large numbers of students flocked to Brugh and were introduced to the body's energy fields and shown how to work with them.

At that time the energy had to do with healing. Hal was not interested in becoming a healer per se, but Brugh opened the world of energy to him, and, over the next few years, Hal developed his own style of energy work, which he called *field clearing*. It has always been a significant part of our lives and our work, and has helped us move through difficult physical challenges both at home and, perhaps more important, on our travels.

It was only after we met that we began to consider the world of healing as it applies to personal relationship. Early on in our explorations together, we began to notice that different selves actually *felt* different from other selves. Being with a vulnerable child or a loving parent felt like being in the room with an energy machine that gave off a warm glow that could be sensed and that made a palpable connection. We called that *personal energy*. Facilitating the mind was totally different. The mind generally gave off no energy and we did not feel a connection. We called that *impersonal energy*. One was warm and connected, the other cool with clear, crisp boundaries. These are two very different ways of meeting the world.

We paid more and more attention to what we began to call *the energetics of Voice Dialogue*. Different selves had different energies connected to them. If we were facilitating sensual energy (which we called *Aphrodite energy*) we could sense a tingling in the skin of our whole bodies. If we were facilitating the higher self we could feel a powerful sensation in the tops of our heads, the *crown energy*. Though Hal had learned about energetic reality through the work at the Center, Sidra seemed to have a totally natural connection to it. We began to see that some of the difficulties of our interactions were based on energetic realities we hadn't previously known. Sidra's primary self was personal in those early years, and Hal's primary self was impersonal.

We began to recognize that some of our most impassioned judgments toward each other were based on this difference. When we first starting teaching together, this was a real problem. Sidra said of Hal that if someone in the front row of the audience fainted and fell to the floor, Hal wouldn't notice. Hal said of Sidra that if someone in the last row of the audience got up to go to the bathroom, Sidra would be upset because she felt abandoned or judged.

One time we were teaching, and at the end of the first hour at the break Sidra asked Hal if he had seen the couple in the front row right in front of him. Hal didn't know what she was talking about. She then pointed them out to him and it was a couple that was apparently involved in S&M practices. The girl was wearing a very large metal collar around her neck and metal bands around her ankles embedded with metal rings for bondage. Hal was quite sure that he was the only one in the room who had missed seeing that.

Another time Sidra and Hal were walking on the beach near Santa Barbara, and Hal — in full impersonal energy — was immersed in the ideas they were discussing. Sidra stopped walking and, with a smile, asked: "Hal, would you mind looking around and seeing where you are?" To his great astonishment he discovered that they were in the middle of a nude beach and that all around him there were naked sun worshippers. It was not impersonal energy alone that created this diminished perception, but impersonal energy was certainly a good part of it. Hal's basic primary selves were impersonal, and he just didn't make an energetic connection with the world around him.

In more recent years, we have begun to use the words "linkage" or "energetic linkage" when talking about this energetic connection. When we got into negative bonding patterns, when judgments took over, we lost our linkage. Things felt hopeless between us. Then we did our work with each other. Maybe Hal discovered he had been holding back his reactions. Maybe Sidra discovered she was pushing too hard.

Whatever the case, by doing our work with each other we got back our linkage. We would feel energetically connected again. We felt like newlyweds. This happened over and over again. We were beginning to see with absolute clarity that it wasn't marriage that destroyed love and intimacy. It was the development of negative bonding patterns and the ensuing loss of linkage.

Repeatedly, Hal's feelings would get hurt. Maybe he was jealous of Sidra at a party when she was energetically connecting with other men. If he didn't share his jealousy, his vulnerability — whatever forms that sharing took — his inner child disappeared from view. He used to joke about it disappearing into the universe about a hundred light years away when this happened. What we realized was that linkage ended at that moment. Linkage is real. When it is lacking it is very lonely and the relationship feels terrible. And — unless you know about what you have just lost — it's not so easy to get it back.

We began to examine the nature of peoples' linkage. You can be linked to your dog or cat. You can be linked to a child. You can be linked to your work, or your computer, or your book, or your television set, or your secretary, or to money, or to worry, or to your to-do list, or to alcohol, or to drugs, or to food, or to exercise. You can even be linked to your spiritual practices or to your consciousness process.

In relationship work we began to see that if the primary linkage wasn't between the two people in the relationship, then there were problems. The primary linkage might go to one of the children, creating a kind of psychological marriage between the parent and that child. This happens with great frequency, and then, if the marriage breaks up and the parent meets someone she/he loves, there is a wrenching disconnect from the son or daughter who had carried the primary linkage before the arrival of the new partner. This awareness of linkage introduced a new dimension to our considerations of family relationships, and led us to a deeper understanding of the intense pain involved in step parenting and the introduction of a new partner into a family system.

Our work with energetics was in two basic areas. First, there was the fact that every self could be experienced energetically and that the awareness of this was of utmost importance. We saw clearly that the effectiveness of the facilitator was dependent upon the recognition of the energy and the ability to hold this. We realized that the best facilitators worked at an energetic — rather than verbal — level. They paid more attention to maintaining the energetic integrity of a self than to asking it the "proper" questions.

There is another aspect to the facilitator's sensitivity to energetics. If the facilitator was able to use energetics, then he or she could often help a self to emerge by a process of energetic induction. This works like a tuning fork — you strike the tuning fork and set it down on a sounding board. The sounding board then vibrates at the same frequency — giving off the same note. The facilitator operates like a tuning fork, calling up a specific energy within him- or herself and the subject responds with the same. In this way, and when appropriate, the facilitator can help to induct a sought-after energy. This is particularly helpful when helping people learn how to use personal and impersonal energies.

This was a whole new world to explore. We also began to teach the Aware Ego how to bring into itself, or channel, the different energies, and here again it was the awakening of a whole new world. We literally taught people how to "play their own instruments," how to affect their own energy fields. This work was particularly important because it was a way of strengthening the Aware Ego Process and empowering the individual.

The second area of our work with energetics was exploration and experimentation with linkage. We looked at linkage as it related to bonding patterns and saw how it led to an increased understanding of the dynamics of family systems.

Hal has one strong memory of an experience with Sidra that catapulted him to a new understanding and appreciation of linkage. A good many of the negative bonding patterns he got into with Sidra had to do with his feeling left out when she was with her children. Since her basic energies were personal, the linkage with her daughters was very strong. One day they were alone in their home in Southern California; it was the first day that all of the children were away. They were sitting on the two ends of the couch and there was a very strong energetic linkage — they could feel a buzz between their hearts. Hal was a very happy man. This process went on for five minutes or so and suddenly stopped completely.

Hal asked Sidra what had happened. Sidra then said something that was truly remarkable for Hal. She said that she was doing an experiment. She wanted to see what would happen if she visualized her daughter in the next room. When she did that, the linkage between them ended totally and her energies automatically (or unconsciously) went to her daughter.

Hal had been working on his judgments about Sidra's mothering for a long time. Suddenly he understood at a very deep level how this process works. If a mother has children, and if one or more of those children is near her, then her primary linkage is going to shift to the child. We don't mean every time but we do mean most of the time. What Hal saw is that the mother is hardwired to link with her child. This is not a conscious choice, so if we want to be very clear, we call it *unconscious linkage*.

If Hal wanted quality time with Sidra away from the children, he had to learn how to go to her with his own intimacy needs and make them clear to her without sounding either like a whiny victim child or a killer judgmental father (he had an advanced black belt in each, but they were not very useful). Sidra then was able to become aware of where her energies were and was able to handle them in a more conscious way. She could reinstate her linkage with Hal — and she could even maintain her connection to a child at the same time. We call that *conscious linkage*.

This was a turning point in Hal's life, and interestingly enough, as we might well expect in this kind of process relationship, Sidra was able to more effectively look at her own linkage issues with her children. Because she now knew what was happening, she finally had some choice and was able to begin to control where her energies went.

With these kinds of experiences, everything changed in the work and in the theory. For the newer person, Voice Dialogue may well look like a simple technique: just ask the right questions and you'll get to the self. For anyone who senses into the underlying energetics of the work, it becomes something quite different. Experienced facilitators are able to work at deeper and deeper levels as they become more at home with the energetic realities that are in us and that determine so much of what happens in our lives and in our relationships.

So it was that we began the practice of helping people develop mastery in the world of energy. Sidra describes this process as teaching people how to play their own instruments so as to be able to meet the world within and the world outside with ever-increasing levels of subtlety and imagination. And, as we age, we find this ability to dance with the energies is truly one of the loveliest gifts imaginable.

Recently Sidra had a dream in which three women in their mid-'90s came to our home to teach us about aging. What they taught is that as we get older our relationship to energetics becomes more and more important. We had to learn at ever-deepening levels how to run our own energies, how to call up the necessary energies to do whatever it is that we needed to do.

Thus it is that learning to play our energetic instrument becomes an integral part of Voice Dialogue and the Psychology of Selves. We have not written a separate book on the energetics of relationship, but it is included in our book, *Partnering,* and in the CD sets *The Aware Ego* and *Partnering: The Art of Conscious Relationship.* For the energetics of Voice Dialogue, see Robert Stamboliev's *The Energetics of Voice Dialogue.*

The Seventh Element – Partnering

In the last ten years, we've begun to think of our kind of relationship as a partnering relationship. A partnering model of relationship is a nonhierarchical way of being with someone. This way of thinking about relationship can be applied to all relationships, but its primary focus has particular application to ongoing primary relationships. In addition to being nonhierarchical it is also seen by us as being a serious Joint Venture in both a personal and business sense.

As part of this Joint Venture, both people must be surrendered to some level of a psycho-spiritual process in their own personal lives and also surrendered to such a process in their relational lives together. It is important here to understand that the surrender is not to the other person but to the relationship itself.

The ability and willingness to surrender to the process of relationship has a number of major consequences. For one, your partner/friend

Collaboration in recent years—on our back porch at sunset.

becomes your teacher just as you become her/his teacher. Another way of thinking about the Partnering Model is simply to think of it in the sense of Relationship as Teacher.

There is another consequence to this process. We gradually learn to embrace the disowned selves that we carry for each other. This happens over a very long period of time. Ultimately we come to the discovery that in each of us lives an introject of our partner. Sidra is learning about the energy configurations in her that correspond to Hal. Hal is learning about the energy configurations in him that correspond to Sidra. This is a very exciting process and one that allows a continuing conscious separation of the two people, yet a deeper clarity regarding the whole issue of bonding patterns.

There is an extensive ongoing learning process in which both people must learn the basics of the Psychology of Selves, the Aware Ego Process, the consciousness model, the work with bonding patterns, the understanding of energetic realities, and the relationship to the physical body.

There evolves an ever-deepening relationship to the spiritual dimension and, hopefully, there is some connection to the dream process that is shared in the relationship. We have seen that, over time, the dreams can become an increasingly powerful inner teacher both in our lives and in our relationships.

The concept of a Joint Venture also has major consequences. Every aspect of relationship involves a joint decision-making process. There is nothing wrong with one person being responsible for taking care of finances. It is simply that the other person cannot abdicate responsibility for finances. The other person must not become an unconscious daughter or son just because someone else is taking the major responsibility for a particular area. In a partnership, both partners are liable — even if one has a special expertise or interest in one aspect of the business of living.

In this light, an ongoing partnering relationship can be seen in part as a serious business venture between two people, one that requires a good deal of time and energy. We strongly recommend business meetings in which the business issues of life can be dealt with. That may sound unromantic, but if there aren't regular business meetings, then the business of life — the requirements of everyday living — have a tendency to invade all available space and to be handled unconsciously.

We live our lives most of the time out of our primary selves. This changes as we do our psycho-spiritual work. We begin to have a choice about who is going to live our life — or, as we like to say, who is going to drive our psychological car. As partners we must decide over and over again who is going to do what and when. Who is going to call the friends about the party? Who is going to take the clothes to the cleaner?

Primary selves decide whatever partners do not decide consciously together. This is analogous to the default position on a computer. The computers we use came with default settings for each application; there are hundreds of default positions. They work, but they're generic. If you want to use your computer in a more personal, creative and artistic way, then you must learn how to change these settings so that you have real choice as to how it will operate.

If you wish to have a more creative, imaginative, and sensual connection to each other, you need to be constantly handling the business and personal decisions — determining what belongs to each of you at a certain time and then working out who does what. In this way, you do not live your relationship via default positions, which simply means through your primary selves. Instead, you are a team — constantly working together to support the Aware Ego Process in each of you. The gradual integration of whatever it is that the partner carries for us greatly enhances our ability to make conscious decisions and choices.

The psychological work is essential to discover who is running our lives and who is living our relationships. The spiritual work is essential because without a sense of spiritual reality/God/Higher Intelligence our lives cannot expand beyond purely personal considerations. The work with energetic reality is essential because for a truly satisfying relationship, the primary energetic connection must be between the two people involved.

All of this is an ongoing process that can last forever. One of the greatest surprises and delights of our aging process is the amount of change, creativity, and intimacy that remains for us in a true partnering relationship. The continuing support of our dreams is truly awesome, and the profound power of the Intelligence of the Psyche becomes more and more of an everyday affair accompanying our ongoing and ever-present dance with the world of bonding patterns.

The Eighth Element – Dreams, Daydreams, and the Intelligence of the Unconscious

As we mentioned earlier, dreams and visualization have always played an important part in our explorations. At the very beginning, Sidra, in particular, was deeply impacted by a series of visualizations that initiated her into some of the very deepest waters of the unconscious. With time the work with visualization became less important to us as Voice

Dialogue and the dream process became more primary. And in recent years we have found ourselves placing an ever-increasing emphasis on the dream process for ourselves and with our clients. We have also enjoyed working with daydreams as we discovered how daytime fantasies provided a gold mine of information about what is happening in people's lives (including ours).

What we first became aware of was the fact that when people began to develop an Aware Ego Process and were able to stand between opposites, the nature of their dreams began to change. They became clearer. They became more organized. We have always known this at some level, but somehow our understanding and appreciation of this process changed. We watched clients begin to decode their own dreams in relatively short periods of time, depending, in large measure, on the strength of the Aware Ego Process.

As this process continued, we saw that the intelligence of the unconscious began to manifest in an ever more powerful way, and we found that the dream process itself was becoming the teacher for people. We had experienced this earlier in our own lives as we watched how the unconscious organized itself and seemed to have its own agenda for our development.

What is this intelligence? Where does it come from? What does it want from us? And how does it manifest in our lives?

We became aware of the fact that the dream ego, or how the dreamer appears in his or her own dream, gives us a picture of how the primary self is behaving. This seemed to be true of most dreams, though not all of them. Occasionally the dream ego would represent not the current Primary Self System (or operating ego) but instead, the disowned self.

Then we began to ask for people's daydreams or daytime fantasies. These are different from the visualizations of guided imagery. They are not deliberately sought after like visualizations; instead, they are going on much of the time even though many people have no awareness at all that they are, in fact, daydreaming. These daydreams play like background music — and nobody knows who put it on.

For example, imagine that you are driving in your car and someone

Morning mists at our home in Albion.

passes you and then cuts in front of you. You are angry, and in your mind you begin to talk to that driver, expressing your outrage at what happened. This can go on for a long time and can totally destabilize you. Some people will continue this daydream and imagine that they drive after the other person and deliberately crash into him and hurt him. Others will have just a momentary flash of fury or a fleeting image of destruction.

The "you" of the daydream generally gives us a picture of your disowned self. Your primary self may be calm, controlled, and rational. The disowned self that emerges in your daydream is an energy that carries the rage, anger, and resentment that is generally kept under control. We found that by listening to people's daydreams and by making them aware that they are having daydreams, they begin to get a picture of a disowned self.

Once the picture is clear, then there is the chance to explore the self. In this example, there is a chance to learn how to stand between the control and rationality of the primary self that continues to drive carefully and the more uncivilized part of us, the angry, destructive self that can be so frightening to the rational, controlled side.

Rather than trying to change ourselves — which is always a problematical thing to do — what seems to be required of us is a surrender to the unconscious itself as we learn to trust that the intelligence it makes available to us has a plan and direction for us. The surrender we refer to is not that of a passive child who gives up all responsibility. It is, rather, a surrender to a kind of knowing that is not ordinarily available to us. The deeper problems of life can seldom be solved by the rational mind alone. We need the mind, it's true, but it is only one of our resources.

The ignition of this intelligence is not the same as having a particular religious, or enlightenment, experience. Instead, it is an ongoing process that seems to clarify and deepen the Aware Ego. It wants to help us see who it is in us that is living our lives so we can learn to take over from that part (or self) and live our life with ever more choice. This is not short-term work. It is a process that continues forever!

We are well aware of the fact that not everyone remembers dreams, and we can only be grateful that there are so many different approaches to consciousness that can be utilized in the journey of personal growth. Yet we cannot help but be amazed at how often the act of standing between opposites will initiate a dream process or deepen an already existing one.

All of this leads to a natural and organic movement within us whereby the unconscious itself becomes our teacher, and gradually the bonding to the outside teacher diminishes in strength. The role of the outer teacher changes to that of a consultant to process. Finally, even this is no longer necessary and the inner teacher takes over completely. We have had the deep satisfaction of watching this happen to more and more people. And so it is that Hal has revisited his Jungian roots, and this work with dreams and daydreams has become one of the basic elements of Voice Dialogue and the Psychology of Selves.

One of the greatest surprises for us as Hal approaches his eightieth birthday and Sidra approaches her seventieth is the ongoing nature of this intelligence as it continues to unfold and bring to both of us new understandings of matters both personal and transpersonal. It has helped us prepare for aging, and it continues to help us with all the gifts and challenges that come at this time of life.

God, the Greater Intelligence, the élan vital, the Organizing Principle of the Universe, whatever you prefer to call it, manifests in many ways. We feel privileged to have been a part of this manifestation in the work we have shared over the past thirty-five years. And, as we observe the various manifestations of this intelligence all around us, and as we feel the organizing principles behind them, we cannot help but feel assured that God is indeed a mathematician.

Others have discovered this organizing mystery in their work — whether it was with mathematics, the cosmos, the subatomic world, "the field," the physical body, the structure of cells — or in a variety of spiritual practices, both ancient and modern. For us, this intelligence has found us, as we have found it, in the depths, the complexity and infinite richness of human relationship.

Section II

Voice Dialogue and Other Modalities

The Body: A Path to Presence

J. Tamar Stone, MA, RPsy

B e here now. Wherever you go, there you are. Chop wood, carry water. Indeed, the present is where the entire world resides. But to be fully present in our life, we must reside in our body. After all, what's chopping the wood, what's carrying the water? What's taking you wherever you go? What's being here now?

In the mind-body-spirit trinity, our body tends to be the least valued as we travel the spiritual path. We devote lots of time and money to stretching and exercising our mind, feeding and renewing our spirit, but think nothing of skipping meals, checking office email while on vacation, using toxic products in our home. Whether or not we choose to actively expand our knowledge and consciousness, our body remains the breathing, blood-pumping organism that moves us through our life. It is the place of integration, of grounding, for mind and spirit.

Your Body, Your Selves

Bodies are as individual as snowflakes, externally and internally. Our body is a reservoir of information — a blueprint of our genetics, our personal and ancestral history, and our sense-based preferences. It is a delegation of parts, each with its own personality, opinions, and perspectives. The

Body Dialogue Process invites conscious communication with the body's overall voice and the voices of its parts. Hearing and valuing the body's own knowledge base is essential to cultivating a healthy relationship — an intimate friendship — with our body. Imagine the kind of relationship you have with your significant other or best friend, a connection based on mutual respect, effective communication, and pleasure in each other's company. This possibility exists with your body.

The Body Dialogue Process was inspired by The Voice Dialogue Process, the Psychology of Selves, and my personal experience with a physically disabling illness in my late twenties. Body Dialogue uniquely helps bridge the divide between mind and body — a chasm, for some, reinforced by Western educational and socioeconomic values.

Our body and its many parts want to be recognized for the significant role they serve in our overall well-being. Our body wants to be heard when it expresses its likes and dislikes — with respect to food, temperature, environment, fabric, furniture, exercise, touch. A seeming diehard machine of invisible and involuntary functions, our body often goes unappreciated and unacknowledged. We forget that we, and all our sub-personalities, or selves, exist and speak, in and through the container of the body. Without the body, there would be no selves.

What we disown we attract, so explains the Psychology of Selves. For example, someone who's overly responsible and refuses to take a break likely attracts into her/his life (and is irritated by) seemingly irresponsible or lazy people. Those "lazy" people, however, may actually be embodying a message that the overly responsible person needs to hear: "Relax! Take a load off!"

Such messages can also come to us internally. For example, a body revved up or driven by our overachiever self may attempt to get our attention by creating a little tension, a headache, eventually a cold or flu. If we don't read these early warning cues that the body gives to help us, our body must resort to screaming to get our attention.

That very situation catalyzed my discovery of The Body Dialogue Process. While I, ironically enough, was working at a Health Maintenance Organization, my type-A self established a daily routine of taking the eight-flight stairwell to and from the cafeteria for exercise. What that self didn't factor in was my high-heeled pumps. Night after night of intense muscle cramping in my legs apparently was not enough to alarm me.

A diagnosis of rheumatoid arthritis did get my attention — and launched me on my healing journey. To minimize my joint pain, I had to sit, stand, walk, and lift a glass more consciously, and in doing so I learned how to move my body according to its natural alignment. At the same time, I'd been curious about why only certain parts of my body hurt. To get some answers, I decided to adapt The Voice Dialogue Process to explore the overall voice of my body and the voices of its parts. When I asked my hands why they ached so much, they said, "We're furious. Your boyfriend doesn't appreciate our touch." They also told me, "We're exhausted from all the paper-pushing. We crave a creative outlet."

The Body Dialogue Process is one of those outlets. My hands love that I do for others what I did for them. A client of mine came in one day with an over-acidic stomach, an increasingly frequent condition for him. In giving voice to his stomach, we discovered that it had become part of an information feedback system and would burn whenever he didn't express what was really going on with him emotionally. Tracking some incidents in his life, he realized the validity of his stomach's message. Shortly thereafter, he reversed the lifelong pattern of his accommodator self — a people-pleaser afraid to "rock the boat" — by speaking his truth in the moment to his girlfriend, mother, and brother.

Your Body, Your Path

When we have a conscious relationship with our body, we eat when we're hungry, sleep when we're tired, and exercise or move when our body feels the impulse to. The authentic voice of the body doesn't demand to eat to feed our emotional needs the way the inner-child self does. The listened-to body doesn't need to drink coffee to generate a second wind. The appreciated body exercises because it feels good, not because the culturally programmed internal critic says it should be thinner.

The Body Dialogue Process exposes those selves that hijack our relationship with our body and increase our vulnerability for injury and illness over time. Establishing a line of communication with our body (and its parts) allows us to more proactively manage our well-being rather than live at the effect of our counterproductive unconscious patterns. One client's critic was so obsessed with aging that she, at fifty-seven, scheduled a facelift. When I asked her body how it felt about this decision, it replied, "This isn't necessary. For me, aging is natural and inevitable. But if she's absolutely committed to doing this, I want her to give me the right food and rest for my recovery, and to quickly detox me from the anesthesia and pain medication."

A life of presence means honoring not only our body's needs but also its preferences — for example, choosing clothing for comfort and style rather than style at the expense of comfort, creating a home environment that soothes and rejuvenates, and blocking out time for rest, recreation, and reflection.

Your Body, Your Nature

Our five senses are the doorway to being fully present in our body. And when we're present in our body, we become more connected with our surroundings and the larger world. Living in the body isn't a perfected state, but rather being with *what is*: seeing, hearing, touching, smelling, and tasting life as it arises in the moment. When we perceive from the lens of the body as a whole, it's like a seventh sense — a synergistic experience of all the senses. The whole *is* greater than the sum of its parts.

The body wants to be related to as the physical being that it is. We humans are a physical species, members of the animal kingdom. As our culture has evolved industrially, then technologically, we've gone from working the land to working the assembly line to working the mouse. The more we've gotten into our head, the more we've lost connection with our inherent physicality and instinctual nature. Animals, wild and domestic, fascinate us: they spend their days watching, hunting, eating, napping, moving according to their primal urges, creatures of the moment. Similarly, professional athletes captivate us, in part because they demonstrate superhuman physical abilities, but also because they're more connected with their innate animal nature. Repressing or disowning our instinctual energies over time suppresses our body awareness and natural vitality, and may lead to injury and illness.

In my Voice Dialogue and Body Dialogue workshops and trainings, I dedicate a couple of hours to exploring our disowned animal nature. Playing a particular piece of music, I invite the participants to move instinctually, allowing the animal self they most need in their life at this time to emerge. I facilitate each animal self, giving voice to its unique perspective and why it's showing up now. A bird self shows up when someone needs more objectivity, more "big picture" perspective. A marine-animal self shows up when someone needs more flexibility and flow. A jungle-animal self shows up when someone needs more grounding and personal power. We have as many animal selves as there are animals!

Your Body, Your Being

Nurturing a relationship with our body takes commitment and attention — as does any relationship — and ongoing neglect of that relationship can lead to breakdown, from acute ailments (headache, cold, flu), to chronic conditions (arthritis, diabetes, cancer). Because divine mystery plays a part in directing the steps of our path, however, judging illness as a less desirable path to presence is misguided. It is also counterproductive to the healing process. Pain, injury, and illness are rich opportunities to explore possible underlying psychological, emotional, or spiritual imbalances while responsibly addressing the physical symptoms. Body Dialogue supports the overall healing process by directly accessing the psychophysical patterns that may have given rise to the condition. Honoring our body's voice creates greater health, pleasure, and capacity to hold its many selves. All we have to do is learn to listen.

DANCING WITH THE SELVES

Dassie Hoffman, PhD

During our training as Voice Dialogue practitioners and teachers, we have often heard the phrase "the dance of the selves." This article will explore an expansion of the idea: the possibility of actually dancing with the multiple sub-personalities that become available to us during our exploration of the Aware Ego Process. I'll discuss how full body movement is a natural extension of teaching Energetics, which is an integral part of Voice Dialogue. Also, I'll present examples of the ways in which we (at The New York Voice Dialogue Institute) have integrated movement into our annual training program — Voice Dialogue Training for Mental Health Professionals.

It is important to understand the chronological evolution of these theories, and the impact of various events upon their development. The ideas originated thirty years ago, while I was working as a dance/movement therapist at a small psychiatric hospital in Connecticut during the early 1980s. In New York City I attended a workshop in which Hal and Sidra Stone introduced the ideas of Voice Dialogue to the East Coast. I was so intrigued by the workshop that I began to attend Voice Dialogue training groups, which were led by Anna Ivara. I attended these groups for several years, driving down from Connecticut to attend them on

Monday nights.

The Voice Dialogue classes presented many new ideas, which I hypothesized could be applied to my dance/movement therapy work. The conceptualization of the Psychology of Selves offered answers to my many questions about what was actually occurring in my movement groups at the hospital.

My observations indicated that patients moved and danced differently in various stages of their hospitalization. Patients who were acutely psychotic danced in one way; as they became healthier, their movement vocabulary altered, and then shifted again as they prepared for discharge. There was no material in the dance/movement therapy literature that addressed this phenomenon.

If, however, one theorized that there were different selves (sub-personalities) present within each person, then one could understand that there would be alterations in movement as patients became healthier (or relapsed). Early Voice Dialogue theory introduced the concept of primary and disowned selves. In my mind, these concepts offered new ways of understanding the changes in the movement patterns of my patients. And the patients in the hospital often verified my theories. One patient said that she was "Pepper" when she felt confused, and could explore that in motion. When she felt better (clearer), she would call herself "Beverly," and dance in a completely different fashion. If we understood that Pepper and Beverly represented primary and disowned selves, we could observe the actual shifts in movement as the selves changed, as this patient became healed and ready to leave the hospital. My hypothesis was that there were selves that moved patients into improved health, and other selves that pulled them back into older, unhappier ways of thinking and moving.

The concept of selves in motion continued to intrigue me. One day I was working with a group of patients who were about to be discharged. I observed a tremendous amount of tension in the room. These people were more physically "uptight" than when they had been psychotic and had first joined my group. I invited them to place their Inner Critic in a chair and have it sit there for a moment. Then I invited them to try to dance again. We were all surprised and delighted with the results. Once the Inner Critic had been moved aside, people felt more permission to move their bodies as they chose, and they danced with pleasure.

After the movement segment of the group, I asked the participants to return to the chairs on which they had left their critical selves. I reminded them that they would need to be able to access their Inner Critical voices in their lives outside of the hospital. However, they now knew kinesthetically that they had an Inner Critic who lived within the body. They had also demonstrated to themselves how good it felt to move without the restrictions of that critical self. I found this an excellent learning experience, proving to me that the Voice Dialogue model could be employed safely within a dance/movement therapy session.

The Residential Voice Dialogue Summer Kamps (1988–1994) offered me another venue in which to explore the place of movement within a Voice Dialogue session. I was invited to be the resident dance therapist, with whom campers could work on their personal issues using movement and music. This was an unusual opportunity to explore in greater depth and detail how to integrate dance/movement into the framework of an individual Voice Dialogue session.

I was clear at the outset that to add movement into Voice Dialogue sessions might feel frightening to the participants. Being in a self (subpersonality) implies working in an altered state of consciousness. However, every self has a number of verbal defenses available, or a Protective Self to rescue it if necessary. When a person is asked to work nonverbally, using primarily movement as a vocabulary, he/she can feel unprotected and vulnerable.

Therefore I devised a theoretical framework for my participants, combining the theories of a dance/movement therapy session and a Voice Dialogue session. It is the careful blending of the two that provides safety and a unique therapeutic experience. In a dance/movement therapy session, we always have certain elements present: there is an introduction (warm-up), a theme, an energetic discharge (release), grounding, and closure. These elements may be expressed verbally, nonverbally, or in combination.

When we employ movement in a Voice Dialogue session, the introduction is usually verbalized by the subject as we check in with the Aware Ego. The movement portion is implicit, since the subject is in our office or room; i.e. some part of them has brought them this far. It is essential to speak with whatever primary selves have feelings about the participant "doing this kind of work." In this manner, we can learn which selves support or feel resistance to our proceeding.

It may be necessary to assure the primary self that the movement exploration will be time limited, and that the subject will be returned safely to the Aware Ego. A primary self may also request that the subject be returned to a specific space after the movement portion. This needs to be respected.

The primary self may often reveal the theme of the session. The facilitator can then begin to consider the music or props that could be useful with this theme. If the primary self is the one that actually intends to dance, it can be asked directly about music. On the other hand, if the sub-personality that needs to move is a disowned self, then the facilitator will have to wait until it actually appears in the room before selecting music. The utilization of a drum in a non-rhythmic fashion provides an excellent support at these times.

When a sub-personality — the moving self — emerges, the facilitator needs to make an energetic connection as quickly as possible. My preference is to make a gesture of opening myself up physically (head up, smiling, arms and shoulders widening), and then, by stepping back, enlarging the space between us. This both provides a welcome and creates an area in which to work. From this moment until the conclusion of the movement work, the facilitator must remain in eye contact with the subject, maintaining an energetic linkage at all times.

The moving sub-personality may now be addressed directly about music and/or props. Generally, these selves will speak to you directly, or might indicate nonverbally what their needs are. It is better to wait in silence, while continuing the energetic connection, than to guess incorrectly. A newly emergent self can be frightened away or angered by a facilitator's mistake.

As the thematic material emerges, the facilitator must intuit how much of the movement work to join. My preference is to become an active, energetically linked participant, changing levels if the subject does so, but moving only minimally. There have been occasions when the subject signals a need for more physical involvement from the facilitator. If the self appears to be in physical danger during the movement, and seems unable to request help, the facilitator must move into their space at once, hand outstretched. It may be necessary to touch the subject on the shoulder or back to offer concrete reassurance. The moving self will continue to express its needs (verbally or nonverbally), until it has completed its story.

The theme of a session will vary with each participant, but usually there is a tale that must be told. Many of these stories are revealed nonverbally because the subject would be unwilling to discuss them in words. Themes are highly individual, but include the most private material, such as dreams and nightmares, daydreams, buried fears, and family secrets. The ability to move around the room allows Inner Children, Spiritual Guides, and Instinctual Selves to find a comfortable place to reveal themselves.

When the theme is completed, the subject will experience some form of energetic release. The facilitator can observe this when the moving self rolls away, or turns its back, or shifts into stillness. Sometimes, the energetic connection between the subject and the facilitator feels severed abruptly. Whenever this occurs, it should be noted by the facilitator, and honored quietly.

When the subject initiates the connection once again, it is time to begin the process of grounding. It is recommended that the self be shifted back into that place in the room in which it originally appeared. In order to re-ground the subject into reality, it is imperative that a discussion take place between the facilitator, who has witnessed the movement, and the sub-personality who has moved. This timely conversation allows the self to verbally complete the work that was done nonverbally. This is also the time to explore any additional feelings still felt by the self. When we shift the subject into the Aware Ego, further discussions are appropriate. To revisit the session from a nonverbal place, we carefully guide the subject through Awareness, to observe once again what has occurred during the session. The final visit to the Aware Ego allows the participant to move out of the altered state she/he has visited, and offers the closure required.

This offers a picture of how the Voice Dialogue session can be combined with a dance/movement therapy session. I have learned over the years of combining these two modalities that the theoretical framework of the Voice Dialogue session offers a sufficient amount of structure and safety for most participants. I believe that inclusion of the visit to Awareness, and the additional review held in the Aware Ego (now known as the Aware Ego Process) provides a strong framework for the sessions, even when they include movement.

These discoveries have led me further, permitting exploration of how the expansion of my Energetics training can actually lead into asking the selves to move within a group setting. During the first few years of Summer Kamp, I worked only with individuals. During the later years, I originated an Aphrodite Day movement ritual that became a regular event on the Summer Kamp calendar. All of the women at Kamp were invited to participate and to dress as their Aphrodite Selves. Many of them brought special clothes from home to wear, or shopped for them locally.

As leader, I consciously channeled Aphrodite energy, and appeared in full stage make-up and costume for this event. I provided the flowing scarves and the music for these nonverbal ritual occasions. The theme was always to get in touch with the Aphrodite Selves within each of us.

When the music began, we moved together as a group, warming up in a large circle. We could watch each other and allow the excitement and energy of the group to support us as individuals. At some point during this ritual, one of the women would step forward into the circle. She would become her own version of Aphrodite, moving in her own unique fashion. The other women in the group would cheer her on, shouting encouragement and clapping together as she danced. The energetic connections between the group members were contagious, and almost palpable. One by one, each member of the group would dance her own version of Aphrodite.

The final segment of the Aphrodite Day movement ritual was a traditional Voice Dialogue wrap-up. All the participants were asked to move (in this case physically) from their places as Aphrodite into their places of Aware Ego. We spent considerable time in this part of the ritual, attempting to insure the physical and psychic safety of the group members when they reentered the Summer Kamp environment.

The Aphrodite Day Movement Rituals were great fun for the participants, and a tremendous learning experience. For this Voice Dialogue teacher, they provided an illustration of how much group support and linkage can enhance energetic training, particularly when used with movement. Energetics work has become an essential part of contemporary Voice Dialogue training. As teachers, we stress the main energetic components of the Voice Dialogue sessions, the ways in which the selves initially identify themselves nonverbally the first time they appear during a session, and later in the Voice Dialogue process. We highlight the facilitator's energetic repertoire and the need to create and maintain energetic linkage with the sub-personality being facilitated. We train our students to observe and feel the energetic shifting that occurs when a subject moves from the Aware Ego into a sub-personality.

We often fail to take the next step: to encourage the expansion of the energy of a self into movement. In my experience as a Voice Dialogue practitioner and teacher, as well as a dance/movement therapist, each of the sub-personalities has its own movement vocabulary and repertoire; however, in order to observe and capture these often-elusive movement fragments, we must train ourselves in another level of energetic observation.

At the New York Voice Dialogue Institute, we have been training mental health professionals for many years. Although East Coast participants often appear to be resistant, even dismissive, of energetics training, we have continued to feature this essential aspect of Voice Dialogue training. During our yearly training workshops (Levels I and II), we train our participants in the many aspects of Energetics. We seek to develop their sensitivity to their own Energetics repertoire, as well as to heighten their awareness of other energetic occurrences in their work.

For example, our training syllabus includes a special warm-up segment for the period after the lunch break. We invite our participants to "warm up" for the afternoon facilitations by using a combination of music and movement exercises. This post-lunch movement period has become an integral part of our trainings. The expansion of Energetics into movement as a group can include a pre-facilitation introduction into the facilitation training of the afternoon. Participants may be asked to move as one of their primary selves, or they may wish to move with a self from a dream or with a disowned self they seek to know further.

The safety of the environment is provided by the two trainers and the increasing connection that group members have with each other. (During our trainings, Level I is taught over three weekends, and continues into Level II, which is another three-weekend course.) Expanding Energetics into movement may feel easier and safer within a group environment, and once participants have become familiar with the process itself, they seem to glide into larger and more expansive movements. These movements allow the participants to fully integrate the Energetics of the selves into the whole body, and, because of the totality of the kinesthetic experience, these lessons are not lost or forgotten.

Here are some examples of the ways in which we have expanded our Energetics training sessions into movement. Perhaps we have spent the morning teaching the Energetic aspects of the Personal and the Impersonal Selves. Then we ask our students to select which self they will work with during the afternoon facilitation training. We put on music, lead the group in a physical warm-up, and then everyone is asked to move with the self they intend to explore that day. This instruction allows great freedom to locate the self within the body, to discover individually how that feels, and what relevance it might have in their upcoming facilitation.

Furthermore, if we have featured the Personal and Impersonal during the didactic portion of the Energetics session, we have also discussed the concept of energetic linkage. Then we can easily expand upon those ideas and provide the participants with a demonstration of the physical experience of linkage between the selves as they move through the room. The individual group members may elect to move as Personal Selves and link with others, or as Impersonal Selves who do not link with others. Since these exercises are done nonverbally, the interactions between the selves in the room are very intense and can be very educational.

Another important aspect of our Energetics training is our presentation about the importance of *shielding*. We lead the participants in a series of exercises that highlight the experience of a variety of shields or the defensive use of Energetics. Group members can develop their own brick walls, or force fields, or glass covered coaches, or suits of armor. Once they have created their own type of shield, they are invited to move through the room within the shield, to learn how that feels. Participants can assess the usefulness of their chosen shields, and are invited to bring their ideas back into the group for discussion.

These are only a few of the ways that Energetics training can be expanded into full body movement. Many of the senior Voice Dialogue teachers have started to explore and expand upon these ideas as they work with their students. I encourage all of them to continue on their explorations. I believe that we enhance and support the theoretical basis of the Psychology of the Selves with this expansion into movement.

Doctors Hal and Sidra Stone's Work Revolutionizes Performer Training

Jason Bennett, BFA

Before finding the work of psychologists Hal and Sidra Stone, I had studied essentially all of the well-known, 20th-century performer-training methods. Each is brilliant in its own right, and this work trained a generation of American performers. I noticed, however, that many of the traditional methods were seemingly at odds with one another. Some helped some kinds of performers but not others. Most schools of thought rejected the other schools and could not see how these varying approaches could be unified and evolved.

The work of Drs. Hal and Sidra Stone allowed me to synthesize and continue to evolve the training of performers in a way that honors all of the traditional methods. The birth of this process permitted me to realize that each method appealed to the archetypal make-up of certain kinds of performers but left out others. The Stones' work allows all of these archetypal systems to be unified for the first time in history.

This is because the fundamental and deepest aspects of the Psychology of Selves and Voice Dialogue are so expansive. All the tools and processes I've ever come across can be re-envisioned by adapting Voice Dialogue and the theory of the Psychology of Selves to performer training. This includes the most recent focus of the Stones' work: the Aware Ego Process, Bonding Patterns, and the Energetics of the many selves and archetypes found within the human experience.

Energetics access and dimensionality are at the heart of great performance. The Stones' work allows a combination of movement-based, imaginatively based, emotionally based, rationally based, and vocally based training methods to be brought together, which basically encompasses all traditional methods. The approach yields such amazing results that it has sometimes been criticized as impossibly ambitious to achieve, but, using the Stones' work we are able to help further develop virtually any kind of performer trained in any kind of way.

Voice Dialogue and the Psychology of Selves are not the only body of work performers should have exposure to, but the fundamental axioms of the Psychology of Selves explain, in large part, why performing is always interesting. Without the many ingredients listed below, the performance or production is most likely to fail to entertain.

1. Action is dramatic when primary selves fight with the disowned selves of another. (No primary selves versus disowned selves, no dramatic conflict.)

2. Action is dramatic when the primary selves within us fight with our disowned selves inside. And the disowned selves burst forth to the surface in the most charged moments.

3. Action is dramatic when the underlying vulnerability is revealed in a character, or between characters, often bursting forth.

4. Action is dramatic when an extreme positive bonding pattern flips to a negative bonding pattern or vice versa.

5. Action is dramatic, or the resolution of a story occurs, when the birth or the development of an Aware Ego Process occurs in a character or between characters.

6. Action is only dramatic when specific and transpersonal archetypal energies are accessed, often causing cataclysmic love affairs or wars between characters, within a character, or within groups of characters. (This all applies to cultural conflicts, too.)

7. The only way to access the transpersonal realm in a healthy, reliable way is through honoring the primary self system. And by doing so, developing an Aware Ego Process. This takes varying degrees of time, depending on the performer's development.

It is an elegant, practical, and deeply experiential approach to performer training. Two primary selves sitting in a room agreeing with one another would certainly not yield any dramatic action for an audience to experience. And with no vulnerability at stake, we would see a boring performance. Only the clashes between the archetypes and selves, and the underlying vulnerability have a chance at being great entertainment!

It is worth noting that almost all traditional acting tools exist as preparation tools for the purpose of accessing selves, archetypes, and vulnerability. There is no other reason for these preparation tools; but with the increasing development of Aware Ego Processes, the less of these "tricks" a performer needs to embody energetic dimensionality in performance. The more developed the Aware Ego Process the more instantly, reliably, and magically a performer can access anything.

Great Performers Are Energy Masters

Acting is an extremely high-energy sport, and great actors are energy masters. The best actor training helps you deepen your energetic awareness, stamina, and vocabulary. Ultimately, all effective storytelling is a high-stakes exchange of energy between actors and the audience. Many aspiring actors come to actor training blind to these energy exchanges and are unable to call forth intense and sustained levels of performance energy.

Talent can be defined as the ability to manifest the specific energies the audience needs to receive from the story being told. Actors feed audiences energy. Every human interaction is, in fact, an energy exchange. Master actors are master communicators and are expert in manipulating energy.

In acting terms, energy is difficult to precisely define. Other words that are similar, but not the same, are impulses, moods, qualities, emotions, states-of-being, archetypes, points of view, selves, sub-personalities, and vibrations. Energy encompasses all of these.

Audiences receive an energetic "feeding" while attending any kind of performance event. In fact, as you read this article, you are feeding on the information in it — a relatively limited kind of energy exchange. This information triggers associations and fantasies within your unconscious; the information you are receiving is a catalyst for energetic reactions within you.

When it is most intense, the energy exchange between actors and audiences feels like magic. Actors are like magical scientists. The best actors facilitate audience members' access to all kinds of intense or repressed archetypal energies that the audience members' ordinary lives may not provide the opportunity to experience. Connecting with energy is the fundamental reason audiences attend performance events.

When a performance is successful, the audience is literally getting to know themselves through these energy exchanges. In this sense, as an actor you are a teacher, helping audiences reconnect with energies they probably felt more of a connection to when they were children. As we "grow up," we are socialized out of the connection to many of the universal energies, because we may identify with or disown various selves.

Because of all this, you must expand your imagination as much as possible in your training to be an actor. Your imagination is the most sophisticated playground of all kinds of energy. The imagination can be organized into archetypes — the universal energy patterns hardwired into your brain. Successful actors must easily access all kinds of archetypes.

An "archetypal education" is a fundamental goal of actor training. The more archetypes you learn about the more you can communicate with specificity and dimensionality, thus the better your acting becomes.

Each major human archetype within you is a specific energy pattern — expressed uniquely through your body and voice. The voice and body must be connected to the imagination, freed from tension, and "stretched" so it can call forth and release many kinds of archetypal energies. And ultimately, this must happen spontaneously and profoundly, with no conscious effort.

This kind of energy training is intense. Most actors are not born able to do this in the manner of a professional actor, while some actors' life experiences train them well for this kind of energy mastery. The great news is that energy awareness and mastery can be taught, to a large extent, using the Stones' work adapted for performer training. Access to a wide range of energy was always a goal of most traditional actor training, though teachers of the past often were simply unaware of the energy dynamics of their training. They didn't have the vocabulary to talk about this. Actor training that leaves out the cultivation of consciousness about archetypal energies should become more evolved; however, scene study classes sometimes omit this essential work.

Cultivating Energy Consciousness On Your Own

You can work on energy consciousness on your own. Start paying attention to the energy exchanges between you and others. Notice how some people "change the room" when they enter with their powerful energy. Perhaps you can change the atmosphere of a room with the energy you radiate. Experiment with altering the energy you radiate as you interact with people.

Find adjectives to describe energies you see people radiate as they interact with others. Notice how energies evolve when interactions get intense. Play with energy. Find as many words as you can to describe the diverse energies you experience in yourself as you journey through your life. Any descriptive word or phrase is fine if it has meaning to you — from energy that is "like a lion," or "like Britney Spears," to energy that is "frantic" or "lonely."

Imagine yourself radiating intense energy into the world. Choose what kind of energy you are radiating at different times of the day. Notice how different activities elicit different kinds of energy within you.

Pay attention to your dreams and daydreams. Notice how each image in your dream "feels" differently from another. Each image in your dreams represents an archetypal energy pattern within you. As you are working on a character, the dream images you have will correspond to different energies the script calls for. Sometimes, the connections will be symbolic and not overtly logical or obvious. The energetic intelligence of dreams is profound.

You can practice "acting" from the different images within your imagination. Perhaps you have an image of an elephant in a dream or daydream. What does it feel like to move down the street "from" the energy of the elephant? How does it change your voice to allow the image of the elephant to influence your vocal energy? Where can you feel this elephant energy in your body as you connect to this image?

All this might sound unusual, but your psyche is actually made of images. In other words, *you* are made of images — fantasies and memories. Anything you can imagine is a part of you, and it can change the way you think, feel, speak, and move. Your imagination creates your reality. That's an amazing concept with profound ramifications for your life and your acting. The best actors know this and use it in their acting. You can practice connecting with the energies of your images all day long.

As an actor, you have to be able to choose to experience specific kinds of energies, at extremely high intensities, for long periods of time. This takes training. We have all kinds of exercises in our classes designed to cultivate these kinds of energetic "muscles," and these exercises are more effective than traditional 20th-century actor training. This means our work can help many more actors.

Anthony Hopkins, Angela Bassett, Daniel Day Lewis, Denzel Washington, Dustin Hoffman, Meryl Streep — these are energy magicians, energy masters. They understand and can communicate what it means to be human on the most profound levels. They are teachers, and their teaching is, in large part, energetic. The processes they use in pre-rehearsal, rehearsal, and performance can be taught. The actor's ability to harness, manipulate, and express energy is more teachable than ever before. And the work of Drs. Hal and Sidra Stone allows us possibilities I never dreamed of when I first began professional training.

Look for actor training that is far more profound than the simple intellectual analysis of a character's objectives and obstacles. This type of old-fashioned training can be shallow compared to modern training, which integrates all the great acting methods into an approach that includes growing energetic consciousness. Look for acting teachers who do work on themselves to learn about the energies within them, who are accountable and practice what they preach.

Finally, acting is play! It is high-energy play. What an exhausting privilege it is to play like this. But it is vital play. Our culture could not survive without the arts — and we need the performing arts now more than ever.

It is we artists who are "speaking truth to power" with our storytelling. I'm so proud of the myriad movies released in the past few years that deal with so much of what our world is grappling with. As actors, our lives are devoted to exploring humanity, to exploring right and wrong, to exploring what is really going on right now on this planet. But to do that, you need to master your own truth — which is ultimately an imaginative, energetic truth. Master the energies within you and you are well on your way to becoming a successful professional actor. This is the journey of a lifetime. If you pursue the journey with respect, love, safety, and most important by honoring the primary self system the Stones' have so eloquently advocated across the world, no matter where you get off the train, you are a better person for this journey — and, we hope, the world is a better place.

Conscious Body and the Energy Medicine of Selves

Judith Hendin, PhD

A physical symptom bears a gift from the unconscious as powerful as any dream. Through pain or illness, the body collaborates with the unconscious to lead us to inner selves that have been disowned and buried inside. When we discover the particular self that is lying behind a symptom, this self offers medicine that may actually heal the body, as well as bring transformation in life.

Part I. Background

Hal Stone has long taught that pain and illness are often calls from a disowned self (Stone & Stone, p. 135). Some of these selves are familiar to us. A Relaxed self may counterbalance a hard-working Pusher as it tries to prevent exhaustion or a heart attack. An outspoken Straight Talker may want to speak up as it tries to balance a Pleaser, and this may heal indigestion or insomnia. When people work with their primary selves and develop an Aware Ego process that honors both the primary and disowned sides, the body often gets well. But what if the disowned self behind the illness is elusive? What if a physical condition has no obvious connection to a particular self?

Ten years of exploring ailments through trials and experiments led to the birth of the comprehensive psychodynamic technique I call the Conscious Body process. The next ten years were devoted to understanding the discoveries. Conscious Body employs the principles and wisdom of Voice Dialogue and the Psychology of Selves, as well as my background in body therapies, psyche-soma modalities, cultural anthropology, and theatrical dance. Conscious Body evolved intuitively; rational understanding came later.

The Conscious Body process has been used with hundreds of client symptoms, and with forty symptoms of my own, both major and minor. Client symptoms ranged from rashes to headaches, insomnia to cancer, musculoskeletal pain to intestinal distress, ovarian cysts to sexual impotence. The Conscious Body process can be used with any physical symptom, or with any physical component of a psychological condition, such as the rapid heartbeat of a panic attack. An analysis of Conscious Body client records over a ten-year period, published in the *USA Body Ppsychotherapy Journal*, shows the effectiveness of this work: 63% of symptoms disappeared; 22% improved; and 15% saw no change (Hendin, 2009).

Conscious Body has three aims:

1. Discover the self behind the symptom.

2. Move the energy of this newfound self through the body to possibly generate healing.

3. Ignite an Aware Ego process that honors the newly discovered disowned self and the associated primary self.

A Conscious Body session has a distinctive dramatic arc: the methodical pace of Thinkers; the questioning reluctance of Gatekeepers; the quiet stillness of relaxation; the slow, mysterious revelation of symbols from the unconscious; the amping up of energy as the self behind the symptom comes into view; the full-throttle expression of this energy through the body; and, finally, the denouement, as the subject reenters everyday reality and the Aware Ego process begins.

Four types of disowned selves generally appear from physical symptoms:

Opposites – Classic primary-disowned pairings of selves often appear, such as Pusher-Relaxed, Caretaker of Others-Cares for Self, Pleaser-Straight Talker, Rational-Sensual, Rulemaker-Independent, Special-Ordinary, Responsible-Carefree, Inner Critic-Inner Ally, and Inner Patriarch-Inner Power. As in Voice Dialogue, any unique self, with its opposite, may also appear.

Inner Child – The Inner Child frequently appears in its various forms, including such Children as Playful, Lonely, Sad, Frightened, Needing Touch, the Inner Baby, and "I exist!"

Emotions – Anger, sadness, fear, and even joy arise. The Conscious Body process treats emotions as selves.

Trauma – Adult trauma or childhood abuse, whether sexual, physical, or emotional, can manifest through body symptoms. In each case, a Wounded Child and many other selves need to be heard. If trauma emerges from a body symptom, the facilitator can either continue the work or refer the client to an appropriate therapist.

These four groupings of selves can overlap. An Inner Child can have emotions; trauma recovery can involve opposites, the Child, and emotions; and so forth.

The facilitator does not necessarily jump into Conscious Body right away. For example, if someone has intense pain throughout the body, and they suspect a history of trauma, it is prudent to work with the primary selves first. A disowned self that arises from the body may point the way to months, even years, of inner work.

Of course, physical symptoms may not necessarily be a result of disowned selves. They can derive from nutritional, environmental, hereditary, and lifestyle factors, or the natural aging process, among other causes. The Conscious Body process is a diagnostic and therapeutic tool that accesses the rich psychodynamic component of symptoms.

Part II. Conscious Body in Action

Let's step into a session with Nora. Actual dialogue illustrates the Conscious Body process.

Talk to Thinkers

Nora is outgoing and friendly as she tells me about herself and the history of her condition. A young woman, Nora works as a legal consultant for nonprofit companies. Her family (husband, two children, two cats) brings her joy and contentment. Several years ago, Nora's body began to tingle and twitch. The sensations started in her left arm and spread around her body. Doctors at a leading research hospital ran, in her words, "every medical test," yet all the results came back normal. When Nora extends her hand to shake mine, her whole body is slightly trembling.

◆

The Conscious Body process begins with an intake, which is simple. The facilitator asks the subject to share everything she or he knows about the symptom. The purpose of the intake is not to diagnose like a medical doctor but to allow the Thinkers to speak. Gathering rational information at the beginning allows the subject to drop deep into the unconscious later.

Three Thinkers appear in relation to body symptoms: The first, the Rational Mind, holds factual information about the symptom. When did it begin? What medical treatments have been tried? What were the results?

The second Thinker, the Psychological Knower, also plays a major role during intake. In today's world, people's Psychological Knowers have many ideas about why illness has occurred. Maybe someone needs to take time off, or maybe someone needs nurturing care. As logical as the suppositions of the Psychological Knower may sound, when the self behind the symptom finally appears, it is usually completely different. The client senses *Yes, that's it.*

A third Thinker is the Alternative Medicine Knower. This self holds information about chakras (energy centers), meridians (traditional Chinese Medicine), doshas (Ayurveda), and other schools of body wisdom.

Two of the last selves Doctors Hal and Sidra Stone added to the pantheon of the Psychology of Selves were the Rational Mind and the Psychological Knower. The Stones emphasized how influential these parts are in personal relationships. When working with the body, these Thinkers are also crucial.

Here is a brief example of the three Thinkers speaking during intake.

FACILITATOR. I'd like to hear everything you know about this condition. Is it okay if I take notes?

NORA, *speaking as the Rational Mind.*   Sure. The tingles and tremors began four years ago. I've had nerve conduction tests, electrocardiograms, MRIs, and blood work, but nothing showed up. The tremors have gotten worse over time. I have difficulty sleeping, so I feel tired a lot. I can't exercise much, though I really want to. I've tried changes in my diet and I've added supplements. I've also tried alternative therapies, like acupuncture and massage. They give relief for a day or two, then I'm back where I started.

FACILITATOR. Complementary therapies often bring relief or healing to the body. I use them myself. But they don't seem to be working for you right now. Do you have any ideas about what may be causing this condition?

NORA, *speaking as the Psychological Knower.* I can be very uptight. I hardly ever relax. The shaking might be my nervousness.

FACILITATOR. Is there anything else you think might be connected to the trembling?

NORA, *speaking as the Alternative Medicine Knower.* The energy flow in my meridians is probably blocked.

As the facilitator interviews the Thinkers, an energetic connection is developing with the self behind the symptom. Neither facilitator nor subject yet knows who this self is, but the facilitator energetically conveys interest in looking for it. The facilitator can sometimes feel it looking back.

Greet Gatekeepers

Week after week, Nora comes to sessions, ostensibly to work with her body. She speaks about many issues, but never wants to talk directly about her physical symptom. One day I ask, "Could there be someone in you who might not want to do this work with your body?"

People have many reservations about investigating their body symptoms. Conscious Body honors this by speaking with a part called the Gatekeeper of the bodypsyche. (I prefer my term "bodypsyche" to the commonly used "bodymind." Bodymind can imply involvement of the Rational Mind, whereas bodypsyche represents the space where body and psyche intermingle — not real, physical space, but psychodynamic space with all the bounty the psyche brings.)

In Conscious Body a Gatekeeper is always present. The Gatekeeper's role is to stand as sentry at the gate and not let anyone pass into the inner realm. There is a discerning element in the Gatekeeper. It is concerned for the subject's safety. A primary self may also function as a Gatekeeper, such as a Pusher that keeps a person too busy to do inner work. I have met over thirty versions of Gatekeepers of the bodypsyche, such as the Skeptic, the Tough Guy, and Fatigue, a Gatekeeper who yawns whenever the topic of the body is broached.

The facilitator speaks to the Gatekeeper using regular Voice Dialogue. The subject physically moves to a new position, which allows this inner character to come forth and speak as a real person. When the Gatekeeper feels that its concerns are respected, it often opens the gate. The challenge for the facilitator is not to take the Gatekeeper's apprehensions personally.

A note about changing positions: In Voice Dialogue, the subject always moves to a new position when contacting a self. Purely because of logistics, in Conscious Body, such movement is optional. When the subject is lying in a horizontal position, moving sideways is awkward, and often there is not much room. So, the facilitator can say, "Let yourself become this part" or "Let this part be here." This works effectively. Any time the facilitator wants more separation, the subject can move an inch or two to one side to let a self be present.

FACILITATOR. Do you have any concerns or reservations about doing this work with the body?

NORA'S GATEKEEPER. (*The Gatekeeper crosses its arms and legs, glares at the facilitator, and speaks in a formidable voice.*) You're damn right I have concerns. I don't want to do this. I'm skeptical of the whole idea that the body might reveal "someone inside." It sounds preposterous. I have other concerns, too. What if Nora loses control? I don't even know what's going to come up, so how do I know that you, as a facilitator, can handle it?

FACILITATOR. I understand, and I'm glad you're talking with us. (*The facilitator addresses each of the Gatekeeper's concerns, and then continues.*) Ultimately, it will be up to Nora to decide whether to go forward. If we do go forward, do you have any advice or guidelines for us?

GATEKEEPER. Go slow, very slow. If something difficult comes up, don't barge ahead. Give her time to get accustomed to it.

FACILITATOR. We will follow your advice, I promise.

The facilitator respects the Gatekeeper, asks its advice, and invites it to join the team. Then things proceed smoothly. If a person jumps into Conscious Body without first meeting the Gatekeeper, it usually turns up later in the process. Honor it at the beginning, and the gate often stays open.

Enter the Bodypsyche

Nora lies down and relaxes deeply. She focuses her attention on the energy of the symptom, and waits for images, feelings, or messages to appear.

The first two steps, Thinkers (intake) and the Gatekeeper, are easy and straightforward. The next two steps, which follow symbols and find the self behind the symptom, are subtler and require finesse.

The subject lies down on a sofa, bodywork table, or the floor, softened by carpet or cushions. The facilitator sits on a chair, a stool, or on the floor near the subject. The facilitator ushers the subject through a whole-body relaxation.

The subject then focuses attention on the *energy of the symptom*, which is connected to the energy of the self behind that symptom. Facilitator and subject do not know any more about the energy than that, but that is enough. The energy of the symptom, whatever it is, will lead to the self.

Together, facilitator and subject step into the land of the unconscious. When traveling in any foreign land, it's good to appreciate the local language. The unconscious speaks in the language of symbols — animals, places, colors, objects, people, spiritual figures, and fantastical creatures. We know this from dreams. The bodypsyche speaks in the same symbolic tongue. Nora shows how this unfolds.

FACILITATOR. Let your attention focus on the energy of the tremors. Be open to any image, feeling, or message that may arise, in any form, even if it makes no sense.

NORA *in the symbolic realm (breathing slowly, eyes closed, body relaxed).* I'm in a cave....

FACILITATOR *(repeating Nora's exact words, keeping the rhythm slow and deep, so Nora stays in the bodypsyche and does not shoot back up to the head).* You're in a cave.... What do you notice next?

SYMBOLIC REALM. It's not dark. There's a glow. It's like white on black. Now I see that the source of the glow is a dim light.

FACILITATOR. Stay with the dim light. What do you notice now?

SYMBOLIC REALM. The cave is being illuminated. There are carvings on the walls. One of the carvings is of a calf.

FACILITATOR. Stay with the calf. What do you notice next?

SYMBOLIC REALM. The calf is mooing and butting its head against another cow.

The facilitator can swim with confidence in this symbolic realm by recognizing a few common occurrences.

If the emerging symbol has even the slightest hint of rational connection with the symptom, the facilitator questions it. Nora's actual physical condition involved tingling, twitching, and trembling, and doctors thought her nervous system might be implicated. So, if Nora's symbol had emerged as electrical wires, that would be very close to a description of the *actual body part*, her nervous symptom. Also, if Nora's symbol had been a quivering branch, that would be very close to a description of her *actual symptom*, the tremors. Other practitioners do excellent work speaking to body parts. In a Conscious Body session — even though it may be counterintuitive — the facilitator actively stays away from any symbol that closely describes either the actual body part or the actual symptom. In such instances, Thinkers may be interfering with an open connection to the unconscious. If this happens in a session — and it often does — the facilitator simply explains that the Rational Mind may be helping, but that Conscious Body aims for a different level. Subjects readily understand this. Then the facilitator begins again and asks for images, messages, or feelings, *even if they make no sense* — actually, *especially* if they make no sense.

Symbols arise on sensory channels. The two most frequent channels are the visual and the kinesthetic. Nora saying, "I see a light," is a visual symbol. Kinesthetic symbols can arise internally ("I feel like there's a light in my belly") or through movement ("I feel like throwing a light bulb against a wall"). Other sensory channels are the auditory ("I hear a light being turned on"), olfactory ("I smell a burning match"), or gustatory ("I taste a burning match").

The facilitator's task in the symbolic realm is to follow images as they arise, without interpretation. The symbol may come immediately, or it may take time to develop. Eventually, a symbol crystallizes. This is worth waiting for. Like Nora's calf, the image pulsates with life.

Discover the Self behind the Symptom

Nora remains in deep relaxation. She stays connected to the calf that is mooing and butting its head against another cow.

The facilitator and subject will soon glimpse the self behind the symptom. They focus on the symbol a bit longer to allow it to bloom into the self.

FACILITATOR. Stay with the calf. What's happening now?

NORA *in the symbolic realm.* The calf is furious.

FACILITATOR. What is it furious about?

SYMBOLIC REALM. It's furious because this cow is not listening to what it has to say.

FACILITATOR *(sensing that the self behind the symptom is becoming clear, the facilitator asks for more details).* Is there anyone in particular that isn't listening to it?

NORA *in the symbolic realm.* The calf's mother never listens to it, ever.

The self behind the symptom has appeared. The symbol has developed into something that has a character, a feeling, a distinct point of view. For Nora, this is a part of her that is angry about not being listened to by her mother.

Medical research has shown that buried anger is often connected to illness. Anger about what? Finding the particular issue for a particular self is crucial because it allows the specific energy to move through the body. Nora's fury about not being listened to by her mother is pinpoint-specific anger. Specificity is the key to healing that may come.

One more note about symbols: sometimes a symbol is clear, but the self is still unclear. In Nora's case, this might have occurred if the calf appeared but said nothing. When this happens, the facilitator can talk directly to the symbol. Anything can speak — calf, light, cave, anything. One may wonder why a calf or a cave would bear a message from the unconscious. "Why?" is a question of the Rational Mind. Interesting as it is, the question is not useful at this moment in the Conscious Body process. It is more important to remain attuned to *energy* rather than *interpretation*.

When the self eventually emerges from a symbol, the facilitator dialogues with the self briefly and then swiftly moves to energetic expression — unless the primary self needs to be heard first.

Acknowledge the Primary Self

Nora's disowned anger was beginning to percolate. Would it be able to come forth?

If there is one rule in Voice Dialogue, it is always: Start with the primary selves. This makes the work organic and safe. Yet, body symptoms usually lead to disowned selves. To maneuver respectfully on this terrain, the facilitator listens for clues about the primary self. A simple statement like "I never get to be angry" implies a pair of selves: the disowned self who wants to get angry, and the primary self who does not allow it. In Conscious Body work, sometimes a disowned self is free to express itself without first contacting the primary self. At other times, it is necessary to dialogue with the primary self first, and then ask permission for the disowned self to speak:

NORA'S SELF BEHIND THE SYMPTOM (*might have said*). I'm furious because my mother is not listening to me, but I can never express my fury.

FACILITATOR (*recognizing the reference to a primary self*). There may be someone inside who says it is not all right to express fury. May I speak with that one? (*Nora lets herself become that part. The facilitator addresses this primary self.*) For you, it's not all right to express fury. Can you speak about it?

NORA'S PRIMARY SELF. Life should be safe and comfortable. I'm afraid if Nora gets angry, people will reject her.

FACILITATOR. Do you have a sense of when you came into Nora's life?

PRIMARY SELF. Early. Her parents yelled a lot, and I decided never to do that. It was too hurtful for everyone.

FACILITATOR. I understand your decision never to express anger like her parents did. At the same time, a part of Nora is coming up now that wants to get angry. It seems important to her body, and perhaps to her life. How would you feel about that angry part being here, even just a little?

PRIMARY SELF. I suppose it's all right, but only here in the session, not with other people, not yet.

FACILITATOR. We'll definitely follow your guideline. Now let's go ahead and meet this other self. You can go back inside (*or Nora can move over*), and we'll let the other part come through that wants to get angry.

When emotions that have been disowned and buried begin to surface, a primary self often appears. When one self wants to express emotion but another self does not, the containing, primary self is the Gatekeeper of Emotion. Nora experienced this. Her Gatekeeper of Emotion did not want anger expressed. The Gatekeeper of Emotion appears with sadness and fear as well. For example, the self behind the symptom may plead, "I need to cry, but crying is not allowed." The disowned self that wants to cry is referring to the Gatekeeper of Emotion that does not allow tears.

In such instances, the facilitator greets the Gatekeeper of Emotion as any other primary self, listens to all its concerns, and respectfully asks permission for emotional expression. Usually the Gatekeeper of Emotion grants this permission, emotions flow freely, and symptoms often disappear. This simple, effective approach of treating emotions as selves has profound implications for medical research that has found correlations between buried emotions and illness.

The Gatekeeper of Emotions is only one of an uncountable number of primary selves that emerge with body symptoms. Remembering the four types of selves that appear from body symptoms — opposites, the Inner Child, emotions, and trauma — the facilitator can interpret anything that arises from the bodypsyche.

Whatever arises, maneuvering between primary and disowned selves that arise from the body requires finesse. It's essential to stay true to the precepts of Voice Dialogue by honoring the primary self first and foremost. The facilitator should never pressure a disowned self to express itself if the primary self has reservations.

Move the Energy

We return to Nora, who is still lying on the sofa. The new angry part she has discovered wants to come to life. Its energy wants to move. Facilitator and subject are heading toward possible healing. The energy of the self behind the symptom needs to surge through the body. From here on Conscious Body is rooted entirely in the energetic aspect of selves. Nora is eager.

FACILITATOR (*addressing the new part that is angry and wants its parents to listen*). If you could express yourself fully, what would you do?

THE ANGRY SELF BEHIND THE SYMPTOM. First, I'd stand up and spread my arms out wide, with my finger splayed. Then I know people would see me.

FACILITATOR. Would you like to actually do that? (*At this point, the new self is so engaged that it usually welcomes the opportunity to express itself.*)

ANGRY SELF. Yeah, I'd like to try. (*The self stands up and stretches its arms out to the side.*) I feel twice as big! I'm stretched so far I feel like I might burst. Now I want to open my mouth wide, like I'm a dragon with fire coming out of my jaws.

FACILITATOR. Go ahead. I'll mirror you. (*The facilitator stands, stretches out her arms, and opens her mouth, too. This is a literal matching of energy that is spoken of in Voice Dialogue facilitation. The facilitator keeps her own energy slightly lower than the subject's, so the subject is in the spotlight. The purpose of the facilitator's involvement is to make the subject feel comfortable, and to support and amplify the subject's energy so it surges through the body.*) What do you want to do now?

ANGRY SELF. I want to walk around this room with huge strides. Along the way, I'll speak to mother and tell her a thing or two.

FACILITATOR. Let's go.

ANGRY SELF (*striding, then pausing, arms still outstretched*). Here she is. You know what I want to say to her? 'Shut up! You always talk-talk-talked. You asked about the events of the day, but you never really listened. You didn't care. I have a lot to say, and I want you to shut your mouth and listen to me!' (*Turning to the facilitator*) I like this.

FACILITATOR. You're doing great. Keep letting the whole body do whatever it wants.

ANGRY SELF. Mother used to recite a jingle, 'Better to stay silent and be thought a fool, than to speak and remove all doubt.' You know what I feel about that? (*The Angry self lifts her arm like a boxer winding up to pummel an opponent.*) I want to punch mother right in the nose.

FACILITATOR. (*The facilitator, prepared for this kind of expression, grabs a thick pillow and holds it in front of the Angry self.*) Would you really like to punch mother?

ANGRY SELF. Can I? You're never supposed to hit your mother....

FACILITATOR. You're not actually hitting your mother, nor are we suggesting that you ever do this in real life. This is simply a way to let the energy move fully through the body.

ANGRY SELF. Then I want to do it! (*The Angry self wallops the pillow-as-mother with all her might, over and over.*)

FACILITATOR (*speaking in rhythm with the punches to support the energy flow, the facilitator interjects a suggestion*). Let the anger flow directly from the tremors. Let the anger flow through them and from them.

ANGRY SELF (*Nora pauses and focuses on the tremors. Her arms shake a little, and then these shaking arms resume punching. The energetic expression continues until it is completely spent and the self droops, with a smile on its face*). That felt soooo gooood.

At this point, the energy of Nora's self behind the symptom has been fully expressed. As the facilitator matches and encourages the emerging energy, this energetic contribution adds voltage to the energy surging through the subject's body. Not every self is this dramatic, but the energy of the self behind the symptom, grand or miniature, carries medicine that may accelerate healing.

Other possibilities for the expression of disowned selves are vast. Here are a few examples from the thousands of Conscious Body sessions I have conducted:

- In a case of chronic fatigue, disowned Confidence emerged. The client paraded up and down the office as she experienced this new confident energy in her muscles and sinews. Her chronic fatigue disappeared.

- From an intestinal disorder, a Frightened Child emerged who needed to cower behind a bookcase. The Child, shy and shuddering, did exactly that. The fear flowed through the intestinal disorder, and the symptom vanished on the spot.

- From extreme hip pain, where there was a history of sexual abuse, a fresh, delicate sensuality blossomed forth. As this new sensuality wafted gently through the hips, the pain diminished.

- A man with leg cramps fearfully recalled a teacher that used to strike him on the legs with a ruler. That fear poured through his legs, and the cramps released.

- A woman with an ovarian cyst discovered disowned grief about witnessing her father abuse her brother. As she wept, she directed the tears to flow through the cyst. A subsequent sonogram showed the cyst had dissolved.

The energetic palette is limitless. Selves are energy flowing through the body. Once subject and facilitator have discovered the precise self behind the symptom — from following the wisdom of the unconscious to the exact self that is calling — the subject can direct this precise energy through the symptom with intention. Healing results can be significant.

Conclude the Session and Plan Follow-up

Nora returns to her regular waking consciousness. She takes a few minutes to reorient herself as she comes back into her whole body, into the present time, and into the reality of the office.

At this point, facilitator and subject can decide how much they want to talk. If the energetic shift has been substantial, it is best not to talk much, but to let the energy continue to move through the body. The energy shift is paramount.

The facilitator can briefly ask how the subject is feeling. The facilitator needs to be sure the subject is grounded, clear, and ready to transition into everyday life. Any immediate questions can be addressed. Analysis of the session can wait until the next meeting, at which time discussion of opposites, further Voice Dialogue to develop an Aware Ego process, and practical applications can be taken up.

FACILITATOR. How are you feeling?

NORA. I feel good, a little tired. But I'm concerned. Am I supposed to go out and talk to my parents, or other people, with that kind of anger?

FACILITATOR. Not exactly. A *part of you* is calling for expression. It has been, as we say, disowned. Right now you may feel the excitement of the discovery of this self. At the same time, it is important to honor the primary self in you — in this instance, the Gatekeeper of Emotion — that has contained this part. That primary self specifically said it does not want you to bring this new expression into your life yet. It's important to respect and abide by that request. Eventually, you can learn to hold both sides and make choices. What's important for your body is to let some of the energy of this newly discovered self gradually continue to flow.

Follow-up is essential. A person like Nora can run the gamut of the Conscious Body process and discover a disowned self in one session. To integrate the newfound energy into the body, and develop an Aware Ego process in life, takes time.

Nora's tremors subsided in two months. When the tremors occasionally returned, she learned to turn up the energy of her new self, and she could dissipate the tremors in a minute or two.

Conclusion

The connection of symptoms to selves is built into the bodypsyche. With body symptoms, someone is knocking at the door. Any physical symptom may be the call of a self crying for life. The Conscious Body process, distilled over many years of exploration and research, leads us to this vibrant self. When this new self expresses its energy with full gusto, actual healing, as well as colossal insights, result.

References

Hendin, J. *The self behind the symptom: How shadow voices heal us.* Easton, PA: Conscious Body & Voice Dialogue Institute, 2008.

Hendin, J. The self behind the symptom: The energies of inner selves and body symptoms. *USA Body Psychotherapy Journal*, 8(2), 21–30, 2009.

Stone, H., and S. Stone. *Embracing our selves: The voice dialogue manual.* San Rafael, CA: New World Library, 1989.

Acknowledgments

Judith Hendin wishes to acknowledge her colleagues Shakti Gawain, Kate Lampe, Jane Winter, and Dassie Hoffman for inspiration and/or creative collaboration.

Voice Dialogue DreamWork

Carolyn Conger, PhD

I can't imagine doing DreamWork without Voice Dialogue. In the thirty-five years I've been facilitating psycho-spiritual workshops and individual sessions, the Psychology of Selves and Voice Dialogue method have helped me and my clients dive into deeper, clearer waters than the standard dream interpretation techniques. We are able to get to the core issues and energies of the dream quickly and organically, bypassing the wandering intellectual expeditions that prevail in dream interpretation. Rather than assigning meanings to individual symbols and images in the dream and checking them off as complete, using Voice Dialogue engages the dreamer at an energetic level, bringing the images alive and opening the exploration. It's the process, not an assigned content meaning that's important. The interaction of the dreamer with his dream is active and vital, affecting all levels of body, mind, and spirit.

Following is an excerpted session that will demonstrate the use of Voice Dialogue with DreamWork, and how it fits seamlessly with other modalities the facilitator may choose.

Gilbert is a middle-aged professional who consulted me because he had a series of dreams that kept him from sleeping. He explained they all were about failing to perform well. He dreamed he was not prepared for a history test or was behind in school lab experiments or didn't have the finances accounted for at work in time for a meeting. In each one he worried about not being prepared. In these dream scenarios, his whole life was hinging on the outcome, and his agonizing question was "Am I going to make it?" No wonder he couldn't fall back to sleep.

Gilbert shared his latest dream:

I am driving toward a high mountain pass. It's one I know well from childhood, Balsam Gap, on the road between Waynesville and Cullowhee in the Smoky Mountains of North Carolina. There are never any other cars on the road and I don't know where I'm going. Maybe a road to nowhere.

I am myself as I know myself now. Sitting beside me in the passenger seat is a dark, shadowy figure wearing a black hoodie with a pointed tip at the crown. He never says one word or moves from his stationary position. I don't know who he is, what he wants, or why he is riding with me.

As we curve higher and higher to the pass, I look to my left through the woods and see a white clapboard house filled with visitors, happy and laughing. I can see through the large front windows to every room in the house. Everything is white — furniture, appliances, books, everything — including the visitors' clothing. There is a white bus parked in front with a blue sign in cursive letters over the front window that reads, Pressley. It's like a church bus and the people are having an event. Presley is a real town in this area, so in the dream the name is misspelled.

We drive higher toward the pass, and occasionally on each side of the road I see other white clapboard houses through the trees, but these are unkempt in front, and there are no people. I glance inside the windows and see everything disheveled — bookcases tipped on top of beds with bare mattresses, broken furniture, ragged curtains, things piled up in heaps in every room.

As we continue up the mountain, I feel overwhelmed and sad, with a heavy feeling of loss. I'm sad the houses at higher levels are disheveled and the visitors cannot come. It's a lost opportunity. The houses could have taken in visitors and explorers. They are empty guesthouses. What a shame and loss. I don't know how it will turn out.

I ask Gilbert to *title* the dream, and he replies, "Empty Guesthouses." He knows what comes next, and volunteers the *context.* "Nothing unusual was happening in my life around this time," he says. I check again for significant or emotional events, and he describes smooth sailing.

Next, I give Gilbert an art pad and felt-tip colored pens to express anything he wishes about the dream. He draws three white houses to the left and right sides of an upward-spiraling road, with a mountain peak at the top of the page. To the right of the paper he makes bold black strokes to form an amorphous shape. Around the first house at the bottom of the page he draws blotches of yellow color radiating out like the sun. There is not as much detail as he initially described. Some clients like to draw out a scene, mapping the architecture of the action, or draw a character's portrait, while others choose free-form shape and color to represent feelings. Often, people go into a light trance while doing this, which augments the participation of the unconscious. I look at the drawing with interest, but, to keep the field of exploration open, I do not comment or ask questions about his art at this time.

"How would you like to enter your dream?" Gilbert doesn't know. "What is the most salient part, the part that catches your attention? We could start there," I say. He tells me the shadowy one pulls at him just a little bit more than the empty house. So the first *character* we choose for Voice Dialogue is not the Gilbert in the dream, or the visitors or the houses or the road or the mountain pass, but the literal shadow figure. Since it is not wise to immediately engage a shadow element, I first dialogue with Gilbert's known sub-personalities. Ben, a tough sewer-maintenance worker type, wants to kill off the dark guy and bury him. Eliza, a purely intuitive part, wants to love him into a good person with droplets of light. Kenny, a two-year-old energy, is afraid until a superhero comes forward to offer protection.

We work with Gilbert's primary selves and with their opposites, and then discuss the Aware Ego process that develops between pairs of opposites. He understands that without an Aware Ego, the primary self will grab control again. Gilbert says he feels safe in the Voice Dialogue structure and language. He likes getting to know himself in this way. Finally, Gilbert and all the parts agree it's okay for me to talk to the shadow figure.

I ask him to move to another part of the couch.

"I'm ShadowMan, the dead part of Gilbert," he offers. "I won't allow him to create happy guesthouses anymore. The end of the road is near. All the houses — everything — is dead from now on. There's no hope. My other name is Death, and I'm taking him away from all that was good in life."

I am silent for a moment, letting the words and heavy energy of this sub-personality permeate the atmosphere. We continue the dialogue slowly, revealing valuable material. ShadowMan finishes, and I ask Gilbert to become present, to move to his original place on the couch. When he is ready, I invite him to share his *feelings* about ShadowMan now, and his feelings when he was in the dream. He said the part was much more frightening and powerful during the dialogue than in the dream, that his words were chilling and true. The horrible knowing that ShadowMan is always there with him, quiet and strong, is difficult for him to bear, and he cries. He shares general feelings about other elements in the dream, again, when he was having it and as he works with it now. Gilbert is wide open, stunned by the strength of ShadowMan. I honor the process by steering away from interpretation, helping Gilbert to focus on the pristine elements of the dream.

He says the energy of Dream Gilbert is coming up for him now. I encourage him to move to a different part of the couch. "I'm driving, but my body is stiff," he says. "I know this dark shadow thing is sitting beside me, but I don't engage him. Maybe I'm ignoring him so he will go away." The Dream Gilbert continues in a soft monotone. "I'm just driving, that's all. Don't know where and I don't care. I'm like the shadow, can't move much." After exploring why he's not moving (he's forgotten how,) I ask him if he wants to try to stand and move. He rises and shuffles to the center of the room like a bent, crippled old man. We continue the dialogue as he slowly walks. He explains that he is frozen and can only plod forward with effort. It contains him and makes him feel safe, he says. I move him back onto the couch to the present-day Gilbert, the one who contains all the parts of the dream and more. From this perspective he shares that he knew his life had gotten more contained and frozen, but didn't realize it was so bad. He said he'd given up going for walks and swimming, which he used to enjoy.

After sharing about Dream Gilbert, ShadowMan, and other parts of the dream extensively, he responds to my prompt of *associations* to parts of the dream.

"ShadowMan reminds me of the devil. He's evil, and the point on his head is like a horn. He also reminds me of my uncle, who raised me. The son of a bitch beat me and kept me out of school to run errands from his mechanic's shop that dealt in stolen parts. He wouldn't let me have any fun. Made me stay in my room when I didn't work for him. Once I did sneak out and went to a Mormon picnic with a girl from school. That first house with all the people reminds me of that time. Loving people and fun and happiness."

Gilbert talks easily of other associations. The white color is goodness, which ShadowMan destroyed in the broken houses. It's also his spiritual connection to life. He believes the mountain pass is a critical portal, where he won't be able to turn back, where he enters the land of the fully dead. At this point Gilbert goes back to his artwork and draws a gate intersecting the road toward the top of the page, making a stop sign and a guardhouse. Both are bright red, outlined in black. He writes the words "Balsam Gap" on the guardhouse wall. He touches his pens as he surveys the painting, but does nothing more.

I look at the clock and see we've been working for one and a half hours. I tell him we've done enough for now, and that he did great work. He sighs and leans forward. " I know the next step," he says. "Is there any *action* to be taken now?" "No, not yet," I answer. Often, clients are ready to bring an insight from the dream into their daily lives, i.e. Gilbert might choose to wear a black hoodie one day to symbolize his new connection to his shadow self. I say that if he wishes, we can work with the dream more in our afternoon session. Perhaps we'll explore whether the *theme* of this dream relates to the series of his dreams about not performing well. But I don't need to plan anything — Gilbert's wisdom will know how to begin.

Voice Dialogue DreamWork can be used in a group setting. The basic Voice Dialogue is done with the dreamer after he shares his dream, similar to the example of Gilbert's session. The other group members observe, and afterward, if the dream teller wishes, the *Dream Council* makes offerings for the dreamer to consider exploring further. We assume an attitude of respect toward the dreamer, not needing to interpret or rush insight. A typical offering might be, "Gilbert, if it were my dream, I'd check in with ShadowMan regularly by centering, moving into his energy, and writing down anything he had to say to me." Or, "I'd want to do Voice Dialogue with the happy visitor people, just to hang out in their vibration. It might help unfreeze me."

Often, I will use the group to augment a disowned self we've dialogued with. Everyone has felt the energetics of that part in the dream, and everyone has some variation of that energy within, so I put on slow, ambient music and we intuitively move with our eyes closed, from a centered place, to expressing ShadowMan's energy. Via body movements, each person practices moving back and forth between these two dimensions in a comfortable way. I usually demonstrate first, reminding them that this is not dance, it's *intuitive movement* initiated by a connection to the vibration of that particular self. Gilbert benefits from being immersed in the matrix of ShadowMan energy, and from the group sharing afterward. The insights from each person about oneself are often surprising, and readily available.

Another technique for working with dreams and Voice Dialogue in a group is what I call *DreamDrama*. This is a tool for amplifying the connection to a sub-personality that emerged during a prior individual or group Voice Dialogue session. I usually wait at least a few hours before reengaging these energies, so the dreamer can practice connecting to that self from a fresh viewpoint.

Gilbert shares his dream with the group, and I ask him to choose a part of the dream that invites further exploration. He decides that the part where the houses higher up the mountain are disheveled, keeping visitors away, holds the most sadness and loss of hope. I direct him to stand in the middle of the circle and pick five people from the group to represent the visitors who didn't have the opportunity to be in the guesthouses. Gilbert carefully chooses and places the people in the center of the circle in a way that is right for him. I tell him the rest of us sitting in the circle's periphery represent the houses.

I face Gilbert and guide him into his dream Gilbert self. His features change into a visible sadness as he enters the energy. Gilbert knows how to do DreamDrama, and he trusts his unconscious will produce important material through active imagination. The "visitors" are instructed to follow their intuition in the drama while also drawing on the elements of Gilbert's dream. They too enter an altered state that connects them to Gilbert's unconscious. This intuitive, telepathic connection of everyone's unconscious while doing DreamDrama always expresses valuable material for the dream teller, and is something the facilitator can rely upon.

When he is ready, Gilbert says, "Action," and the drama comes alive, with the visitors wandering around to examine the houses, shaking their heads, and speaking to one another about how they can't stay in these broken-down homes. At first Gilbert watches, then begins sobbing, at which point the visitors go to him. Some comfort him, and others beg him to fix the houses so they can stay there. The drama goes on for five minutes; when the exchange lessens, I call, "cut."

All the players stay in place, as I ask Gilbert, then the others, to share what they felt and understood by being in the embodied dream. In addition to the weight of his sadness and despair, Gilbert realizes that the visitors are the energies within him who can repair the guesthouses, that they are strong and motivated to make changes. He feels there are many of them, a whole village of selves ready to work together to repair the old and even build new homes. I ask him if he's curious about what new parts of himself will visit and inhabit the restructured guesthouses, or renewed Gilbert. He responds that he's excited about this. Then the rest of the group in the outer circle, the "houses," share their observations and feelings as that part of him. Gilbert takes in all the sharing and sometimes responds. The session ends with him thanking us all and saying he will never forget this experience.

Finally, Voice Dialogue DreamWork has been a primary tool for my counseling of people with chronic and terminal illness. These people are plunged into a confusing emotional morass, and working with their dreams offers them hope — perhaps not for physical healing, but hope that they can identify and learn to manage the contradictory dynamics their psyches exhibit under duress. And when death beckons, the numinous dream elements present themselves. Dialoguing with them is extraordinary. Facilitating a dying person's introduction to and energetic infusion of the numinous figures, symbols, and experiences is my humblest privilege.

A Journey Into the Realm
of the Unconscious:
Voice Dialogue Sand Play Work

Miriam Dyak, BA, CC

At the Stones' last Summer Kamp in Philo, California, in 1994, John Swinburne from Australia offered to do Voice Dialogue sessions incorporating sand play figures. I signed up to try it out, and I was immediately entranced! I did not at first grasp all of the potential in using small figures and objects to represent the selves, but I could feel right away that there was something wonderfully powerful in having a tangible, visible representation of the self as I moved into it and separated out from it. I caught the spark before I could understand all its implications (as we so often do). Then I spent the next few years combing second-hand shops, flea markets, etc., to build up a collection for Voice Dialogue Sand Play while I waited to have a place where I could do this work. My boxes of crazy kitsch were bursting at the seams when the room across the hall from my office became vacant. I rented it, put up shelves, purchased two trays and the right kind of sand to put in them, and began what has been a deep and magical journey of Voice Dialogue Sand Play work with my clients and students.

Before I started with Voice Dialogue Sand Play, I anticipated that it would be adventurous and a lot of fun, but I never imagined how extraordinarily profound an effect this work could have on my clients. In many cases, I saw people go through significant life changes in a surprisingly short time with the accelerating energy of this process. Who would guess that a "bunch of props" in a pile of sand could induce such a transformational experience? I began to see that adding Sand Play to Voice Dialogue was a match made in heaven. However, to my knowledge, only a few Voice Dialogue facilitators in the US and in Australia have incorporated Sand Play into their practices thus far. The figures we used at Summer Kamp were remnants of Hal Stone's sand tray collection that he had used in his days as a Jungian analyst, and most Sand Play (or Sand Tray) therapists around the world are Jungian based. I have so far encountered little interest in the mainstream Jungian Sand Play community in learning about Voice Dialogue Sand Play, and only a few brave Voice Dialogue facilitators have already jumped in and started building a Sand Play collection. I hope to provide an introduction to the possibilities of this work that might inspire more curiosity and excitement about combining Voice Dialogue with Sand Play therapy, and I am happy to be available for consultation with any facilitators who would like support in developing a Voice Dialogue Sand Play practice of their own.

What Exactly Is Voice Dialogue Sand Play?

The simplest explanation might be that it's a Voice Dialogue session in which the person being facilitated chooses a number of objects, arranges them in a tray filled with sand, and then uses them as representations of her/his own inner selves. For example, a female client selects a large bear, several trees, an old woman, and a boat. She positions these in her tray wherever it occurs to her to put them, perhaps digging down in the sand to make a pond-like place for the boat. The trees are next to it, and so is the bear. The old woman is alone on the opposite side of the tray. The client and her facilitator have a conversation about what is in the tray — the same kind of conversation they would have in a regular Voice Dialogue about the different selves and which one might need to speak first. Perhaps the client decides that the old woman in the tray is a primary part of who she is, a familiar known quantity, and the facilitation might start there. As in a regular Voice Dialogue session, the facilitator would ask the client to physically move over in order to be the self that is represented by the old woman. What is different from other Voice Dialogue work is that the client would be moving over to become and to speak as this particular figure of an old woman. This approach to Sand Play, I should point out, is very different from the traditional Jungian-based Sand Play work. Only in Voice Dialogue would the client move, embody, and speak from the voice of any of the figures in the tray.

What are the Advantages of Working with Voice Dialogue Sand Play?

I suspect that each facilitator who explores this way of working with selves will develop a list of favorite aspects of the work from their own and their clients' experience. For me, the main advantages of Voice Dialogue Sand Play are the enhanced separation, access to the Unconscious and the archetypes, the recognition factor, and what I would call *real-time change*.

Enhanced Separation: Identifying a self with a tangible, visible object in real space and time gives a concrete reality to the self that is not necessarily as clear in a regular Voice Dialogue facilitation. In Sand Play, when the subject comes back to Aware Ego he/she can see not only the place in the room where the self was located, but also an actual object as a vivid physical and energetic representation of that self. The sensual reality of the self/object is undeniable, and consequently the separation is most often more pronounced and long lasting. That is to say, that the client is more likely to understand, feel, and remember their separation from the self as real.

In addition to separation from the selves that are facilitated during the session, there is also a separation from the other selves/figures in the tray because they are also real, solid, visible, and clearly physically separate from the Aware Ego even if they didn't all get a chance to speak. Just observing them creates a separation that wouldn't be available in a regular Voice Dialogue session with selves that are mentioned but not facilitated.

At the end of the session, we take photos of the whole tray and of the individual pieces, giving the client clear evidence of all the selves that were in the tray. Instead of a vague idea of other selves that might be in play around the client's focus for the session, there is a full picture of the energies/beings — what they look like and where they are positioned in relationship to each other. I encourage clients to continue the work on their own, using the photos as a way to remember the selves, experience their energy, and let them speak through journaling exercises or other forms of self-facilitation.

Access to the unconscious and the archetypes: Sand Play objects are closely related to the selves/energies that show up in our dreams. A client reaches for a green tree woman standing on the shelf. It looks like a woman whose feet are roots, whose body is a tree trunk, and whose arms stretch out into branches and leaves. Halfway through the session, when this tree woman is facilitated, we discover she's not only gentle and green, but also has a bright-red snake coiling up her back. Almost every Sand Play figure brings surprise, something the person being facilitated didn't realize at first when they chose it, and with that surprise comes deeper revelation about the inner self who is connected to the figure.

As with dream work, Voice Dialogue Sand Play also gives us greater access to archetypal energies. I often see a client bring a wild animal or a fireman or a red convertible sports car or a mythological being into the tray and be amazed (after the fact) that they have called in a real spirit, a live energy. When people feel this aliveness, then it often can and does call them in turn into a greater level of being. After such an encounter with the essence of an energy, the client and I both are changed, and go forward from this moment in a new and sometimes transformative consciousness.

Because of this almost guaranteed access to the Unconscious, Sand Play work can be especially powerful and helpful when the client's process has plateaued, when dreams are scarce, or when the client comes in without a clear sense of where to focus next. In these instances (in almost every case) I have found that Sand Play creates an opening to a deeper level of the work.

The recognition factor: What I am calling the recognition factor is simply what happens when a person spots a particular figure on a shelf and suddenly recognizes a part of themselves. In fact, it's often the self that sees itself reflected in a pod of dolphins leaping over waves, or in a raggedy little child, or in a fierce black panther, or even in a simple lotus seedpod. One moment the figure is just an ordinary statue sitting on a shelf, and the next it comes alive through the spark of recognition. In that moment the self emerges, perhaps for the first time ever, into this person's consciousness. I have seen a client reach for an object and suddenly burst into tears, or hold a figure in their hand, and break into an ancient dance they had no idea they knew. This same recognition factor is part of why people "fall in love" with a piece of jewelry or a kind of car — it holds an energy for them that reflects a self that has been missing or hidden. Walking into a Voice Dialogue Sand Play room is like walking into a dream world where inner selves can find their outer reflections, and as a result feel honored, acknowledged, even redeemed.

Real-time change: What I mean by change happening in real time within the context of a Voice Dialogue Sand Play session is that movement in the tray is not only symbolic but often constitutes real and lasting change in the person's life. This already occurs in regular Voice

Dialogue work— separating from a self physically, energetically, and psychologically creates an actual opening in the moment in which the Aware Ego Process can come into being and grow.

This same separation occurs and is also enhanced in Voice Dialogue Sand Play. The work often reaches transfigurative moments where a self/figure opts to move itself to a different part of the tray and/or to newly align itself with other figures. For example, a child figure might be under the uncomfortable wing of a threatening parent figure. Across the tray is a large, ferocious-looking lion representing both a threat that the parent uses to scare the child and the instinctual energies the parent wants to socialize out of the child. If there is a revelatory moment in which the child self suddenly sees the lion as an ally, and moves across to tray to be with the lion, that is a moment of real shift in the person's life. I find that these kinds of movements that happen spontaneously in the course of Voice Dialogue Sand Play work create profound and real change in the person's process. We essentially have a new starting point from there on out.

What is Required to Work with Sand Play?

The essential requirement for all Sand Play work is a collection of objects from which one can build a world: animals of all kinds; people of all ages, races, occupations; gods, goddesses, supernatural beings; vehicles of all types; furniture; buildings/houses of many kinds; cartoon characters; miscellaneous objects such as children's wooden building blocks, colored glass "pebbles," mosaic tiles, cloth scraps, ribbons, artificial flowers, and objects from nature such as shells, seedpods, driftwood, and stones. All of these have to be small enough to fit inside a tray of sand that is not larger than one's peripheral vision is wide. (I try to keep my objects in a range from one to twelve inches in height.)

One also needs to have space — shelves, drawers, baskets, etc. — to display these objects in a room where one can work privately with clients and where there is a space for one or more trays to hold sand. The tray should have a base under it, preferably on wheels so it can be moved easily. And, since Voice Dialogue Sand Play is done mostly with adults, it helps if the base brings the tray to about waist height of a standing adult (see references for online sand tray sources). That way it's easy for the subject to arrange the pieces in the tray without having to get down on the floor to do it, and it's also possible to sit in a chair and have everything in the tray easily visible. I usually have at least two chairs in the room, three if I'm working with a couple.

The sand to fill the trays should be clean, not so fine that it might be dusty and cause breathing problems for you or your clients, and preferably earth toned so as to give a sense of ground. I use a type of sand called *Lapis luster, 2nd to finest California beach sand*, which I bought from a local mineral company. The grains are small but clearly visible, and comprise a mixture of colors from light beige to dark brown that overall give a mottled earth-tone impression. If you know of Sand Play therapists in your area, it could be helpful to ask them what they use and where they bought it. Sand that you yourself gather from beaches might bring unwanted animals and substances into your Sand Play space that could possibly be harmful to your collection of objects.

A Comprehensive Guide to the Use of Sandtray in Psychotherapy and Transformational Settings by Gisela De Domenico (1988, 1994, 2000) is one of the best all-round guides to setting up a Sand Play environment, complete with descriptions of the kinds of pieces needed and how best to display them. A core principle is that there should be enough organization to the display of objects so that the client is not overwhelmed by chaos. It should be relatively easy to find things; i.e. all the animals are together, all the natural objects together, all the household objects together, etc. At the same time, it's important that the organization not go so far as to prejudice the client's perception of the figures. For example, one could group all the Christian figures together, all the Hindu figures together, all the Jewish figures together, etc., but it would not be a good idea to group all the religious figures by one's own idea of good and bad, angelic and demonic. Similarly, it's a good idea to group people by men, women, children, and families, but not to influence the client's choice by making groupings of what I, the facilitator, think might go well together.

Characteristics of Voice Dialogue Sand Play

Every Sand Play facilitator or therapist will create his/her own unique collection of figures. The collections truly reflect the creativity and personality of each person who does this work, and no two collections are exactly alike. At the same time, there are two major differences between Voice Dialogue Sand Play and most other Sand Play work. First, the majority of Jungian-based Sand Play work is done with children, while Voice Dialogue Sand Play is usually done with adults, since it is not generally helpful to encourage children to separate from their selves while they are still developing a Primary Self System. Second, the figures are used in Voice Dialogue to represent a wide range of inner selves. These two factors together may result in a greater proportion of human and mythical figures in a Voice Dialogue Sand Play collection, as well as more "adult content" in the collection overall. In my own collection, for example, men, women, couples, families, children, gods, goddesses, and supernatural beings easily take up almost half the space in the room.

I have included sexually explicit figures and antique items that would be either inappropriate or liable to get broken in a collection used with children. I also do not have a wet sand tray for molding into sand castles, etc., as many of my objects would not survive that kind of play.

How Much Do I need to Get Started?

De Domenico's book does give a clear idea of the basics needed for a successful Sand Play environment, but you really can begin with a lot less than she recommends. You need your collection to be big enough to give people lots of choices. Optimally it should include too many pieces for the rational mind to catalogue and remember, which means clients can't think their way through their choices. Intuition and feeling have to come into play. It pays to start somewhat small and inexpensively, and let the bulk of figures come from garage sales and the less expensive second-hand stores such as Goodwill or Value Village (in the United States). The toys your children (or your friends' children) have outgrown can also be an inexpensive way to help you get started. Once you begin collecting for Sand Play, you'll start seeing potential selves everywhere you go, and the temptation will be strong to graduate to antique malls, gift shops, and online catalogs, and to keep adding pricier items to your collection. A good strategy is to begin working with the process before you invest too much. That way you can discover which kinds of pieces get used the most, and you'll also learn which pieces clients ask for that you don't yet have in your collection.

The most essential tools are your imagination and your delight in working with the unconscious. This process, like dream work, calls for a love of archetypal energies, an ability to think symbolically, and a true appreciation of the unexpected. Oddly enough, the pieces you collect will be most useful if they also capture and express this imagination. I look for expression in figures, ones that look real and alive, and I avoid those that are vapidly sweet or too generic in their energy.

How to Structure a Voice Dialogue Sand Play Session.

It has been an ideal setup for me to have an office for regular Voice Dialogue work and a separate room just for sand play. I always begin a session sitting with my client(s) in the regular office, talking about what has been happening since the last session, what the selves are up to, and where the client feels she/he wants to go with the work. A client might come in saying she feels it's a day for Sand Play work. More often than not, though, something in what she's saying about her life and her process catches my attention, and I have an intuitive feeling to suggest taking the session into the Sand Play process. That might be well received, or the client might decide, "No, not today." Sometimes, though, we run up against a self that has strong judgments or fears about using the Sand Play process. If that's the case, as always with Voice Dialogue work, we start where we are, and we honor the self that doesn't like the idea of Sand Play by moving to it and listening to what it has to say. In doing that, a whole world of understanding may open up and we might leave actually working with Sand Play to another time (if at all).

When we do decide to take the session into Sand Play, I pretty consistently follow these nine steps in working with this process:

1. Introducing the Sand Play room

2. Choosing a tray

3. Grounding

4. Choosing the figures/objects and placing them in the tray

5. Conversation about the world that the client has created in the tray

6. Facilitating figures/selves

7. Working in Aware Ego

8. Photographing the tray

9. Putting away the figures.

1. Introducing the Sand Play room: It can be overwhelming to some selves to walk into my Sand Play room. Shelves and baskets and parts of the floor are overflowing with so many energies! If the client has never done Sand Play work before, it helps to let them know that there's intentionally more stuff in the room than they can possibly see all at once, and that finding the right pieces will be intuitive and a process of discovery. There are often selves worried about "doing it right," so it helps so assure them that they really can't go wrong.

2. Choosing a tray: If you have only one tray, then you would bypass this step, but it's good to come into the Sand Play space and focus first on the tray as the ground for the work. With two different trays, the client picks one, and I wheel the other out of the room to make more space.

3. Grounding: I guide my clients in a grounding meditation before they choose any pieces and begin the work. This is something that I have developed and added to the process. As far as I know, it has no counterpart in Jungian-based Sand Play. We take the lid off the tray, and both the client and I, standing across from each other, place our hands on the smooth sand. We both close our eyes, and I guide them in a meditation (about 3–5 minutes) that's a bit different every time I do it, but usually begins with breathing down through the body into the ground and feeling truly supported by the earth. I add, "When we go to meet the unconscious, it's good to do that from a grounded, supported place, held by the earth, held by the universe."

Once we've established that grounding, I guide the client in feeling how their current focus is living inside them. Perhaps, for example, I might be working with someone who came in talking about an ongoing frustration and miscommunication in their family. After deciding that Sand Play might really shed some new light on this issue, and after grounding, I would direct their attention to the story they had been telling me about the family. I might remind them of a few specific things they said earlier, and then direct them to bring their attention inward so that they could begin to feel "how the story is living inside them." We would follow that attention through their different levels of being — how the story is living inside their physical body/being, emotional body/being, mental body/being, and spiritual body/being.

Once the person has had an opportunity to become aware of how this story is affecting them on these four levels, I instruct as follows: "While you have been focusing on your story and how this story lives inside all the levels of your being, the energy of your focus affects the environment around you. It affects all the little beings in this room, and some of them "wake up" to your story. In a few moments (not yet), when you open your eyes and look around, you'll find that everything looks and feels a little different than when you first walked in. Some pieces will seem to almost reach out to you and say, *Take me!* And some of those you'll look at and think, *Why of course, that makes perfect sense!* Others you might look at and think, *Why on earth would I ever want that thing?* I recommend that you be open to both. We're working in sand, not stone. Everything is changeable. When you're ready, open your eyes, look around, and see who or what might want to come be in your Sand Play world today."

4. Choosing the figures and placing them in the tray: Moving through the space and selecting pieces flows naturally out of the guided process. The client is now tuned into her selves in a deep way, and from that awareness everything really does look different to her than when she first came into the room. I sit in a chair and focus on keeping my energetic linkage with her while she explores mostly in silence. At some point I offer the possibility that if she finds herself looking for something specific, it's a good idea to ask, as I might be able to help her find it. Clients often ask if there is a limit to how many pieces they can choose, and I always reply that they are free to pick as many or as few as they like. As in a dream, everything in a Sand Play world has the potential to reveal information. A hugely crowded tray heaped with lots and lots of objects reflects a reality in the psyche different from a world in which only one or two or three figures reside. It's important that the facilitator does not attempt to influence the client's choices on any level.

5. Conversation about the world that has been created: Once the client feels the tray is complete, she needs to find a place to stand or sit in relation to the miniature world she has put together — this is where operating ego/ Aware Ego will be located in the room. Then the facilitator and subject need to have a conversation that will help identify what is primary and what is disowned in the tray so they can determine where to begin talking with the selves. I like to ask some version of these three questions:

- ◆ Which piece(s) here in the tray seems most familiar to you, most like the way you usually are? (If they've done a lot of Voice Dialogue work, I might say, "most primary.")

- ◆ Is there anything here you find repulsive or frightening? Something you feel is definitely not you?

- ◆ What are you most curious about? Is there a particular piece you'd most like to explore, one where you'd be disappointed if we didn't have the time to talk with it?

One important note here is that as we discuss the pieces in the tray, I make sure that I am sitting slightly off to one side to avoid placing myself in the client's direct line of vision. I don't want to be in the way of her/his view of the tray or to insert myself into the dream reality she/he has created.

6. Facilitating figures/selves: The first self to be facilitated might not be one of the figures in the tray at all. As with any Voice Dialogue session, we need to start with what is most primary and/or the self that has the most reservations about the process. It's not unusual for a client to step back, look at the tray, and say, "I don't like any of this!" The beauty of the work is that one can have the client move over into that self, and honor it by listening not only to what it doesn't like about the figures in the tray but also what else in the person's life it finds disturbing. If I ask if there is a figure that might represent this self, it may actually say that one of the pieces in the tray does represent its energy, or it may pull another piece off the shelves and put it where it wants to be. Once we have some Aware Ego in relation to this gatekeeper, the way may open to talking with several of the other pieces in the tray.

Facilitation of Sand Play selves is very much like all Voice Dialogue facilitation, with some additional possibilities. Often the person being facilitated will move a lot in the manner suggested by the figure, or physically strike a similar pose, which means the body can become even more active than usual in bringing through the energy of the self. As facilitator, you can point out certain aspects of the figure and ask questions about them. Perhaps in talking with a monster that has a lot of chains attached to it, you could ask how the chains got there, or with a clown holding a hoop, you could ask if he expects anything to jump through it. It's possible to ask Sand Play figures what they would like to change in the tray, and what would have to change in the person's life to make that possible. They may or may not be able to go ahead and make the change right on the spot. Sometimes a particular self might also go to the shelves on its own and bring in a new figure/object — something to represent either a supportive force or oppositional energy. It's also possible that the first figure representing a self was really chosen by another self that judges it. The self may say, "This isn't really me or what I look like." I then might ask the self then to find a figure that does represent its energy accurately, and put that in the tray instead. The possibilities are abundant; I've mentioned just a few.

7. Working in Aware Ego: In Sand Play work as with all Voice Dialogue work, I have clients move back into the Aware Ego after each and every self. It's always important to remember that our primary purpose is the development of an Aware Ego Process. Because of the enhanced separation from selves in the Sand Play work, you may find a new solidity in the Aware Ego, and a heightened ability on the part of the client to tell the difference between the experience of being captured in a self's energy and that of being at center in the Aware Ego. I use the Awareness position less often with Sand Play because awareness seems to some extent to be built into the visual and physical separation from the figures/selves in the tray. Bringing energies into Aware Ego, and learning to regulate and blend them, sometimes seems easier to do in Voice Dialogue Sand Play. This is probably because the selves become hyper-real in this way of working, and the energies are so clearly defined.

8. Photographing the tray: Photos are great for the client to have and work with. They also help the facilitator remember the session. I always ask the client if they would like photos, and if the answer is yes, I take digital photos to send to them via email. I wheel the tray to a corner of the room where there is a blank wall for background, because I don't want to include random other pieces in the picture. I begin by taking a photo of the whole tray from the same angle that the client's Aware Ego was seeing it. Photos also include a view of the whole tray from the opposite side, and then views of individual pieces and/or small vignettes of objects. It's not unusual for a person to discover a whole new aspect of the figure/self while looking at a close-up photo.

9. Putting away the figures: A client may or may not want to participate in putting the figures away at the end of the session. I leave that option open without implying that this is something for which they are responsible. With or without the client's participation, it's very important that all the pieces are returned to the shelves or containers where they were found, the sand smoothed over in the tray, and the lid put back on the tray so that all is ready for the next session.

Using Voice Dialogue Sand Play in Couples Work

I am always in awe of what happens in all Voice Dialogue work, and am amazed by the rapid changes that come as the result of separating from selves. Working with couples in Voice Dialogue Sand Play can be doubly exciting in this way. Everything a couple decides to do in the context of Sand Play provides rich information for the process. They may put their figures together in one tray or each select her/his own tray. Either way, the facilitator will have a graphic and tangible picture of their respective selves and how they do or don't interact. The most moving and enlightening moments for me are when a pattern of interaction in the relationship suddenly becomes totally clear to the selves involved, and completely visible to everyone in the room.

One person may have complained all along that the other is not giving them enough space, but now that his giant octopus really is half burying her little Volkswagen bug in the sand, he really gets it. The reports I hear from couples in later sessions often confirm that the realizations in the Sand Play session carry over into daily life, i.e. that he really is more conscious now of how he takes up space, and she's become more conscious of keeping her vehicle on the road. Hugely helpful as well is the humor that comes out of the experience. Once the couple can joke about his "eight arms getting in the way" or about her needing "to upgrade to a larger vehicle," they are on their way to more Aware Ego Process in their relationship.

In summary I would like to reemphasize that Sand Play adds a profound and magical quality to Voice Dialogue facilitation. It allows for great imagination and creativity on the part of both client and facilitator, and it brings many if not all the benefits of dream work, regardless of whether the client is able to remember her dreams. Furthermore, even though collecting figures for Voice Dialogue Sand Play can become a passion, one truly can start with a fairly small collection and only one tray of sand. I have found that different clients may see the same piece in a great variety of ways — for example one person's wicked stepmother may show up as another person's symbol of positive feminine power. With each piece carrying the potential for such varied meaning, your small collection may carry many more energies than you might assume at first glance.

The story goes that the entire field of Sand Play work was actually started by a child or children who were in therapy with a Jungian therapist. The therapist had a box of sand on one side of the room and some toys on the other, and it was the children who put them together and began creating "dream worlds" out of their own psyches. The therapist caught on to the significance and potential of this process and Sand Play/Sand Tray was born. I have no way to verify this story, but I have seen over and over again the inner selves of all ages light up with this work. The selves seem excited and honored to be represented in this way, which makes facilitating them all the more satisfying and inspiring.

References

De Domenico, G. *Sandtray-Worldplay: A Comprehensive Guide to the Use of Sandtray in Psychotherapy and Transformational Settings.* Oakland, CA: Vision Quest Images (1988, 1994, 2000).

Online resources for Sand Play equipment:

Uniquity (www.uniquitypsych.com/index.html) has equipment and books for sale. They offer the standard rectangular trays used by most Sand Play therapists.

Ron's Trays (www.sandtrays.com) makes wonderful trays and stands including an octagonal wooden tray that has been everyone's favorite. Nine times out of ten clients choose the octagonal tray.

Section III

Practical Applications in Everyday Life

Tending our Aware Ego Process in Daily Life

Martha-Lou Wolff, PhD

We have Voice Dialogue sessions to get to know our selves and gain the awareness we need in order to have conscious choice in our relationship to them. We experience our selves with this process by embodying them, sensing their energy, seeing the world through their eyes, and hearing their beliefs. We separate from them when we move back to the center, and notice that what we sense there is different from when we were in the self. During a session we have an opportunity to step away and witness what occurred. This increases our awareness. Each time we return to the center, an Aware Ego Process (AEP) is ignited.

Voice Dialogue facilitation initiates this process, but it is not actualized until we use it in our everyday life. We can set intentions in a session; however, our ability to be conscious comes into being, moment-to-moment, as we make choices while respectfully taking into account the selves that have opinions about, and are affected by, each choice. Every situation we are in gives us an opportunity to practice our Aware Ego Process.

We have found that we cannot be aware continuously. Most of the time we are on autopilot, using habitual ways of being. Then, we have a moment of awareness and can reorient ourselves. So far, no amount of work establishes a permanent state of conscious choice. The change we hope for is an increased fluidity in our access to our Aware Ego Process.

This ability can be strengthened if we pay regular attention to it. In fact, we are learning from neuroscience that not only our thoughts and behavior can change, but also the substance of the brain can be modified with repetitive intentional activity, such as meditation. As Daniel Siegel says in *Mindsight* (2010), "The intentional focus of attention... stimulates new pattern of neural firing to create new synaptic linkage." With this in mind, it is possible to approach our Aware Ego Process with the same effort as people who meditate, knowing that the continual practice of it leads to the most fruitful results. *If we want lasting transformation, what we do daily is as important as having Voice Dialogue sessions.*

Keeping our AEP Happening

Facilitations can be powerful experiences, and they have immediate impact, but this often fades over time. If we systematically follow a session with activities that repeat it, the effect can be prolonged. To offer a variety of exercises for this purpose, Lawrence Novick, Marsha Sheldon, and I wrote *The AEP Workbook* (2005).

One of the exercises we recommend is writing a summary of what was experienced in each self, what it felt like to return to the center, what perspective was gained by witnessing from the Awareness Level, and finally, how it felt in the center at the end. By having this description of these steps, a session can be re-experienced during the days after the session. This may take only a few moments. Some people choose to record their sessions for a more thorough review. Either of these techniques can supplement gains from the time spent in the session itself.

Most of us do a great deal with our AEP in our daily lives. I believe that people who incorporate it into their way of being are the ones who fully appreciate its value. But mostly we do this without thinking much about it. I ask a colleague if he practiced his Aware Ego Process regularly. He had to take a moment before he realized how aspects of it had become routine for him. It is important for us as teachers and facilitators to explicitly encourage a personal practice of the AEP, so that the work done in sessions is reinforced in daily life.

Specific Exercises

Any time that we feel the tension of the opposites that were facilitated, we can have a tune-up by literally redoing the session briefly: Sit in the center, move to a self and return to the center, then move to another self and return to the center, move to a witness position to observe, and return to the center to see what you experience. We gain new appreciation for the selves and our relationship to them each time we do this.

After a session we know that Primary Selves have a huge gravitational pull. We continually return to their domain. When we become aware of this and wish to reconnect with the more disowned self, we can repeat the session on our own. By so doing we intentionally create an energetic adjustment.

Another way to keep up our relationship with our selves is to practice dialing in their energies by choice, experiencing them in varying degrees. Sitting in the center, imagine a pair of opposite selves on either side of you. Begin with one of them, bring in the energy a very little bit, like 10%, which is a good level to check in with a self. Then tune it up to 50%. It begins to feel like it has the whole truth, but you are still present and can consult with it. Then imagine a situation in which this is the self that you want to carry. Dial in the energy 80% or 90%. At this level the perspective, energy, and intention of this self are fully accessible. At the same time, you are present to monitor it, and to move it out when you feel the time is right. Finally, thank the self, and separate from it by dialing its energy down to 0%. Repeat this procedure with the opposite self. When you finish you may want to step away to the Awareness Level and observe what you experienced. Return to the center and experience how the shift takes place. Each time we do this, we gain another small increment in our capacity for an Aware Ego Process with these two selves.

It may seem like doing these exercises on our own is artificial. I remember the first Voice Dialogue sessions I had. I thought when I moved to a self I would be faking it, but soon the reality of selves became clear. In the same way, allowing oneself to do some exercises soon reveals the power of understanding that comes with regular practice.

A number of other exercises, including consultation and negotiation with selves, are described in *The AEP Workbook* (2005). It is a guide for deepening our AEP.

Since writing the book, I have begun to explore the idea of setting boundaries with selves. A friend asked me recently, "Can I fire a primary self?" I suggested, as I usually do, "Probably it's better to give it a hug and thank it for giving you what you needed to get to this point in your life. Tell it you have some new ways of being you would like to try now. Then promise to check in with it continually as you make your choices." After that I read an article for mothers about setting boundaries with their toddlers. I began to think that primary selves, in a way, are like children: They have their absolute beliefs, energies, and strategies that they want us to follow. Perhaps there is no harm in being more forceful with them by expressly drawing a line. I think it reassures them to know we are developing the capacity to be in charge, in the same way this is comforting to children. Consciously choosing a very specific boundary, consistently maintaining it, and showing the self our life is going well often leads to new ways of being and calms the primary self.

In my own life, I have had to do this with the part of me that does not want me to have a sexual relationship unless I am married. It was born in the 1950s, and this part lives on strongly in me. When it is facilitated, this self says that it is worried that I will be running around chasing sexual partners and that I will lose my dignity. I have had to reassure it that running around is not what I have in mind. I will continue to be monogamous. The new specific limit I want to set is that I do not have to marry someone in order to have a sexual relationship, but I will be as faithful as if I were married. Establishing this boundary and repeatedly, intentionally setting it has allowed enduring change.

Another specific exercise is to create cues to alert us to observe our Aware Ego Process. One cue I am particularly fond of is guilt. We feel it when we have acted on the urgings of one self without taking into consideration the self with an opposite point of view. By noticing when we feel guilty, we can immediately describe the two selves at hand. One is telling us we did something bad, and the other was in charge when we acted. After noting this pair of opposites, we can begin to be more conscious of them, have facilitations of them, and eventually when we are in a similar situation, we can choose our action after consulting with both sides. Besides helping us be aware of our Process, this practice decreases the amount of guilt we have in our lives.

Expand

Having precise cues like this to focus our attention increases the likelihood we will practice our Process frequently.

Just for the fun of it, we can create experiments in which we use specific selves in a new way. We can pick a situation and decide to bring in a self we would not normally have present. After consulting with our primary selves to be informed of the potential pitfalls, we can negotiate a plan. Often the outcome is quite different from what the primary selves believed, and gives us a reality check on their assumptions. For an entertaining and thought-provoking read of an extreme experimenter, see *The Guinea Pig Diaries* (2009), by A. J. Jacobs.

Capturing the Support in our Dreams

Dreaming is another regular occurrence to which we can pay attention because it sheds light on our Process. There are many profound and illuminating ways to work with dreams. These are especially useful in the context of therapy with someone experienced with them. Incorporating dream exploration into a daily practice often intimidates people who do not feel capable of dream interpretation on their own, or who are not willing to spend much time on dreams.

In order to respect this reluctance, I suggest a simplified approach, a question to ask as we are remembering a dream. It is possible to focus on a specific scene in the dream (or the end of the dream) and ask, "What self was being inducted at that moment?" We have just been feeling a self. Making an effort to describe the experience builds our vocabulary and our ability to characterize the qualities of that self. We can rely on the wisdom of the unconscious to invite us to get to know the most relevant selves for a particular time in our life.

If the self is unknown or feels threatening, it is good to have a facilitation to experience it and gain more clarity about it. If the self is already familiar, and the induction of it is a reminder to pay attention to it, then it is possible to be extra alert to this self during the day. We can ask, "How is it influencing me?" and "What does it need me to know?" and "How can I honor it?"

Making a daily practice of noting one self that is contained in a dream gives us a rich explorative palate. If we look at dreams as free Voice Dialogue facilitations, we can capture a brilliant insight into what parts of us are in need of attention. It is possible to reap a gift from a dream every time we remember one.

Developing a Practice Community

This is an inward voyage to map and experience our landscape, and an outward search to compare notes with others. Being able to speak about our reflections during the day in this way reinforces our Process and enhances the transformation we are making. I believe that those of us in the early training groups who established facilitation buddies to trade sessions and share dreams with between classes sailed with what we were learning with much more agility. I generally recommend that my students find someone at their level to practice with, or at least share their dreams with, to have some outside reflection on them. This can be done in person or on the phone. Often people travel a long way to participate in a training, and then return to their homes where they are isolated. Having someone to discuss their dreams with helps this work to become a regular practice.

Connections with other people who engage in this work also provide an excellent opportunity to observe our interactions and to study our bonding patterns with them. When someone else knows about the interpersonal dynamics of selves, we can explore these by referring back to an encounter together, diagramming the movement of energy. Sometimes we are able to stop the action midstream, step back into a place of Awareness, and review what has just happened. Doing this too often definitely interrupts the relationship, but done from time to time, it provides us an opportunity to harvest invaluable understanding of how we interact. These connections we create and maintain with others play a significant role in supporting and sustaining our practice.

We do this work to gain the benefits of ongoing change. We do not achieve a sustained state of conscious choice, but over time we notice our blind spots more quickly and enrich our adeptness at engaging our Aware Ego Process. Intentionally using it in our everyday life goes a long way to help us nourish what we have learned on this journey and to continue learning.

References

Begley, S. *Train your mind, change your brain: how a new science reveals our extraordinary potential to transform ourselves.* New York: Ballantine Books, 2007.

Jacobs, A. J. *The guinea pig diaries: my life as an experiment.* New York: Simon & Schuster, 2009.

Siegel, D. *Mindsight: the new science of personal transformation.* New York: Bantam Books, 2010.

Wolff, M-L., L. Novick, and M. Sheldon. *The AEP workbook: practical exercises for deepening our Aware Ego Process.* California, SCVDI, 2005.

ADVOCACY AND THE
PSYCHOLOGY OF THE AWARE EGO

Ruth Berlin, LCSW-C

If I am not for myself, who will be?
If I am only for myself, what am I?
If not now, when?
— Hillel the Elder, 1:14

I never planned on being a middle-aged environmental health advocate — certainly not after more than two decades as a psychotherapist. But life writes its own script.

In 1990 I was living in Los Angeles, married with a four-year-old son. I was deeply involved in learning and practicing Voice Dialogue with Drs. Hal and Sidra Stone, as I had done since 1984. In June of that year, however, the California Department of Agriculture sprayed the pesticide Malathion to eradicate fruit flies in parts of Los Angeles County. Initially I thought nothing of the spraying, which was taking place over fifteen miles from my home. I was ignorant of the fact that the sprayed pesticide drifted for miles. Like most people, I believed the officials who stated that only those living in the immediate areas being sprayed should remain indoors during the aerial applications. Consequently, my family spent our usual daylight hours enjoying the great California outdoors as much as possible, and paid no heed to the spraying.

But as the pesticide drifted for miles and miles, carried by the winds, it became more toxic as it transformed into its breakdown product, malaoxon, impacting many people, my family included. My son went into anaphylactic shock, which, thankfully, he survived. I became very sick with memory loss, chronic fatigue, joint pains, and more. Eventually I discovered that all my symptoms were listed under potential adverse reactions to the class of neurotoxic pesticides that includes Malathion.

For the past sixteen years I have been the executive director of the Maryland Pesticide Network (MPN). Running MPN, a coalition of twenty-five Maryland organizations concerned about the impact of pesticides on public health and the environment, is now my second full-time job. My first is my full-time private psychotherapy practice of nearly forty years. In both jobs, Voice Dialogue and the Psychology of Selves are essential to my work. This chapter focuses on applying the Psychology of Selves and Voice Dialogue to the world of activism and advocacy, and the importance of inner work for success in this critical arena. By identifying and working with our primary and disowned selves, as advocates of a "cause," we can circumvent the potential for self-righteousness and polarization that leads to failed attempts and frustration.

The Back Story

My physical reaction to Malathion was hardly unique. Pesticides can cause a wide range of acute and chronic illnesses. Low-dose, short- and long-term exposures to pesticides have been linked to cancers, reproductive dysfunction, developmental disabilities, immune system disorders, asthma and other respiratory diseases, and neurological and behavioral disorders.

In July 1990, shortly after our pesticide poisoning in L.A., my family moved to Annapolis, Maryland, where I got increasingly ill each year from May to October for what seemed no apparent reason. After three years, I learned that Malathion was being seasonally sprayed for mosquito control in my county. This catapulted me into a state of rage and a whirlwind of research and consultations with experts and organizations working on pesticide-related issues.

Deciding to act, I organized a public meeting to address the toxicity of the pesticide being used in the state's mosquito-control program, and the lack of notification to residents regarding the hazards of exposure. Media coverage of the well-attended event and a consequent meeting with the Maryland secretary of agriculture resulted in the state's halt of the use of Malathion and the substitution of a less toxic pesticide.

> *Each of us will know, in a deep and essential way, what*
> *part of the restoration of the natural world we have access*
> *to and what part we are responsible for preserving.*
>
> — Eisenstadt

Not long after, a pest-control operator sprayed my son's school while the children were in class. Once again my son had a life-threatening reaction. I contacted the Maryland PTA's legislative chair and asked if she knew that kids and pregnant moms and teachers were being exposed to these toxins. She did not, and was horrified by the prospect. That phone call in 1993 birthed the MPN. My environmental advocate self had now become a new primary self. Until that time the extent of my environmental consciousness and advocacy was a preference for organic fruits and vegetables, primarily for health reasons, but now, being an environmental health advocate was an identity I fully embraced.

Our coalition of twenty-five organizations lobbied for five years to pass the groundbreaking *Integrated Pest Management in Schools Law* that made illegal a repeat of what happened in my son's classroom — despite legions of pest-control industry lobbyists working against us. Prior to each year's legislative session, I had moments of doubt as to whether the Inner Wise Woman voice that prompted me to go forward was not just some Inner Masochist masquerading as Wise Woman, since it seemed that despite our best efforts we failed to pass legislation. But by the time the law passed, we had the support of an overwhelming number of legislators, as well as that of the governor.

Today, thirty-two states have similar laws, all modeled after the Maryland law. This was also the initial model for a federal bill still being debated in Congress, and for which I continue to lobby on Capitol Hill. When asked by the media what I think is the key to our success, I note the strength of our diverse coalition, teamwork, and our willingness to work with everyone — even those who did not consider themselves part of our team.

Over those five years, many seasoned lobbyists told me that we did not have a prayer of passing the bill given the corporate big guns aligned against us. What they didn't know was that my tool box included Voice Dialogue and the Psychology of Selves.

My first few years studying with Drs. Hal and Sidra Stone were very special. I was excited about incorporating their work into my psychotherapy practice. I had been a psychotherapist since 1972 and had studied Psychosynthesis for several years, but nothing had as profound an effect upon me and my work as did Voice Dialogue and the Aware Ego Process. Nor has anything since, yet I never imagined that this work would become essential to maneuvering the political and advocacy world that has become such a large part of my life, just as it has been to my personal evolution and psychotherapy work.

MPN has evolved into a highly regarded entity in Maryland's political, scientific, and public health arenas. MPN publishes a well-respected journal for healthcare providers, produces widely disseminated educational publications for the general public in English and Spanish, and conducts a pilot project with fourteen healthcare facilities, including Johns Hopkins and Sheppard Pratt hospitals, to reduce/eliminate their use of pesticides. In addition, MPN facilitates the *Pesticides and the Chesapeake Bay Watershed Project*, a 115-stakeholder project dedicated to reducing the occurrence and impact of pesticides on the bay. We make things happen. But in truth it's not simply a result of blood, sweat, and tears (though there's plenty of that, thanks to Workaholic and Slave-Driver selves).

I give major credit to my immersion in Voice Dialogue, the Psychology of Selves, and the Aware Ego Process for guiding my process as the MPN executive director and consequently impacting the work of MPN.

My spiritual teacher, Swami Muktananda, taught me experientially about the oneness of all creation — that we are but a microcosm of the macrocosm — and the need to honor all life. In my consequent pursuit of a more transpersonal approach to therapy, I entered a three-year training program in Psychosynthesis, a transpersonal psychology developed by the Italian psychiatrist Roberto Assagioli, which ultimately led me to the Psychology of Selves and Voice Dialogue.

> *The need to protect our basic vulnerability results in the development of our personality — the development of the "primary selves" that define us to ourselves and to the world.*
> — Stone and Stone, 1989

When I first became involved as a public health/environmental activist, my very logical Sensible Self (one of my Primary Selves) warned, "You need this like a hole in the head. How could you even consider taking on another project in your life? Do you really enjoy working until midnight or 1:00 am and getting up at 6:30 am to start all over again? Are you crazy?" My Layback Lady complained bitterly. Now there'd be even less downtime to just relax, piddle in the garden, paint her nails, read a book, pet the dog, hang out with family, sit in the sun, or watch her favorite TV shows.

So, I reflected on these words of wisdom. I dialogued with a bunch of my inner/Primary Selves and reflected on whether it was some self's need for recognition (perhaps my Savior/Rescuer, or my Pusher) that drives me to fill up precious time with more work. After much dialogue and reflection, I came to some realizations. I was aware of a rage-filled part of me that wanted to destroy the pesticide and pest-control industry for what it did to me and to so many others. And I wanted to do my part as a child of Holocaust survivors in confronting the poison the Nazis used to kill 6 million Jews, including much of my family. (The Nazis originally developed many of the pesticides employed today, for use in their death-camp gas chambers.) This angry self, which clearly bought into fantasies of David and Goliath and *Star Wars*, was actually a voice of revenge. Thankfully, I was able to separate out from her and, thanks to the Aware Ego Process, was able to use a small percent of her energy — a homeopathic dose, as the Drs. Stone often say — to transmute her vengeful anger into a willingness to firmly and powerfully confront opponents when appropriate.

Without a doubt, I realized the Savior/Rescuer in me would probably have a ball each time that potentially lifesaving legislation passed. She loves that kind of stuff; however, I did not want to be an advocate that would be unconsciously led by this self. I also realized that I feel a tremendous sense of rightness and peace in my advocacy work — a sense of destiny. These feelings are born out of my Healer and Wise Woman selves. Strengthening the Aware Ego Process (through separating out from my opposite primary selves) allowed me to chart a more balanced way of meeting the needs of my disparate selves.

Over the years, despite the disappointment when our efforts failed to pass sensible, life-protecting legislation, there has been a continued deep satisfaction and sense of purpose doing this work. I have worked, and continue to work, consciously to balance the needs of my Inner Child, Mystic, the Layback Lady, Wife and Mother, and others, with the needs of my Worker Bee in my two full-time jobs. I have mostly succeeded.

The World of Politics, Advocacy, and the Disowned Selves

> *Seeing ourselves as separate is the*
> *central problem in our political thinking.*
>
> — Gore

Pesticides catapulted me into an alien world, the strange world of politicians and advocates, breeds unto themselves. Legislators and environmental advocates alike often fervently believe they have a corner on Truth and Justice. Focused as they are on garnering power and attention, their language tends to be devoid of introspection. Environmental activists (not unlike legislators) focus on overcoming the world's "bad guys," and the need to battle and defeat them to protect public health and the environment, and save the planet. While their language is of climate change, post 9/11 chemical security, minimizing clear cutting of forests, wilderness protection, sustainable growth, endangered species, and the like, they are similar to legislators in that they rarely speak about personal needs, wants, vulnerability, feelings, the Divine force, and so on.

Most activists I know carry a strong identification with the voice of Justice. The well-meaning Activist Self's dedication to its specific cause can lead to self-righteousness that can bowl over friends, as well as perceived opponents. This passion is an essential driving force for service in the world. Unless, however, we are willing to separate out from this Primary Self, truly listen to our opponents from an Aware Ego, and identify the Disowned Selves they represent, we can be just as destructive as those we judge to be destructive because of our unwillingness to see the complete picture. The key, as in a family system or any relationship, is to identify and embrace both our primary and disowned selves to allow for all perspectives from an Aware Ego Process and find a way to work together.

I have come to know many Maryland state legislators over the past sixteen years, and I can say with confidence that most have primary selves that often have to do with being top dog and wielding power. For the most part the psychological, spiritual (as opposed to the religious), and political worlds do not come together for legislators. While many I have known have strong religious affiliations that impact their politics, they tend not to value introspection, and both elected officials and well-intentioned advocates tend to evidence little empathy for their opponents.

I believe that one of the reasons it took five years for my coalition to facilitate the passage of the ground-breaking *IPM in Schools* law was because it took *me* that long to identify and work on separating out from my primary selves and embracing the disowned selves exemplified by so many of my political opponents.

> *Whatever parts of us we try to get rid of in our personality, life will bring to us in the form of people who are exactly like our disowned selves… these disowned selves are like heat-seeking missiles, aimed at us by the intelligence of the universe and find us they will.*
>
> — Stone and Stone, 2000

Activists generally get paid relatively little and work a lot of overtime. They tend not to leave much room for self-awareness or spiritual pursuits. There simply is no time when you're racing the clock to save the planet. As ecopsychology's main spokesperson, Theodore Roszak, wrote, "The environmental movement went about its work of organizing, educating and agitating with little regard for the fragile psychological complexities of the public whose hearts and minds it sought to win" (Roszak, 1995, p. 93). To have true regard for the hearts and minds of others, we need to develop a similar level of regard for the gifts that our disowned selves provide us.

In order to successfully work with disparate stakeholder groups, our own inner work must include dialoguing with our inner disparate stakeholders. We must include such primary selves as my personal favorites, the Visionary, Activist, Inner Mystic, Environmentalist, Layback Lady, and Therapist/Facilitator selves, as well as access the disowned selves represented by our adversaries, such as our Machiavellian (cunning/deceitful) and instinctual energies.

It is important, however, to keep in mind that basic to the Voice Dialogue process is working first with our primary selves, which came into being to protect us. We must first work on separation from our primary selves who have worked tirelessly to ensure that our disowned selves stay disowned. We need to develop awareness of and separation from them prior to identifying and working with our disowned selves.

> *In Voice Dialogue, we honor the primary selves as the gate-keepers to the psyche and as the lifesavers and protectors they have been for our vulnerability. We don't trespass on the territory of the primary selves without their permission and we don't attempt to push past them in order to seek out vulnerable or disowned selves. … This means first working with only the primary selves until the subject has begun to separate from these selves and they are comfortable allowing the work to move into the disowned selves as well."*

> —Dyak

Early on in my activist work, I received a threatening note in my mailbox consisting of words clipped from magazines. It said, "May a swarm of mosquitoes nest in your hairy armpits." (I guess the writer believed female activists don't shave their underarms; for the record, I do!) In hindsight it sounds like one of those funny Yiddish curses, but at the time the note unnerved and incensed me. Clearly its author was identified with a rage-filled self that wanted to destroy me. In truth, were my own instinctual energy let loose, it would similarly be happy to rid the planet of a few people — in my case, people who knowingly poison children! Fortunately, a homeopathic dose of this energy in me has been a great resource in my work. It has allowed me to embrace the notion that even one person can be powerful and effect change and to own my desire for survival and my Warrior Self.

> *If you think you are too small to be effective*
> *you have never been in bed with a mosquito.*
>
> — Larned

Many extraordinary people have been instrumental in effecting social and political change without necessarily combining a psycho-spiritual approach with an activist vision. However, attempting change with a conscious perspective from an Aware Ego Process can provide additional strength, courage, and inner wisdom to act effectively and appropriately in a challenging situation. It can also provide one a sense of being at peace with the process and of being replenished while doing the work. Making strategic decisions from an Aware Ego is not a stressful process, as we are separate from the various selves that have opinions on the matter, some of whom carry a range of emotions such as anger and fear, which can cloud our ability to honor the perspectives of other selves. As "chairman of the board," the Aware Ego enables us to figure out the appropriate blend of energies to bring forth. It allows us to transition from an us-versus-them paradigm to a collaborative perspective that makes effecting change more viable and powerful.

As MPN's executive director I am often called upon to mediate differing opinions among coalition members. When lobbying for legislation, I am also called upon to mediate among various legislators on strategy and possibilities. As the facilitator of our *Pesticides and the Chesapeake Bay Watershed Project*, which includes federal and state agency scientists, commercial fishermen, environmental groups, farmers, and representatives of the pest-control industry, I and the entire MPN staff are challenged to work for consensus among a diverse group of stakeholders who have never before sat at the same table. I've been told that the breadth of this alliance is unique in our region.

We have the opportunity in a leadership role to model respect and understanding for perspectives very different from our own, once we've gained the ability to do so from doing our own inner work with the selves, and strengthening our Aware Ego process. I strive to do this particularly when dealing with opponents who threaten the changes I work to achieve. One of our five subcommittees in the *Watershed Project* is working on educating the agricultural community on why it needs to reduce the use of pesticides. For the most part, conventional farmers are very suspect of organizations such as MPN. Half of this subcommittee's members come from a mostly conventional perspective that considers pesticides necessary for food production and not harmful to public health. I believe that holding the tension of the opposites (primary and disowned selves) within me from Aware Ego has allowed for others in the group to find their way to consensus, and to produce a groundbreaking information kit for farmers that encompasses the range of perspectives reflected in the group's membership.

To truly accept the other side's perspective regarding the "benefits" of pesticides, I needed to find the voice within that could envision pesticides as a positive for mass food production and an antidote to widespread insect-borne diseases such as malaria. While there is a primary self who worries about children exposed to the pesticide-laced mosquito nets in Africa used to protect them from such diseases (and believes that there are far better ways to protect them without pesticides), I can access the previously disowned part of me that can see the benefit these nets have in protecting the children from malaria at a time when other, less toxic, methods are unavailable to them. From Aware Ego, I am able to hold both perspectives, and energetically, as well as literally, allow for all perspectives in the working group in a way that creates harmony between conflicting perspectives and sometimes results in a group coming up with new and innovative solutions that satisfy all parties involved.

> *Disowned selves can carry "new ways of looking at the world, new information and creative solutions to old problems."*
> — Stone and Stone, 2001

> *No self is completely good and no self is completely bad. Each has something to contribute to the system and each person in the relationship has something important to teach the other. What is important is that we develop an ability to stand between those opposites and learn how to use them both in a new way.*
> — Stone and Stone, 2000

MPN's work with prominent healthcare facilities such as Johns Hopkins is groundbreaking. It was previously unheard of for such institutions to allow an outside advocacy group to spearhead their transition to pesticide-free environments. I believe this occurred partly from finding "their shoes within me to stand in," so that I could truly understand a facility manager's resistance to changing an entrenched (toxic) protocol. Hospital managers are so overloaded, dealing with one crisis after another, that trying to go pesticide-free can be an unwanted burden when pesticides appear to offer a quick, albeit dirty, solution. While the Judge in me may label their behavior lazy and uncaring, accessing the lazy part of me allows for compassion toward their behavior. It amounts to owning my Lazy Self, which fails to do what is right because it is at times too much effort, like "forgetting to recycle" and throwing a plastic container in the garbage instead. Empathizing with the part of them that wants to maintain the less work-intensive status quo allowed me to help them access their "Go Green Facility Manager Self." Over the past few years, several of the healthcare facilities we work with have gone pesticide free, a revolutionary step in the industry.

The focus of my application of Voice Dialogue in advocacy work revolves around my own inner development. I do not outwardly use it with others I work with in this arena or for conflict resolution. The folks I mediate among or work to educate are not in any way consciously using Voice Dialogue technology. The gift of this amazing process is working with various groups and systems from an advocate's Aware Ego Process.

We all perceive a situation based on our limited vision, usually defined by our individual pieces of the puzzle. For the most part, our opponents feel the same passion and rightness that we do about what they are working toward. For example, I know that the pesticide industry and members of the pest-control industry are passionate about wanting MPN to disappear or fail, as they passionately believe in the necessity of pesticides for food production, not to mention the passion they feel about maintaining their jobs and income.

Justified outrage about any one of our ecological, public health, or social crises is a great motivator to action, and looking at an issue from "their" point of view helps us move out of (justified) anger and to a more transcendent perspective. "Keep your enemies closer" is a phrase that suggests being congenial with your opponents; However, from a Psychology of Selves perspective it can be understood as looking within for your disowned voices that are personified in your "enemy," and then owning their inclusion in your inner family of selves.

Only then can we realistically work toward a joint resolution that does not compromise our basic beliefs and that truly works. There are two or more sides to any debate. Being committed to understanding the other side's position in no way implies compromising what we hold dear. In working on the disowned selves our opponents represent, we honor the positive intent behind the opponent's and our disowned self's thoughts and actions, no matter how unsavory their actions may appear. Even behind the evil of a Hitler is the positive intent to express power, which may be used for positive or negative ends. Understanding this does not in any way condone or excuse negative behavior, especially when it enters the realm of evil.

According to Psychosynthesis, the action, and the part of us from which we carry it out, are degraded expressions of a higher quality such as justice or power (Ferrucci, p. 52). This is an important concept in moving out of the adversarial paradigm so common in activism. For example, in exploring the positive intentions of my opponents in the pesticide and pest-control industry, and consequently my disowned selves, I understand that their (and my) intentions often have to do with survival, autonomy, and power. These are important human qualities. When we work with our disowned selves we are able to access these motivating higher qualities. We can then hold that understanding and vision when interacting with those who personify our disowned selves.

A Maryland legislator who strongly opposed one of the bills I lobbied for became a friend, despite actually having voted annually against the bill, including in the year it finally passed. Though vehemently opposed to anything to do with more centralized government control (an effect of the bill I supported), he came to like and respect me, as I did him. During vigils outside legislative committee rooms, waiting for hours to learn the results of closed debates, this delegate would periodically come out to the public waiting area to let me know what was happening; whether I needed to reschedule my psychotherapy clients to free my time to await probable legislative movement, or could go home because nothing further would happen that day. We clearly did not see eye to eye. In fact I thought of him initially as not very smart, provincial, motivated only by self-interest, and insensitive to what I considered best for society. These judgments guided me in my inner search for my disowned selves. By accessing my very Independent-minded Self that believes in "survival of the fittest" and "every man for himself," and which doesn't really give a damn about ensuring the welfare of anyone other than my loved ones, I came to understand and respect his passion. Claiming a small percent of this energy in me translates to self-love and, at times, putting myself and my dearest ones first, which is necessary in balancing out selfless tendencies.

Interestingly, when I was able to access my inner Lawmaker X, Mr. Lawmaker X then seemed to be more respectful of my work and intentions in return, despite the fact that he had not done any inner work on who I represent for him in his inner family of selves. I am a Democrat and generally have the support of Democratic legislators in my work, but in truth I also have a rather conservative disowned Republican within when it comes to certain matters. Exploring who she is has allowed me to engage with Republican legislators in a way that creates a safe space for discussing our differences.

Over the past few years of working with healthcare facilities in Maryland, we have had to work with the pest-control vendors who serve them. Initially, the vendors felt very threatened by our presence in the facilities, as we were reviewing their work and making recommendations to facilities' administrators, including, on occasion, suggestions that they change vendors. My judgment: in my book, pest-control vendors were at the bottom of the food chain along with the pesticide industry. I believe they are all poisoning us, and that they continue to knowingly do so for the sake of profit.

It took a bit of work to access the disowned self of mine that could heartlessly and knowingly poison people for the sake of survival or making money, or worse — for some distorted nationalistic notion of ethnic superiority. As a child of Holocaust survivors, a self that needs to create a just world is rather primary within me. I don't think I have poisoned anyone for the sake of making a living, nor can I envision advocating ethnic cleansing. It is, however, enlightening for me to access and acknowledge the part of me that puts secondary the deaths of innocent Arab children when Israel, the nation in which I was born and to which I have a profound emotional attachment, acts militarily against Arab attackers.

The motivation for survival can be very intense. Pesticide manufacturers are commonly known to hide or distort the science that reveals their products do harm. An "aha" moment for me in this work was experiencing an inner self that also actually manipulates and stretches the truth at times to make a point in my advocacy work. I have at times knowingly glossed over information critical of the studies I cite. I can rationalize this as part and parcel of political strategy, but this particular self, like my opponents here, is more than willing to bend the truth for the sake of my cause. Understanding this disowned self via the Aware Ego Process enables me to be more compassionate, and better allows for honest dialogue with my most difficult opponents.

It has been imperative for me that our project staff approaches the vendors with a willingness to listen to and understand their perspective and challenges, and strive to find points of agreement. Pest-control operators are not necessarily bad guys — they take pride in getting rid of bugs that can carry disease and may be a nuisance. They take pride in their work. They certainly do not set out to make people sick by using pesticides, yet some vendors are willing to ignore the evidence that their product can cause great harm for the sake of their own financial survival. Others simply resist change. Understanding this helped us find common ground. We too want to get rid of vermin, and we want pest-control workers to be able to support their families. There is, however, reason for concern, so how can we ensure their livelihood while also eliminating vermin using preventive non-chemical strategies? Ironically, the more I deeply understand my disowned selves that some vendors represent for me, the more they seem to seek me out wanting to develop a pesticide-free approach. As in any relationship, when we reclaim what the other carries for us, they are able to reclaim what we carry for them. This allows for greater objectivity and a more balanced perspective in relation to the other.

In short, we have transformed the relationship with several major national and local vendors to the extent that we have met with them at their corporate headquarters in order to help them redraft their pest-management protocols to be in alignment with guidelines that call for pesticides to be used only as a last resort. I cannot be a Pollyanna about this; along the way we have made some real enemies who continually seek to undermine our work, but, for the most part, the transformation in our relationship to this industry has been revolutionary.

> *The Aware Ego is not a thing; it's a process. It is an energy in the psyche that moves us toward change. It is constantly requiring of us that we separate from these unconscious selves and learn to use them in new ways. It gets stronger as we separate from more of our primary systems and learn to become aware of and experience our disowned self systems. It ultimately gives us the ability to stand between opposites and live with this tension so that new possibilities can begin to emerge from the deeper — and wiser — parts of our psyche.*
>
> — Stone and Stone, 2001

When I am able to hold this understanding from an Aware Ego Process, my staff and others are inducted to also be empathetic and understanding of the "other," while holding firm on their perspective. Miraculously the "other" also begins to be more understanding of our position.

> *When we do not honor the shadow, we go forth like the thrust of a wave carried along by the power of hidden undercurrents. These undercurrents, operating as projection, denial or neglect represent unconscious shadow challenges to the quality of our inner lives and therefore to the quality of our service. Most of us contaminate our service in each of these ways some of the time. The degree to which we do so depends on our level of awareness.*
>
> — Trout

According to Roberto Assagioli, there are two primary energies, or qualities, in the universe, Love and Will (Assagioli, p. 91). A balanced personal life, as well as a balanced society, is one that manifests these qualities in harmony with each other. In Voice Dialogue language, this parallels the heart/mind voices. The quality of Love is experienced as a state of being. Will is experienced as a state of intention that evokes action or doing. Might be those fifties doo-wop singers understood the critical balance between being and doing when they crooned, "do-be-do-be-do" to our unconscious minds? Each is incomplete without the other. Love entirely devoid of Will may be inconclusive or weak, noted Piero Ferrucci, a teacher of Psychosynthesis (Ferrucci, p. 200). He points out that many "loving" people tend to be shy or too lenient. Conversely, Will without Love can be ruthless; it can lead to isolation, harshness, and destructiveness in the pursuit of power for its own sake.

The balance of Love and Will — consciously accessing the voices of our minds and hearts — allows for Loving Power and Powerful Love. Loving Power translates into responsible action in the world from a place of compassion. Powerful Love is a state of being that impacts those whom we come in contact with. Just being in the presence of people who embody this quality — the Dalai Lama, Mother Teresa, Swami Muktananda — fills one with a great sense of peace and exquisite, unconditional love. Our personal responsibility in this construct is to first work on the issues and selves in the quality we are most identified with, which can then create an opportunity to experience and develop the more disowned aspect of our personality.

Some activists, despite their good-heartedness, positive intentions, and passion, are more identified with Will when it comes to working their cause, their tendency being to "wage battle against their enemy" and to believe their perspective alone is right. When we access our ability for an empathic response toward our opponents by working on the disowned selves they represent, it opens our hearts.

As we work with the disowned selves carried by those whom we are trying to impact, we become open to true compassion for the other. I have found that the Buddhist-based practice of Metta (*loving-kindness*) meditation not only provides me a self-loving practice that helps me stay centered but also the expression, for myself and the "other" of the moment, is deeply rewarding once I identify the disowned selves the other represents. Sharon Salzberg, a renowned teacher of Vipassana Buddhism, writes that in the practice of Metta you repeat certain phrases through the following six categories: Ourselves, a person who has benefited us (including loved ones), a good friend, a neutral person, an enemy or person with whom we experience difficulties, and, finally, all beings without exception (Salzburg, 1995). These phrases are gently and lovingly repeated. Of course you can do it just for yourself and/or someone you love or are having a hard time with. I have adapted this practice as follows for myself and my clients, and use it in my advocacy work:

> May I/you be safe and free from all harm.
> May I/you be free from fear.
> May I/you be happy.
> May I/you be healthy.
> May I/you live with ease.
> May I/you live with peace.
> May I/you be resilient in the face of all challenges, and
> May I/you live with loving kindness in my heart for myself and others.

The key to this practice being most effective is not to deny our unloving, angry, and even hateful thoughts, but to embrace the selves within us that carry those thoughts and the disowned selves manifested in those we react to so negatively. Only from an Aware Ego that can hold the tension of our opposites can we authentically practice and experience true Metta.

> *To see the universal and all-pervading spirit of the truth*
> *face to face, one must be able to love even the meanest*
> *creature as oneself.*
> — Gandhi

In January 1996 I was told that the Maryland House of Delegates' Environmental Matters Committee chairman, a powerful man who represents a strongly agricultural district, was planning to kill our bill for integrated pest management in schools, and that he was upset (enraged, actually) that the bill had resurfaced in his committee for yet another year. His reputation was that of an anti-environmentalist and a force to be reckoned with, and he let it be known that he just wanted the bill to disappear for all time. I considered him a pompous, self-absorbed despot.

Naturally, I'd like to believe that none of those qualities exist within me, and that my life is fully service oriented and that I value humility and the needs of others at all times. Of course that is not the case, so I worked on finding my inner "Mr. Chairman of the Committee," and accessed the part of me that (had my son and I not been adversely impacted) probably would have cared less about environmental issues, let alone the impact of specific pesticides. It took significant inner work to confess my selfish thoughts, wants, dreams, and fantasies. Accessing this energy within me has been a great asset in setting boundaries with my work and with people, in being forthright and confrontational, and not always taking things so personally. As I worked on owning this very important part of me I was able to include the Chairman in my Metta practice.

After accessing this disowned energy, I wrote the chairman a letter asking for a meeting. Surprisingly he responded and offered to meet for not more than ten minutes. We met for an astounding three and a half hours, by the end of which he floored me by saying he wanted to eliminate children's exposure to pesticides in our schools. Over the next couple of months he even decided to draft his own bill for mandatory integrated pest management in schools — a far more politically powerful option than our drafting a bill to be introduced before his committee.

Now, I don't want to turn this into a fairytale or sound politically naïve. I know that politicians often play both sides of the fence, and that the chairman was also capable of this. However, the man who had previously refused to have anything to do with us seemed to have come an unprecedented long way.

What happened to this man who for years fought for a state preemption bill that would make it illegal to pass any legislation stricter than federal law but who came to support our effort that was more stringent than federal law? Other legislators and environmentalists who'd known him for nearly two decades were mystified. During the 1997 legislative session, he structured ongoing meetings with my coalition's representatives, the state Department of Agriculture, and the pest-control industry, to hash out an agreeable compromise bill. During this entire time, I continued to work with my inner selves that he exemplified and with the resulting compassion for myself and for him. The practice of Metta served to enhance my compassion and linkage.

I discovered that the man who so many saw as a heartless, self-serving, narcissistic control freak actually had a primary self with the positive intention of doing good. I held the understanding that he too believes, just as a part of me does, that he knows best and that what he is doing is right. Also I explored what I had to learn from him and his perspective, his belief in less government control and more personal responsibility. While we agreed to continue to disagree on many issues, I came to fully understand the merits of his perspective. We may still disagree on a lot, but I've come to like and respect this man. This was the power of the Aware Ego Process combined with Metta.

More than changing the chairman, the encounter changed me. In 1998 this man was the primary force in our bill becoming law. While it was not all we wanted, at the time it was the first and therefore the strongest legislation ever passed to protect public school children from pesticides in the United States.

In activism, it is very seductive to sacrifice ourselves for the sake of the cause and burn too many midnight candles. When we do so, we can unknowingly be identified with the Martyr that often has a resentful Victim behind it. In some spiritual circles, being selfless is considered an important attainment. But what is true selflessness? If we are truly serving others, should we not also receive the same care and consideration for ourselves that we give to others? Honoring the Server as well as the Self-Serving Self is a critical balance for doing service. Examining the motives for our actions, and holding the tension of the opposites, needs to be a constant practice in activist work as it does in our work as Voice Dialogue facilitators.

Lastly, I need to address nonattachment, a basic tenet in many spiritual traditions. While I certainly have voices that are clearly attached to visualized and hoped-for outcomes in my personal life, my therapy practice, and my advocacy work, my spiritual path is based on nonattachment. When we are attached to our opinions and concepts, there is no room for anything else. Clearly working with and separating out from the selves helps us to access the state of witness consciousness/awareness in which we are not attached. The Aware Ego makes choices based on awareness. It embraces all our selves without attachment to any of them. Ultimately, the Aware Ego Process embraces all the selves and is attached to none. It's the Aware Ego that can put together the appropriate blend of energies and wisdom for each situation that sets the foundation for successful mediation and progress in the world of advocacy.

While I have had, and continue to have, success in my work, I've spent quite a few years working for bills that despite enormous output for four to five months each year of the Maryland legislative session, fail to pass due to agricultural industry opposition. This can be very disappointing. While my therapy practice has very clear and defined boundaries on the hours spent working, my activist work does not; there is simply never enough time or staff to climb out of the weeds. Failure can be difficult to accept after putting out so much effort. It requires attending to those inner voices that grieve the loss and that are angry and frustrated as well as those that see the bigger picture.

Do your work and then step back. The only path to serenity.

— Lao Tzu

My teacher, Swami Muktananda, often said that the bird of life soars on two wings: effort and grace. You put in the effort to the best of your ability, and then you step back and let grace take over. Sometimes what looks like a negative outcome ends up being an important piece of a later and greater win. I spent three years of my life very ill as a result of pesticide poisoning. It was truly a nightmarish period. I was told I would likely never heal. Thankfully I did. It was this nightmare, however, that catapulted me into an arena in which I've found truly passionate service work. The Aware Ego Process allows us to honor all our parts and the perspectives they hold without attachment, which allows for a deep feeling of peace and serenity. My experience has taught me the critical importance of Voice Dialogue and the Psychology of Selves for successful advocacy work and conscious activism.

> *Imagine what would happen if everybody did this. What if, suddenly all over the world, people had to stop whenever they had a judgment or were attacking someone and ask themselves: Why am I so angry and judgmental? What is it that I am missing so badly in myself that I cannot bear to see it in someone else? ... Groups and nations that carry one another's disowned selves could learn from one another rather than fight one another.*
>
> — Stone and Stone, 2000

References

Assagioli, R. *The Act of Will.* New York: Viking Press, 1973.

Dyak, M. *The Voice Dialogue Facilitator's Handbook, Part 1.* Seattle, WA: L.I.F.E. Energy Press, 1999.

Eisentsadt, S. *Jungian Psychology and the World Unconscious.* In T. Roszak, M. Gomes, and A. Kanner, eds. *Ecopsychology: Restoring the Earth Healing the Mind.* San Francisco, CA: Sierra Club Books, 1995.

Ferrucci, P. *What We May Be: Techniques for Psychological and Spiritual Growth.* Boston, MA: J. P. Tarcher, 1982.

Gore, A. *Earth in the Balance,* New York: Plume/Penguin Books, 1993.

Hillel the Elder, *Pirkey Avot/Ethics of the Fathers,* The Talmud, Mishnaic Period.

Larned, M. *Stone Soup for the World,* Berkeley, CA: Conari Press, 1997.

Muktananda, S. *Meditate.* Albany, NY: State University of New York Press, 1980.

Stone, H., and S. Stone. *Embracing Each Other: Relationship as Teacher, Healer & Guide,* Novato, CA: Nataraj Publishing, 1989.

Stone, H., and S. Stone. *Partnering, A New Kind of Relationship*, Novato, CA: Nataraj Publishing, 2000.

Stone, H., and S. Stone. *Voice Dialogue: Discovering Our Selves.* Voice Dialogue International website, from an interview with Gary Zukav on his website, 2001.

Stone, H., and S. Stone. *What is the difference between the "Ego" and the "Aware Ego"? Voice Dialogue International website*, from interview with Gary Zukav on his website, 2001.

Salzberg, S. *Lovingkindness*, Boston, MA: Shambala Press, 1995.

Trout, S. *Born to Serve*, Alexandria, VA: Three Roses Press, 1997.

Tzu, Lao. *Quotes Daddy*, www.quotesdaddy.com/author/Tao+Te+Ching, 2010.

Wolpert S. *Gandhi's Passion: The Life and Legacy of Mahatma Gandhi*, Oxford, UK: Oxford University Press, 2002.

The Inner Eater Selves
Integrating the Parts of the
Personality Involved in Eating

Yolanda Koumidou-Vlesmas, LCSW

The Inner Eater Selves were identified utilizing the Psychology of Selves and the method of Voice Dialogue with individuals who identify with these selves as primary selves and have problems attaining and maintaining their natural weight. Individuals who do not identify with Inner Eater Selves as their primary system were also interviewed and facilitated to understand their relationship to food.

The simple and obvious fact that eating is absolutely necessary in order to fuel one's body makes the misuse of food unique in comparison to similar behaviors. The misuse and abuse of many substances can be addressed through 12-step programs and other support systems whose goal is to quit using a particular substance. Food is different inasmuch as individuals who misuse food cannot quit eating completely. Food is one substance that in its misuse is more akin to behaviors that primary selves use to protect vulnerability in such areas of life as work and relationships. When dealing with the misuse of food, the goal is not to abstain or prevent use but rather to set the mind free from its attachment to food, whether that attachment is to the act of overeating or to the management of food involved in dieting. In doing so, healthy choices can be made that are in tune with the body's needs while preserving the natural enjoyment found in eating that the misuse of food strips away. In addition to these benefits, a significant amount of time and energy is freed to be directed to more fulfilling areas of life. This detachment from food occurs when individuals begin to identify which inner selves in them are actually eating. The group of inner selves involved in eating is called the Inner Eater Selves. The challenge lies in integrating the voices of the Inner Eater Selves through the Aware Ego process while developing the awareness to sense the body's natural signals concerning food.

Natural Weight

Before delving into the Inner Eater Selves it is important to establish some underlying premises from which this work has evolved. All individuals have a natural body type and a corresponding natural weight that is as unique to them as their fingerprints. A person's natural weight might render her/him extra-small, small, medium, large, or extra-large. The natural weight the body carries is based on age, genetics, metabolism, bone structure, muscle mass, and fat proportion. Unfortunately, the body mass index, or BMI, a standard obesity measure that divides weight by the square of height, does not take into consideration all these factors, and in light of recent scientific research is no longer fully accurate. This makes determining natural weight impossible if the only measure used is the BMI. Through the Aware Ego process it's possible to integrate the Inner Eater Selves, allowing individuals to discover their biological natural weight instead of carrying weight that does not belong to them or continuing to pursue an unnatural ideal weight through dieting. (Describing individuals as carrying weight that does not belong to them is a nonjudgmental way of describing the excess weight that an individual has gained beyond his or her natural weight.)

Being in tune with the body's nutritional needs along with an awareness of and separation from the Inner Eater Selves greatly lessens the daily struggle in reaching and maintaining a natural weight. Options are seen and informed choices can be made. As individuals are in the process of discovering their natural weight it is also helpful to enter a state in which they can feel comfortable about their body image without inner conflict. This is especially important when natural weight doesn't conform to society's current definition of what is attractive or when natural weight is not what it was expected to be. Some people carry their natural weight and some carry weight that does not belong to them. It is one thing to be large because of natural weight, and something else because the body is overfed. The gap between the current definition of attractiveness and desirable body type in comparison to a person's natural weight and body type can ruin lives by bringing on depression caused by severe Inner Critic attacks. There are those who take advantage of this suffering over the desire to be like "everyone else": they become rich presenting programs that convince people that they can all be shaped the same. Integrating the Inner Eater Selves through an Aware Ego process can take individuals out of the endless struggle to force their bodies to become something that they are not and instead become what is biologically natural for them. In addition, it significantly alleviates Inner Critic attacks.

The Inner Comfort Eater Selves (ices)

The Inner Eater Selves are composed of two opposite groups of inner selves in one's psyche that are involved with food and eating. Each group has its own philosophy and approach concerning food. The first group uses food as a tool for psychological and emotional comfort, protection, pleasure, or escape instead of for its nutritional value. These Inner Eater Selves misuse food by overeating and are called the Inner Comfort Eater Selves, or simply the ices. This group of Inner Eater Selves takes care of vulnerability that a person may be unwilling, unable, or unprepared to handle directly, and often functions alongside other primary selves that are not involved in eating. When the ices become a primary system, an individual views food as having multiple purposes, the least of which is to feed the body. Often the Inner Comfort Eater Selves act in highly specialized ways, associating certain groups of food and eating behaviors with specific emotional needs. When the ices take control of eating decisions, they override the rules set by the opposite group of Inner Eater

Selves. The ices thus far have all presented themselves as a masculine consuming energy. They are extremely powerful, and this is one of the reasons they hide vulnerability so well for so many people. This is also why misusing food is such a problem for so many. The Inner Comfort Eater Selves never mean to cause harm in any way; they just intend to protect individuals from feelings such as loneliness, desperation, tiredness, depression, rejection, disappointment, anxiety, and jealousy. They always succeed in comforting these feelings, but only while they are in the act of consuming food, and sometimes during the lethargy that follows.

Usually individuals identify and name their own ices, as these may perform the same function for many, but do it in very specific ways for each individual. A type of Inner Comfort Eater Self that identifies with a specific food is very common. For example, an individual might have a Sweet Eater, a self who uses sweets exclusively to provide comfort from loneliness. Some individuals will even focus on a specific sweet, such as a certain kind of chocolate, a flavor of ice cream, a specific desert, or a particular candy. Another individual might have a Carb Eater to provide comfort from loneliness, the only difference being that this self uses carbohydrates to provide that comfort. Again, there can be very specific identification with a certain type of food or a combination of foods like bread and cheese, pretzels and dip, and so on. These Specific Food Eaters follow a few rules that they all have in common. The food must be familiar and practical. Familiarity brings comfort; it is part of human nature to gravitate toward the familiar to feel more at ease. They also believe that the less preparation involved the better; it should be fast and easy to attain the food so that comfort can be immediate. This is why so many Specific Food Eaters gravitate toward junk food.

Another kind of Inner Comfort Eater Self is the Volume Eater. The Volume Eater provides comfort by eating large quantities of food very quickly and does not care what it eats; it is voracious. There is no notion of what is enough with a Volume Eater. Feeling full and then some is one way this Inner Comfort Eater Self provides comfort. Individuals experience the Volume Eater in many different ways. By feeling so full, individuals might feel grounded when chaos is encroaching into their lives; for others this physical feeling may put a lid on top of feelings of vulnerability providing relief from them. For others, the Volume Eater can also act as an activity of escape or as something to pass the time to deal with feelings of boredom. As there is never enough with the Volume Eater, feelings can be protected against for surprisingly long periods of time.

Though they do an incredible job protecting feelings of vulnerability, the ices are limited by the fact that they have no connection to the body, particularly to the stomach, which is a very important part of the body involved in eating. When the ices are active, food is consumed whether or not hunger is felt, even after the stomach is full. There is no savoring the flavor of food, as there is no connection to the tongue either. Instead, food is eaten in large quantities to make up for its being eaten very quickly. This is especially the case with the Pleasure Eater who does not know that food can be kept on the tongue to continue tasting it. Due to its having a masculine consuming energy, it eats quickly, often swallowing before the tongue can fully taste the food. In order to get more pleasure, the Pleasure Eater believes that if the food tastes good it should simply have more to keep on enjoying it.

The Deprivation Eater believes that the individual should not be deprived in any way. Sometimes there are feelings of deprivation associated with food restrictions due to a diet, which can cause severe emotional strain that the Deprivation Eater wishes to comfort by eating the foods that the diet restricts. At other times, an individual may feel deprived in other areas of life. One may feel deprived of a voice and feel that his or her opinions do not matter. One may not feel entitled and is deprived of his or her needs. The Deprivation Eater provides an area in life where the individual will not be deprived. It believes that food can take care of what is missing in other aspects of life, and it can make sure the individual will get what he or she wants with food.

The I Don't Care Eater is especially associated with comforting feelings of hopelessness and desperation. It doesn't care about anything but eating, and as such blocks out everything else that individuals might be going through in their lives. It does not want to hear, see, or talk about anything; its beliefs are blunt, absolute, and rebellious. The I Don't Care Eater does not take into consideration the consequences of its attitude that everything should stop so food can be consumed. Avoiding certain situations can of course worsen them, and the consequences to one's health when this Inner Comfort Eater Self takes hold can be devastating.

The Secret Eater is an Inner Comfort Eater Self that often works hand-in-hand with many of the other ices. The Secret Eater is a self who eats in secrecy, offering relief from the shame of being seen misusing food. It believes it can shield individuals from the shame of misusing food by hiding the action from the sight and knowledge of others. This provides only temporary comfort and relief from the shame; once the eating is completed in secrecy the Inner Critic steps in right on cue. The shame held by individuals who identify with ices as primary selves is a very important part of the way the ices operate. This feeling of shame that the Inner Critic's attacks can cause is one of the Inner Comfort Eater Selves' most serious limitations.

The voice of the Inner Critic enters right after a meal is finished, sometimes first thing in the morning, or while trying on clothes in department stores, when stepping on a scale, or looking in the mirror. These attacks can be severe enough to cause depression over long periods of time. If the ices are identified as a primary self system, food will be misused even more in an effort to deal with the depression and the self-criticism. Consequently, the ices come to the rescue again, thus creating a vicious cycle centered on misuse of food. Since the Inner Comfort Eater Selves (acting as first responders) are always on call to provide comfort from feelings of vulnerability in individuals who identify with them as primary selves, the ices can be used as indicators, or a warning system, that vulnerability is being neglected. If one can learn to identify the ices as signaling neglected vulnerability, it offers an opportunity to pay immediate attention to this underlying vulnerability. Misusing food is a concrete physical action; it is a behavior that one can notice is occurring right away.

Nutrition In-Tune Eater Selves (nites)

The group of Inner Eater Selves opposite to the Inner Comfort Eater Selves is the Nutrition In-Tune Eater Selves, or simply the nites. This group misuses food to achieve weight loss in order to provide comfort from the criticisms of the Inner Critic. The nites want to protect individuals from these criticisms and from other feelings of vulnerability. They do this by effecting weight loss that promotes feelings of pride in one's appearance. When acting as a primary system, the Nutrition In-Tune Eater Selves are focused on the nutritional value of food and how the use of that knowledge can bring about weight loss. The external physical appearance of the body is the main concern of the nites. They are therefore disconnected from the internal workings of the body, and ignore important natural signals from its parts. The Nutrition In-Tune Eater Selves all share some common rules. They treat eating as a strict, serious regimen, categorize food as either good or bad, define correct or incorrect portion sizes, and recognize correct or incorrect food combinations at all times. They have all presented themselves with a stern, domineering energy. Their mission is for the person to lose weight. Achieving weight loss is of the utmost importance in order to mollify the criticisms of the Inner Critic about the weight that an individual is carrying.

The nites help individuals lose weight by following external cues. Most individuals can identify and name their own nites, because they are very specific to each individual. One of the most powerful nites would be the Diet Plan Eater, who adopts the rules of a prescribed diet plan or program. The Weight Watchers Eater is one example. This Self equates food with points, carefully counting and keeping a record every time food is eaten. Another example is the Atkins Eater, who consumes high amounts of protein and a low amount of carbohydrates. Another Diet Plan Eater may merely count calories of all food consumed so as not to exceed the allotted daily caloric intake. The Diet Plan Eater can rigorously follow any diet plan. Following plans requires intense focus, which acts as a very effective distraction from feelings of vulnerability.

Overeaters Anonymous is different from the typical diet plans that
the Diet Plan Eater adopts because they are not solely concerned with
rules around food, and as such have a specialized 12-step Program
Eater. This Nutrition In-Tune Eater Self has an emotional and a spiritual element like 12-step programs, involving a belief in a higher power
that is required to restore individuals to a sane state concerning eating
behaviors. The spiritual element provides another aspect of support for
many individuals against the criticisms of the Inner Critic. It also serves
to protect against the common flip that occurs from the nites back to the
ices. As with the Diet Plan Eater, there is an immense amount of focus
involved in following the rules. This focus acts as a distraction, preventing a person from dealing with the underlying vulnerability that brings
individuals to misuse food.

In contrast, the Healthy Eater is a self who eats only what is considered healthy according to a specific set of standards. This is very
different from the Diet Plan Eaters and the 12-step Program Eater.
It does not attach itself to a specific diet plan, but rather focuses on a
constant informational awareness of the nutritional value of food so as
to lose weight. The Healthy Eater believes in eating only foods that are
considered healthy and nutritious. This Nutrition In-Tune Eater Self
reads labels and considers freshness before buying food. It might also
have a predilection for foods labeled as organic. As there is no set plan
to follow, even more focus is necessary to gain knowledge concerning the
nutritional value of food so that it can then be put into action. Again,
this focus on diet acts as a distraction from feelings of vulnerability.

One of the very common Nutrition In-Tune Eater Selves is the Diet
Missionary. It comes in to lose weight in a certain amount of time for
a particular event. It is very powerful and will let nothing stand in the
way of accomplishing its goal. The Diet Missionary generally attaches
itself to events such as weddings and other celebrations, vacations, new
romantic relationships, and the coming of the swimsuit season. This
Inner Eater Self, though powerful, does not have the staying power of
some of the others. Once the goal is reached (the event having passed or
the new relationship having either ended or lost its novelty), there is no

longer a reason for the Diet Missionary to continue enforcing the rules that brought about the weight loss, so it loosens its grip, allowing other selves to establish primacy with respect to food and eating behaviors.

There is a pride carried along with the nites, equal and opposite to the shame that is carried along with the ices. This pride is centered on control and the results that this control brings. As the nites become successful in their mission, and weight is lost, individuals begin to feel good about themselves and feel pride in their appearance. A newfound freedom is felt, as there is no longer a reason to hide the body, but rather one to show it off. Sexual attention may become more and more pronounced. This brings with it self-confidence and the ability to voice opinion where once it could not. These feelings have a tendency to become feelings of superiority, causing judgment and criticism of people who are viewed as not having the control and pride to lose the weight that does not belong to them. This pride creates an illusion that vulnerability is being handled as it brings pleasure and a sense that everything is okay. In reality the vulnerability is just buried and hidden. When the nites are really successful in losing weight, this pleasure becomes a high that is brought on by intense feelings of pride.

The nites have strict rules, and following these can bring concrete results. Identifying with the nites might very well be the only way for individuals to lose the weight that does not belong to them, thus achieving a goal important to good health (and in extreme situations, saving a life). It is important to note that the nites are not involved in maintaining weight loss, as they are only concerned with *losing* weight. The nites offer extraordinary gifts, as they are able to place food in perspective and enable weight loss. As they are the opposite of the ices, they lack any emotional attachment to food. This is an invaluable gift when individuals are beginning to separate from the ices so that more impartial, informed decisions can be made about eating behaviors. The nites are not just experts concerning the nutritional aspects of food; their weight-loss mission is so paramount that they take it upon themselves to become well educated in other areas involved in weight loss that go along with a diet, especially exercise. They know what should be done to supplement their rules on food to ensure the mission is accomplished.

In using the Nutrition In-Tune Eater Selves' gifts, individuals must be made aware of their limitations and the dangers of disowning the ices outright. A significant limitation of the nites is that they allow for no flexibility in eating. They are constantly mindful of when, how much, and what one should eat according to the rules they adopt. They often require the measurement of food, specifying how many meals should be eaten daily and at what times during the day they are eaten. This consumes a significant amount of energy, often taking that energy away from other important parts of life. These rules all too often remove the natural joy and pleasure that is experienced in relation to the social aspects of preparing and eating food with others. As the nites have no connection to the body, they neglect the taste buds; the choices that are made ignore flavor, which is another aspect of eating in which one should naturally find enjoyment. Another consequence of the nites' disconnection from the body is that the body might become deficient in vital nutrients, as strict accordance to a specific plan may sometimes exclude eating entire food groups. The body knows what it lacks, but the body's cravings are ignored, or even worse, the Inner Critic engages in an attack since these cravings fall outside the nites' rules. These rules the nites adopt as law will result in weight loss, but it might not be healthy or sustainable.

"Them"

There are people who have not developed Inner Comfort Eater Selves or Nutrition In-Tune Eater Selves as their primary system, even though they may misuse food occasionally. Those who do identify with the ices and the nites as primary self systems tend to refer to these individuals collectively in a certain tone. They all seem to center on referring to these apparently blessed people as "Them"; essentially they are identified as outsiders, as different, as the Other. These individuals who have not developed ices or nites as primary systems have more freedom and substantially less attachment in their relationship to food. This is evident in their behavior in social settings where food is present. Their focus is on the companionship, not on the food before them. This behavior is in sharp contrast to individuals with ices and nites as primary self systems, for whom the food is frequently a topic of conversation. For example, they talk about the food in anticipation of eating, about the memories it conjures up, how it tastes and smells, how the food is or should be prepared, how the food is nutritionally rich or deficient, and how healthy or unhealthy it is. The consumption of food or the control of the consumption takes precedence over the companionship of others as well. Individuals with ices as a primary system rarely leave food on their plates. The difference in behaviors in social situations where food is present illustrates just how much time and energy individuals with ices and nites expend, as well as how much time and energy those without them (as primary systems) can focus on other areas of life.

Along with these behavioral differences, these special individuals (who do not identify with the Inner Eater Selves) do not experience shame and guilt to the same degree in relation to the misuse of food. They enjoy the natural pleasures involved in preparing and eating food, as well as the social aspects. On the occasions when food is misused — overly indulged in during a holiday or a special event — these individuals do not experience intense Inner Critic attacks. They simply recognize the misuse of food and adjust for it. They may eat less for the next couple of meals, exercise more, or both. There is just a recognition that steps need to be taken to maintain their health and weight. They are naturally in tune with their body's signals, which is not seen in those who identify with the ices or the nites. What sets these two groups apart is the simple fact that one group develops primary self systems that use eating behaviors to deal with vulnerability, and the other develops primary self systems that do not.

In interviewing these individuals, it was found that their childhood experiences surrounding food were similar to those who do identify with Inner Eater Selves. As a result, it is difficult to predict if the Inner Eater Selves will develop and become identified as primary selves. Both individuals with Inner Eater Selves as primary selves and those without were told by their parents to eat everything on their plates and not waste food. The dinner table and the kitchen were places central to family bonding and celebrations. The parents' relationship to food, whether or not they were overweight, used food for comfort, or had strict rules concerning food, could not be used as a predictor for the development of Inner Eater Selves as primary selves.

When these individuals who do not identify with Inner Eater Selves were asked how they dealt with their feelings, some of them remarked that they would allow themselves to cry. There were also those who numbed and escaped their emotions through several behaviors that included excessive sleep, involvement in infatuations, alcohol consumption, exercise, use of the Internet, work, or keeping themselves busy with activities. When asked if they ever felt bored, the majority stated that they were either never bored or would fill that spare time with an activity. Although those who do not identify with Inner Eater Selves have more of an affinity for physical movement, the activities they chose were extremely varied, some involving physical movement, and others being sedentary. They cited such things as playing with their children, working on their house, reading, or listening to music. Eating and watching TV were the two activities that these individuals rarely used to deal with their boredom or other feelings. Individuals with ices as a primary system have food and TV leading in their list of ways to deal with emotions. Those with nites have the rules controlling food plus the all-consuming mission to lose weight. Thus the main difference between those with and those without Inner Eater Selves as primary Selves is that the individuals without them develop other primary Selves not involved in eating to handle their vulnerability.

A significant number of these individuals hold severe judgments about those who carry weight that does not belong to them. Since they have no experience of what it is like to have Inner Comfort Eater Selves as a primary self system, they are incapable of empathizing with those who do. These individuals do not experience the overwhelming level of shame and guilt experienced by those who identify with ices as primary selves. They never develop Secret Eaters and are unable to imagine that experience. They have no idea of the intensity of Inner Critic attacks, and how that creates a vicious cycle of food misuse. Only through close contact with those who carry weight that does not belong to them and have ices as a primary self system is empathy developed. This is done through the sharing of these experiences and emotions. Those who have this contact lack these harsh judgments.

Facilitating the Inner Eater Selves

The initial step for the facilitator is to identify each individual's Inner Eater Selves and then facilitate them. There are certain areas that need to be addressed and given particular emphasis. One of these is an individual's connection to their body, specifically to the stomach. When either the ices or the nites take over, the voice of the stomach is ignored. Even if the stomach is full, the ices will keep on eating to provide comfort. Alternatively, if the stomach needs more food to fuel the body, the nites will enforce their control over what they think is nutritionally necessary according to their rules.

Judith Tamar Stone has presented a magnificent body of work on the voice of the body and its parts entitled The Body Dialogue Process. She maintains that the body is an entity all by itself. The body and its parts have their own voices, needs, likes and dislikes. When led through the method of The Body Dialogue Process, which has been inspired by Voice Dialogue, the body reveals vital information toward developing an Aware Ego Process in relationship to the ices and nites. In doing Body Dialogue with the stomach, individuals gain insight into their eating behaviors.

When given a voice, the stomachs of individuals who identify with Inner Eater Selves as a primary system often reveal that they are being ignored, that either too much food is eaten too quickly (thereby overfilling and overworking the stomach) or that not enough is eaten to satisfy the stomach's desire to nourish the body. When the taste buds are given a voice, they often mention being ignored, as food is eaten too quickly or foods that do not taste good are eaten. Creating a connection to the stomach (or the taste buds) can give an individual an awareness of their body he or she did not have previously (when the Inner Eater Selves were in control).

Many other parts of the body can be facilitated that are beneficial to creating a connection with the body's natural signals concerning food and eating. Some of these are the eyes, nose, hands, and teeth. With an awareness of the body's natural signals, the opportunity arises to make better choices concerning food and eating behaviors. Honoring the voices of the different body parts strengthens the Aware Ego Process and positively impacts health. When the Aware Ego Process is strengthened in relationship to the Inner Eater Selves and to the body, the struggle with misusing food is greatly diminished. Then real choice is possible, and informed decisions concerning food can be made, thus lessening dependency on external cues.

As the Aware Ego process develops in relationship to the Inner Eater Selves and the body, another process begins where the individual moves toward a new body identity. The length of this transition depends on how developed the Aware Ego Process is in relationship to the Inner Eater Selves and the body, as well as what choices are ultimately made about eating behaviors. The Inner Critic will be an obstacle in this important paradigm shift, as it will try to resist any attempt at change to prevent the shame and pain of failing to attain and maintain this new body image. For example, take an individual who, having previously identified himself as being "fat," lost the weight that didn't belong to him by separating from the ices through the Aware Ego Process. While losing the weight, he began to develop a new body identity more in tune with his natural weight (which happened to be medium). In response to this newly evolving body identity, the Inner Critic resisted the change by saying something like, "That isn't the real you — you're fat. Who do you think you're kidding?" This Inner Critic attack, if not handled properly, could totally undermine all the progress the individual has previously made.

In another case, the movement toward a new body identity may be an acceptance of the weight the body naturally carries. For example, if an individual is naturally large or extra-large, and has most of her life been trying to make herself something she is not (like small or extra-small), the Inner Critic will fight acceptance of this natural body type. Societal and cultural influences often set standards that many individuals cannot meet naturally or in a healthy way. The Inner Critic will fight this change in body identity despite the impossibility of attaining the body image standard set by external forces. Awareness of these types of attacks that are aimed at preventing a change in body identity can help an individual develop the means to handle them. This would make the Inner Critic less of an obstacle in the transition to a new body identity.

For many individuals, the Inner Critic is a major reason why their attempts at losing weight that does not belong to them fail, and why it's such a challenge to maintain a weight loss. The flipping back and forth from the Inner Comfort Eater Selves to the Nutrition In-Tune Eater Selves can occur over years (often the majority of a lifetime) as a direct result of the Inner Critic. Some call this a lack of willpower, but it's not; it is a lack of awareness of the power and function of self-criticism. This power and function can be seen in how these flips occur.

When the ices have been the primary Selves for some time, the Inner Critic's message can become so severe that it causes a flip to the nites. This serves to protect an individual from the pain and shame of all the consequences of having the ices as primary Selves. In order to protect a person from these consequences, and to prompt change, the Inner Critic might say, "You're so disgusting, just look at how everyone stares at you" or "I can't believe you ate all that; get yourself together" or "You really think no one knows you just ate that? Come on, look at you, they know" or "Why can't you look normal like everyone else does? You really need to go on a diet." An individual might choose to make a radical change in behavior to gain relief from being barraged repeatedly by these Inner Critic attacks. This pain produces the flip from the ices to the nites.

Alternatively, after having the nites, with their strict rules, as a primary self system for some time, the voices of deprivation become so powerful that, in combination with the Inner Critic, a flip to the ices occurs. In order to keep individuals from breaking the rules of the nites, the Inner Critic dares them by saying, "You can't keep this diet up, you know you're gonna go back to your old ways" or "Come on, this isn't the real you."

Even though the Inner Critic is trying its hardest to keep the individual from breaking the nites' rules, it is actually being overly critical, and it pushes her/him away from the nites toward the ices. Among the voices of deprivation referred to earlier are the voices of the stomach and the Deprivation Eater, who marshals the battle cry for all those ices that are deprived as a result of individuals living in the nites. These voices might say, "You can't do this to me anymore! How dare you deprive me?" "I will not be deprived any longer. I want what I want and I'm going to get it!" This combination of voices is one of the main reasons why so many individuals have difficulty integrating the Inner Eater Selves.

There are other ways in which a shift away from the nites might occur. Since living in the nites focuses so much time and energy on food (in order to adhere to the strict rules), a shift in focus to another aspect of life that is deemed more important and that demands more attention can cause the nites to lose their grip on dictating behaviors concerning food. This prompts a flip back to the old eating habits of the ices. This refocusing away from the directives of the nites could shift onto work, school, family, or any other aspect of life. Specifically with regard to the Diet Missionary, once its goal of losing weight is reached for an event that has passed or for a relationship that has ended, there is no longer a reason to continue following the strict rules that produced the weight loss. The Diet Missionary no longer has a mission, and if the Inner Eater Selves are not integrated through an Aware Ego Process as the Diet Missionary retreats into the background, the ices can begin to rush in and take over again.

When a flip occurs, previously disowned selves make their appearance and may become primary. There are many examples of this: a Self that carries presence as opposed to the invisibility present with the ices, a Self that carries the pride and confidence of having lost weight, an Aphrodite Self that carries a newfound sensuality, or a Self that holds a newfound voice of entitlement—the opposite of the insecurity and self-doubt that was held along with the extra weight. If the person is unprepared to deal with the attention that these selves might bring from others (especially sexual attention), and with the situations or experiences that these previously disowned selves seek in the workplace or at home, an individual is apt to fall back on the ices for comfort. Gaining a strong voice and confidence can cause extreme stress at work and at home; for example, when an established hierarchy is suddenly disturbed, or when a formerly submissive partner challenges a dominant partner in a relationship. Being prepared for the emergence of such disowned selves will help an individual benefit from the gifts they bring, as well as mitigate any of their limitations or any subsequent harm that these previously disowned selves may cause.

Voice Dialogue facilitations with other primary selves who are not involved in eating are vital in conjunction with the Inner Eater Selves. This is actually quite natural, since working with the Inner Eater Selves brings other primary selves not involved in eating into the process, such as the Pusher, the Responsible Voice, and the Pleaser.

The ices often interact and function along with the Pusher. For example, if one is left exhausted from the unending tasks that the Pusher has demanded be done, then the ices may come in to take care of the exhaustion. They may have the person eat as a way of relaxing, numbing any anxiety due to unfinished tasks, or providing a break from thinking about the next set of tasks to be done. For individuals who carry the Responsible Voice as a primary self, the ices might come in to put a lid on any feelings that might prevent a person from fulfilling responsibilities. For one person, the ices might constantly graze throughout the day, but for another, a Volume Eater might perform this function as each individual uses the ices differently to deal with vulnerability. Therefore the misuse of food can become a ritual at the end of the day to provide relief from a primary self, or it can be used as a tool to assist a primary self throughout the day. On the other hand, the nites often interact with the Pusher by providing more tasks that need to be done during the day, according to their strict rules, in order to affect weight loss. The Responsible Voice may be used along with the nites to make sure individuals take responsibility for the preparation of food, which requires (among other things) careful, detailed selection and accurate measuring of ingredients. The Inner Eater Selves can even provide an opportunity for a disowned self to be present during the day. For example, since the Pleaser's focus is on making others happy, individuals with a Pleaser as a primary self lack the ability to do things that would make themselves happy. The ices offer one area in life, namely food and eating, where these individuals are able to focus on what makes them happy. As this work with the Inner Eater Selves has evolved, the natural emergence of primary selves not involved in eating has come to be one of the fastest, most direct ways of discovering these selves and the underlying vulnerability they protect.

Concrete Benefits

There are numerous benefits in doing work with the Inner Eater Selves. It opens up opportunities to do deep work with other primary selves. Work with the Inner Eater Selves is also another way to help individuals identify other primary selves more easily, and is often a good way in for individuals new to Voice Dialogue. Not only does work with the Inner Eater Selves dissipate Inner Critic attacks on the body but also, with the use of the Body Dialogue Process, a connection to the body can be strengthened and an individual can gain a new awareness of the body's natural signals. Due to this awareness and the development of an Aware Ego Process, decision-making is slowed down and more conscious choices regarding food can be made. As a result, eating behaviors change from within as opposed to being imposed by external cues. The development of conscious choice, along with honoring the ices and the nites for their gifts (and being aware of their limitations), loosens the grip of the ices and the nites on an individual's life. This allows energy that was once bound up in the daily misuse of food to be directed to other areas of life. Doing this work with the Inner Eater Selves also teaches individuals to use the Inner Eater Selves as an alarm system for when vulnerability is being neglected. This is often the fastest and most obvious way to know when vulnerability is being neglected, as behaviors involving food are tangible and noticeable daily. Work with the Inner Eater Selves also aids individuals in losing weight that does not belong to them, as well as finding and maintaining a natural weight. This work also makes it possible for individuals to accept a natural weight that happens to be large by mitigating critic attacks and external pressures from societal notions of beauty as reflected in the media. The physical health benefits gained by doing this work, though listed last, are certainly not the least.

Along with these practical benefits comes the un-tethering of the individual's dreams, inspirations, and wishes that are weighed down by the mind's attachment to food. Dreams fuel a galloping soul, while food fuels the body. Consciously or unconsciously, individuals come to abandon their dreams, but the soul still needs nourishment, and the mind is very convincing in its attempt to sooth the "hungry" soul with food. One hopes that in sharing this ever-evolving work space can open up for inspiration as dormant dreams and wishes are resurrected, creating new horizons for the unfolding journey of the soul.

> *Being a wild horse,*
> *Our soul gallops free across the vastness of the universe.*
> *Yet our mind will tether us to a pole.*
> *Acknowledge it.*
> *Praise it.*
> *Respect it.*
> *But then, learn to direct it.*
>
> — Yolanda Koumidou-Vlesmas

Finding My Stripes

Catherine Keir, BA, CC

It was the late 1970s. Hal and Sidra Stone were leading a weekend training in the Southern California desert. I was still a child in many ways. I felt conflicted, resembling the motion of a Ping-Pong ball moving from "I want to…" to "I don't want to…," often living in indecision, going around in circles. I was looking outside myself for answers. The impression of Hal and Sidra's presence still lingers in my memory. I really had no idea that I could someday become a professional facilitator and teacher.

In the beginning of their book *Embracing Our Selves* (Stone and Stone, 1985), the Stones offer us a tale of an infant tiger left alone in the world by the death of his mother. He is adopted by a herd of goats. He imagines he also is a goat, and stares at the herd so long he becomes one with them. He continues to grow until an older, hungry tiger arrives and shocks the young tiger's known world. This moment of approaching change calls him into what he doesn't know. He submits to a rough teaching delivered by the older tiger, and is dragged to the pond. So certain he is a goat, he denies even his reflection in the water as a young, vibrant, and noble beast. He doesn't see himself as he is. The older tiger waits, and then moves to feed on a goat, demanding that his young friend join him and accept the food he is born to eat. This time the youngster surrenders to the experience. He awakens as out of a dream, and into himself as a real tiger. He responds to the energy that comes through him, his roar of awakening.

In the desert, Hal and Sidra shocked me! They introduced me to a different kind of food, the food of awareness on two levels. Something called me to that place in the desert where we met. I was trying to sort out who I was and what to do next. Being in that room redirected the course of my life.

Mystery had placed me there, and I was in the presence of at least five major teachers who were orienting people toward the healing arts. They were part of a large human potential movement taking place in California, and the opportunity, a taste, was given to me by a turn of fate. My mother had died three months before, and my grief and love for her marked an end, and also new beginnings. In our many efforts to awaken to the life we are born to live, we exist within what we know and do not know. Someone had said to me that life is a process of going awake and going asleep, awake and asleep. This may have been my first conscious glimpse into the idea of opposite forces controlling us. I accepted the fact that both are necessary.

My life truly did move in a new direction after leaving the desert. I cut off my career in theater, for I was unable to bear the vulnerability I felt. I was attracted to employment that allowed me to work in training programs. I liked group settings. I continued my pursuit of Voice Dialogue for myself personally. I was hungry for self-knowledge. Ultimately, trading sessions with friends for years gave me the preparation necessary to successfully perform as a staff member of Hal and Sidra's organizations, Delos and Thera.

The big cats in my dreams began to awaken. Over the next ten years, four significant dreams occurred.

In the first, I witness a disturbing image of childhood and dismemberment, a boy and girl in their fenced-in backyard. The children put their arms through holes in the fence. A large wildcat outside the yard tears off their limbs. There are bloody screams. The mother's protection arrives too late.

In my second dream, there is a pink panther sitting in the passenger seat of an open convertible, smiling. I am assigned to the backseat and get into the car.

In the third dream, I enter a large hall in Egypt. Upon seeing a lioness sitting on a pedestal across the room, I become distraught and hysterical. The lioness moves, preparing to attack. I hear an inner voice: "Let go of fear, shut up, and center." I do, and the big cat settles back down as our gazes lock in through the silence.

In the fourth dream, I am standing near a lone luminous tiger that is white with black stripes. He is shimmering, and he is in the midst of a harmonious kingdom of lush nature.

My teachers have taught me something wise: My development is up to me. My desire is up to me. I must be bold in my demand to wake up again and again, sometimes fierce, fighting with all my strength, sometimes giving up and letting go. My deep longing continues, and as I have learned from my clients, desire is natural. What we do with it is another matter.

Relationships are very important to me. I really wanted to understand Bonding Patterns. I tried to understand the theory in order to fix my indecisiveness. At the same time, I didn't know how to apply the theory in my own life.

Hal and Sidra introduced two questions when they worked with Bonding Patterns: "What am I doing that I don't want to be doing? What am I not doing that I want to be doing?" Naively, I began using these questions to address my ongoing struggle with making decisions. My mind was engaged, and something was left out of the inquiry (just like the tiger who couldn't see himself in the pond). What was I missing? More recently, I have realized that my relationships (and who I appeared to be) were imagined by selves who saw only a fraction of who I am. I didn't understand the limitations of selves. I was bound by selves that wished to be honored, accepted, known, and appreciated. I didn't examine who was in control of my imagination.

Life and death — in the form of an automobile accident — called forth a force in me from the center of my being. Even though my Primary System gave a hundred percent to avoid the impending crisis, it was useless. Enter the first dream. The accident marked the beginning of the dismemberment of all that represented security in my life. I lost my primary relationship and the community that had grown around it. I descended into vulnerability. I couldn't say what I wanted, and frequently settled for what I didn't want. I had turned teachers into partners, friends into lovers, myself into somebody else. In my sleep of connecting via Bonding Patterns, I encountered obstructions in the positive bonding, expecting the other person to be somehow magically psychic. What was I not doing that I wanted to be doing? What was I doing that I didn't want to be doing? And how to stop? The repetition couldn't stop by itself.

Paradoxically, the act of letting go into pain and losing control carried me to a place of authority and self-determination that I had never experienced before. I gave up my life and awoke to an experience of taking command. I was beginning to honor my power.

After the accident, my identification with survival changed. I began to state my desires aloud. My actions produced consequences. Some communications worked well, and some were not so workable. In my efforts to step out of Bonding Patterns, both security and the unknown moved forward together.

Enter the pink panther (my second dream), who knows he likes the open convertible, likes the front seat, and doesn't need to drive the car. I wake up laughing. When I'm riding in a convertible with the top up, I really don't share my experience. Having the top down makes it a lot easier to have fun. Here I am, it's a beautiful day, and I have survived. I have a resolute determination to be happy.

I find the courage to catch myself at unconsciously giving my vulnerability away to others. I don't always have to know all the "whys" of hurting, but I simply know something is hurting me, and communicate my experience. At this stage in my life, I am interested in giving away what I have learned, which is a language that keeps my vulnerability with me.

> *We can relate to the tiger, as it is fierce and commanding*
> *on the outside, but noble and discerning on the inside.*

— d'Sa, 2004

Tomahawk Lady is a part of me, and I challenge myself to stand between my ferocity and my innocence. The vulnerability that trembles in my solar plexus was inherited at birth. Courage, also in my stomach, was present and demanded to be fed. The lioness in my third dream waited in the temple. I work to strengthen my capacity, to contain myself, and to find a stillness that can track subtle movement. This is a posture that can lead to getting food. Once it's there, everyone in the tribe of selves gets fed.

Hal and Sidra delivered another challenging question: "What belongs to me?" I tried to understand this, too, from the domain of my survival system. The tiger in the story settled for grass, not knowing about the real meat he was meant to eat. As a hunter in the domain of aliveness, the fourth dream delivered a spontaneous luminous tiger revealing the living, pulsing dynamic to which I belong — inclusive and embracing. The word "integrity" began to mean wholeness.

In the summer of 2003 I was outdoors at a spiritual retreat, washing dishes in the most ordinary way. Suddenly my perception of seeing opened up into a larger scale of existence, and I experienced the aura of people, plants, and trees. For about an hour, the world in front of me was in illumination. I was experiencing an all-encompassing energy I can only call Love. I don't know how it happened, nor has it happened since. What belongs to me is the consciousness to remember that all the forms we perceive are energy in a package. I have to be updated, much like a computer. My primary selves are precious to me, and they are always there to rally in my defense. At the same time, there is the energy that is unlimited.

When I began teaching, I didn't feel my integrity. I memorized the Voice Dialogue theory, safely hiding behind what others knew. Early on, a mentor-teacher stopped me during a lunch break. He told me that the content was not superior to the experience of the facilitation process. "First, get people working. Then the theory will find its place within their experience."

I flower in the space created by Hal and Sidra, where education includes our life experiences. First in trainings and then as colleagues, working on a Bonding Pattern I have with them is part of what nourishes me.

I am learning that less is more. As the three of us together clear away what is not necessary, I stop being a policeman to my experience, and abandon myself to being alive in their presence. The transformation of an old wound of abandonment requires me to confront our Bonding Pattern from my side. I can see that teachers abandon students; it's a universal law. This law is what makes room for students to surrender to the teacher within. We become the next teacher, and can abandon ourselves to the world as those before us have done. As the tiger story elucidates, every wound has its opposite power, waiting to appear. My wound of loss and loneliness in my personal world is the opposite to the power in me that embraces the world with abandon — to risk, to dance, to love being in the world.

In 1982, I attended a one-day program presented by Buckminster Fuller. Bucky was the scientist and innovator who developed the structural mathematics of the geodesic dome. At one point he brought out on stage a large circle of thin dowel sticks joined together with short rubber tubes. He reduced the size of the circle by removing sticks until only three remained, held together by the rubber tubes.

He held up this equilateral triangle and said confidently, "Stable." He followed with the assertion: "The triangle is the foundational building block of the universe." I walked out that day feeling showered by an awareness of how the universe works.

This impression from Bucky was the beginning of my awakening to what now lives in me, my wish to be stable energetically. Living longer brings with it the ongoing requirement to change. I realize I am faced with a kind of healthy powerlessness to aging. At the same time, I receive strength from a seemingly ageless demand to be in contact with the unique life that waits for me. The Aware Ego Process (AEP) is sensitive and responsive to both sides.

As I mature, my inner conflicts supply the added heat I need in forging an Aware Ego Process. It's up to me to relate directly to my inner battles. Without the pure Awareness of the witness, my body can become the battlefield on which opposite selves struggle with each other. My conscious awareness of the Law of the Triad (the triangle) is my possibility toward freedom. The opposites function within the triangle and are visible; the third aspect is invisible. My mind is continually tempted to see the AEP as a self. The practicality of orienting to life as a process is difficult to grasp. This AEP, this "new kid on the block," as Hal would say, is very sensible. It strengthens my capacity to relate to myself and my own experience, to eat well, to be happy, and to remember to say hello to myself. This third ephemeral quality of inner awareness I sometimes think of as gravity. Although gravity as a force cannot be seen, I experience a freedom in my balance when my spine is moving in harmony with the law of gravity. My attention is connected to my center of gravity.

Always, I am confronted with three conditions:

1. I am, by myself, alone in the world, yet I have, as far back as I can remember, a trust that I am in relation to something. Through my thoughts, feelings, dreams, and senses, I am fed by experiencing more of my experience in the privacy of my own space.

2. In the facilitation process, there I am and there is the other, one on one. We track each other. We listen and we create the opportunity to manifest conscious awareness. We connect. Between us exists a space, free of polarization and bonding patterns, where connection or linkage is available.

3. There is the group of us. In a structured circle with my colleagues, I am one of the "cells" in a larger organism. I belong in the Voice Dialogue community. Most groups germinate from a larger vision, and then move toward it stepwise. At the same time, there are no guarantees that the group will evolve.

In an honest attempt to be present in a group, being confronted with both my primary selves who have learned to behave in groups (the goat), and my own individual possibilities (the tiger), something larger that moves through all of us desires to be brought into form. My commitment to the process and language of Voice Dialogue (and what it offers to the world) is also my response to the desire I see in the general public for this information. Nothing is more practical than working together. I have discovered over and over that, left to myself, I fall toward my Primary Self System and the habits of the past. I can't always see myself. My work with others includes the Bonding Patterns that are difficult or dear to me. Seeing my part in any relationship is half of the struggle. The other half comes from my willingness to experience something that I didn't know about myself, about others, or the world. The polarizing action-reaction dynamic so prevalent in groups is threatening. I suspect Compassion (not mine; rather, the universal intelligent compassion that showers us) feeds our consciousness. I am beginning to realize that because this work is energetically based, I have to be actively open to my experience if I want to sustain my participation. Otherwise, I hold on to right and wrong, or I lose contact with the willingness to continue, or I search for food somewhere else.

The art of facilitation includes grounding, which strengthens my capacity to be with people as they are. Hal and Sidra have brought our attention to what is called the vertical connection. As though dropping down through me, I feel a vertical descent of energy feeding me. For me, the question of what belongs to me now lives in the domain of awakening. Like a grounding rod, I receive the intelligence of the universe in a very practical way. I belong between heaven and earth, and these vertical forces that move through me are the counterbalance to the horizontal opposites I stand between.

I wait at the crossroads. There is a timing that naturally gives way to ideas that can assist necessary actions. Then, with my full awareness focused on what I want to do with this level of intensity, I can be free to care for how I am in life.

People realize the value of quiet time to sit or meditate or contemplate. Some of us enjoy the impressions of nature and her soothing sounds to restore our otherwise over-stimulated nervous systems as we decompress from the stresses and struggles arising from the cultural patterns we live with. In the silence, there is a quiet place where capacity is restored and my container is strengthened to hold more material. This creative allowance, this very silent, very quiet spark is mine to care for, and I find my place in the midst of ordinary life.

For a long time, I have been sensitive to larger forces in the world. I am certain that my experiences of these archetypal forms of energy moving through my body can seduce and bypass my conscious choice. I have learned that not every archetypal desire belongs to me. At the same time, waves sweep through the "tribe of selves," and I need to wake up and decide whether to join in or pass. The goats in our tale knew how to disappear quickly when the old tiger arrived. Being invisible has its advantages.

With age, interest in my personal feelings has transformed. My experience and appropriate expression of emotion are influenced by the agreements and integrity in each relationship. Another level of emotion is impersonal, energy from the big storehouse of human feelings. My heartstrings are played when I feel the depth of pain and loneliness in our world. Intense events beyond my control play the tune of rage. I have begun to hear the harmonics of feeling from within myself. Personal and impersonal energies exist together in me. Life sweeps through and demands we feel the collective toxic stockpile of denied emotion when the Earth needs that rich compost. I continue to value my discernment. What is my personal material that belongs to me, and what is the collective material that is being processed by my organism? Voice Dialogue is an enduring gift that shows me how to move into the ocean of unfelt feeling in the world, and then remember to return to my ordinary personal belongings on the shore, and to rest. For me, this is the art of the AEP.

Though I may not be able to stay awake all the time, the forces and various influences call me. I wake up when I am called. Then I can show up, demand to be fed, and respect my efforts to become more of who I am.

References

d'Sa, C. "Endangered tiger earns its stripes as the world's most popular beast." *The Independent Magazine,* United Kingdom, December 6, 2004.

Stone, H., and S. Stone. *Embracing Our Selves: Voice Dialogue Manual.* DeVorss & Co: Marina Del Rey, CA, 1985.

Conscious Eating Selves Work: Expand Your Self System to Transcend the Status Quo

Mary Disharoon, MA, LMFT

Have you come to the conclusion that diets don't work? Have you tried to diet and then given up before you experienced much weight loss? Have you dieted and lost weight only to gain that amount of weight back and more? Do you find that the only way for you to be successful with weight loss is to live in a chronic state of deprivation?

To be able to get beyond dieting and live in a sustainable lifestyle of health, it is important to understand why diets don't work. Diets create a back-and-forth dynamic between the control of dieting and the release of overeating. The success of a diet is usually short-lived because, if your resolve is relaxed for any reason, overeating appears as an automatic reaction.

Dieting and overeating are interconnected; one actually encourages the other to come forth, and vice versa. This works a lot like a teeter-totter: When one end is weighted, the other end rises up. By engaging in dieting, the weight of your resolve acts similarly to the downside of a teeter-totter. When you inevitably relax the strength of your dieting, your overeating automatically takes over the down position on the teeter-totter with its weight.

If you've ever experienced this dynamic, you know how incredibly frustrating it can be. I know I have, and that's why I wanted to find a way to get beyond this up-and-down cycle for myself and for my clients. I turned to the therapeutic method of Voice Dialogue, the Psychology of Selves, and Aware Ego theory created and developed by Drs. Hal and Sidra Stone. I found that the chronic pattern of dieting and overeating could be transcended when I worked with it as a system of inner selves.

The word "transcend" means "to go beyond the ordinary limits of," and that is what Voice Dialogue can do, since it is a method for expanding consciousness. You can discover, one by one, the different parts that make up your Unconscious Eating Selves. You can also open to and develop some new and valuable Conscious Eating Selves. After working with each self within a pair of opposites, you will be able to energetically hold the tension of their differences, using the balancing capacity of an Aware Ego Process. This expanded experience of consciousness comes with self-awareness, self-love, and self-management.

Here is a list of inner selves matched as pairs of opposites. Between each pair, your ever-developing Aware Ego Process will be able to stay connected to the selves while making conscious choices that support your health and weight-loss goals.

A Series of Ten Voice Dialogue Sessions

Unconscious Eating Selves — Conscious Eating Selves

1. Protector of the Status Quo — Aware Ego Process — Spokesperson for Change

2. Personal Self — Aware Ego Process — Impersonal Self

3. Emotional Eater — Aware Ego Process — Inner Nurturer

4. Carefree Self — Aware Ego Process — Inner Activist

5. Nutritional Dictator — Aware Ego Process — Nutritional Guide

6. Exercise Avoider *or* Extremist — Aware Ego process — Exercise Ally

7. Inner Critic — Aware Ego Process — Inner Teacher

8. Inner Rebel — Aware Ego Process — Team Player

9. Inner Dieter — Aware Ego Process — Body Wisdom

10. Negative Thinker — Aware Ego Process — Positive Thinker

The Unconscious Eating Selves play an active role in your dieting and overeating dynamic. Each of them has a particular way it functions, and together they work as an interconnected system of selves to keep you safe and secure in the status quo of your life. The interesting thing is that they don't actually attend to your vulnerable needs in a direct way. Instead, they use their coping strategies of denial, dependence, numbing, avoidance, righteousness, self-criticism, judgment, rebellion, and control to keep you feeling stabilized enough so that you're not inclined to change.

By using the Voice Dialogue method, and meeting these Unconscious Eating Selves one at a time, you will find it easier to separate from their power and begin to develop conscious choice.

There are four Unconscious Eating Selves that are directly related to dieting and overeating. As you do this work and meet these selves, you will better understand how your overeating is trying to comfort, avoid, or manage something for you (Emotional Eater); how your dieting is trying to control you and your food intake (Inner Dieter); how your nutritional awareness is either overbearing or nonexistent (Nutritional Dictator); and how exercise in your life is conveniently avoided or strictly enforced (Exercise Avoider or Extremist).

The other six Unconscious Eating Selves are generally present in most people's lives, but they have particular roles when relating to the dieting and overeating selves. In doing this work, you will come to know and better understand how this system of selves is trying to keep you safe by preventing you from changing (Protector of the Status Quo); how your open heart helps you feel the satisfaction of connection but carries a sensitivity to being easily hurt (Personal Self); how your free spirit lets you move and explore without taking life too seriously (Carefree Self); how your ability to be hard on yourself can be strong and tenacious (Inner Critic); how you feel entitled to have what you want when you want it (Inner Rebel); and how your negative attitude can fill you with discouragement, which keeps you stuck (Negative Thinker).

An energetic separation from each of these selves will activate an Aware Ego Process. As your awareness grows and evolves, you will have more and more perspective on, and management of, these Unconscious Eating Selves. This separation, as it is experienced (one Voice Dialogue session at a time), will give you the freedom to tap into and develop each of the ten opposite Conscious Eating Selves.

The Conscious Eating Selves will offer you some new ways to think, feel, and act that will counter the familiar status-quo responses. Together, these selves will connect you to a sense of power and authority that is uniquely yours, rather than that of your parents or the societal norms of your culture.

Four of these Selves are particular to the issue of dieting and overeating. You will become able to self-nurture in deeper, more satisfying ways (Inner Nurturer); connect to a sense of authority that lives within your own body (Body Wisdom); develop your own nutritional guidance system (Nutritional Guide); and activate a relationship with an inner friend that will support your commitment to healthy exercise (Exercise Ally).

The other six Conscious Eating Selves are a wonderful addition to anyone's life. In doing Voice Dialogue sessions, you will open to a fuller understanding of the reasons you want to change (Spokesperson for Change); develop your ability to set limits with yourself and with others (Impersonal Self); access your own personal activist who can focus on achieving the goals you want for yourself (Inner Activist); tap into your grounded or transpersonal wisdom as a guide to help you live your life (Inner Teacher); develop your ability to work as a team with your inner selves and any outer advisers (Team Player); and finally, connect with a positive attitude that can fuel a mindset of hope and encouragement (Positive Thinker).

Conscious Eating Selves Work will develop your ability to recognize and accept the fact that you have vulnerable needs, so you can care for those needs in a direct way with an Aware Ego Process. These needs can surface for many different reasons and in many different environments. Sometimes you might be hungry, angry, lonely, or tired; sometimes you might feel disappointed with unrealized expectations, or feel powerless with a triggered memory of past abuse, abandonment, or neglect. Whatever you face, you can make decisions that serve the good of the whole you when you accept your human vulnerability and hold yourself with caring and compassion.

Each of these ten Voice Dialogue sessions concentrates on one pair of opposites. You, the facilitator, can work in the exact order I've listed, or you can change the order once you have completed session number one.

1. There is the *Protector of the Status Quo,* whose overall job is to help you stay safe and secure by remaining the same and never changing. Opposite is the Spokesperson for Change who will offer you the ability to articulate and remember what is motivating you to become a Conscious Eater. Is it for health reasons? Personal comfort reasons? Agility reasons? Esthetic reasons? Vitality reasons? Self-image reasons? Career reasons? For sensual or sexual reasons? Personal freedom and independence reasons? Athletic reasons? Financial reasons? Self-esteem reasons? For personal confidence? To prevent future regret? For integrity reasons? For feeding your soul? For personal empowerment? For any other reasons?

2. There is the *Personal Self,* who keeps you energetically open and friendly, making it hard to say no to food and to what others want of you. Opposite is the *Impersonal Self,* who offers you the ability to set limits and hold a boundary with food, with other people, and with difficult situations.

3. There is the *Emotional Eater,* who can take many different forms but whose main purpose is to exert power, and help you avoid

feelings by comforting yourself with food. Opposite is the *Inner Nurturer*, who offers you the ability to soothe yourself with care and concern so you can feel comforted from within when dealing with the difficulties of emotional pain, boredom, inadequacy, or loss.

4. There is the *Carefree Self*, who is light and airy and keeps you from taking anything too seriously, including changing. Opposite is the *Inner Activist*, who helps you stay focused with follow-through, whether that is planning ahead to purchase and prepare food, writing in your food journal, getting to the gym, making time for a walk, or enjoying a long, relaxing bath.

5. There is the *Nutritional Dictator*, who is strict and unbending when it comes to giving food advice, or who keeps you ignorant about the facts of healthful eating. Opposite is the *Nutritional Guide*, who offers you the ability to help yourself, in a kind and caring way, to make healthy nutritional choices.

6. There is the *Exercise Avoider*, who keeps you sedentary, or the *Exercise Extremist*, who pushes you to burn more and more calories even if it puts your body at risk. Opposite is the *Exercise Ally*, who helps support your health needs with exercise and movement.

7. The *Inner Critic* requires you to meet a standard that is often unreasonable, unattainable, and based on social norms rather than on your own uniqueness. Opposite is the *Inner Teacher*, who offers you the ability to experience your own value and self-worth from a deep inner wisdom or transpersonal presence that can always be available to you if you'll just take the time to quiet yourself and listen.

8. The *Inner Rebel* helps you by protecting your individuality from the authority and standards of others, but its rogue nature can sabotage your commitment to change. Opposite is the *Team*

Player, who offers you the ability to join your other inner selves and outer advisors to become aligned in support of your health and weight-loss goals.

9. The *Inner Dieter* likes to be in control, especially with your food choices, and makes a point of rigidly monitoring what you eat and don't eat. Opposite is the *Body Wisdom,* who offers you the ability to connect with the authority of your body's innate knowing so you can eat intuitively when you feel body hunger, stop when you feel body fullness, and make sensible food choices that agree with your body's desire for pleasure and satisfaction.

10. There is the *Negative Thinker,* whose negative mindset causes you to feel depressed, discouraged, and defeated, all emotions that can trigger overeating as a comfort response. Opposite is the *Positive Thinker,* who offers you the ability to positively support and encourage yourself during any challenges that come your way.

I recommend doing Voice Dialogue with these pairs as a ten-session series, without getting distracted by any other inner selves that might be clamoring for attention. Each pair has a theme, one self representing an established pattern of behavior, and the opposing self carrying something new and different. Staying focused on developing an Aware Ego Process between each of these pairs of opposites will counteract any unconscious sabotaging that may try to sneak in and take you off track.

I suggest two exceptions to this recommendation. One is when some aspect of your vulnerability is ready to be heard, and appears in a session as a self or a system of selves. It is a great gift to your consciousness process when your vulnerability allows itself to be seen. Value your vulnerable selves with time and focused attention, and you will be rewarded.

If you have experienced trauma in your past, selves may show up that relate back to that time in your life. You may have been physically or sexually abused, neglected, or abandoned as a child or adult, or lived through a powerfully frightening experience like a car accident, armed combat, or the death of a loved one. Vulnerable feelings of shame, worthlessness, self-loathing, and terror may live deep inside you. These feelings can unconsciously fuel the addictive nature of a dieting and overeating cycle.

If any of these vulnerable selves becomes available during a session, you can do Voice Dialogue with it. Be sure your facilitator has experience with this depth of work, and then go forward slowly and respectfully. When you are able to meet and listen to your vulnerable selves, you will be able to separate from them enough to hold and manage their needs through an Aware Ego Process.

The second exception is when a different self than you were expecting spontaneously shows up in a session. Everyone's inner self system is unique, so it's quite possible that this will happen. The self may be relevant to the theme of that session, or it may be introducing a new theme that can be a helpful addition to your Conscious Eating Selves Work.

The first exception is pretty straightforward. If a vulnerable self shows up and it feels right, work with it. The second falls into a gray area. Sometimes a self wants to distract your focus, to keep the status quo firmly in place, and sometimes a self comes into a session and is profoundly important to the work. It can be challenging to decipher which is the case. If in doubt, let the self speak.

In addition, I suggest you list the inner selves that show up but never get worked with. They are probably important to your overall consciousness process, so let them speak once you have completed the series of ten.

Here are some other pairs of opposites that you might want to eventually work with. Full and Spacious, No and Yes, Special and Ordinary, Entitlement and Acceptance, Mind and Body, Child and Adult, Giver and Receiver, Pleaser and Truth Teller, Controlling and Laid Back, Inadequate and Capable, Pusher and Aphrodite, Responsible and Free Spirit, Insecure and Confident, Hungry and Nourished, Shy and Assertive, Chaotic and Organized, Concern for What Others Might Think and Self-Authority, Stressed and Content, Procrastinator and Finisher, Heavy and Light, Numb and Passionate, Timid and Adventurer, Hidden and Exposed, Doing and Being, Caregiver and Self-Concern, Victim and Survivor, and Perfectionist and Pragmatist. And, especially for women, there are the opposites Inner Patriarch and Feminine Power.

There are many benefits you will experience from doing Conscious Eating Selves Work. You'll have more awareness of who you are, and you'll be able to value yourself more. You'll be more accepting of your physical body and what you look like. You'll be better able to encourage yourself and appreciate your own effort. You'll begin to recognize old habits when they appear, with an increased chance of changing your behavior to support your new, conscious lifestyle.

You will have more connection to your inner selves because you'll have spent time with them and come to appreciate what they each do for you. This connection will allow your selves to feel like they are part of your team, with less chance of rogue behavior. You'll feel more alive with vitality and inner complexity. You'll recognize that you really do have choices, and you'll feel the freedom to do things differently.

You will notice when you are too energetically open and be able to recalibrate, to protect yourself with boundaries. You'll find it easier to say no to yourself and to others when it's in your best interest.

You will be able to develop your eating intuition. This means staying connected to your body, and noticing when you are hungry, making food choices that will satisfy your desire for certain tastes, textures, and cravings, slowing down your eating so you can make it a fulfilling experience, and letting yourself feel and be informed by your belly's fullness as it comes on.

You will feel less discouraged and more hopeful about yourself and your ability to achieve what you want for yourself. You'll begin to self-nurture in ways that are not fattening, numbing or self-destructive. You'll be more motivated to exert energy, and you'll feel supported from within yourself to take the time to exercise your body. You'll make a connection with your own sense of authority and no longer be so influenced by others' opinions. And, you'll find it easier to connect with Spirit.

As a Conscious Eater, your Aware Ego Process will let you notice the energetic pull of your Unconscious Eating Selves without giving them the full power to run you. And while this is happening, an Aware Ego Process can access the Conscious Eating Selves and effectively use them to enhance your experience of conscious eating and conscious living.

The Final Eighth

Bridgit Dengel Gaspard, LCSW

Creative, talented, dedicated individuals, who are clear about their goals but are somehow impeded from consummating their last few steps, struggle with the phenomenon I call the final eighth. These clients are far along in their process, have been facilitated, and have an Aware Ego Process with knowledge of their primary and disowned selves and their bonding patterns.

Perhaps
their singing voices are finally in shape
they have mourned their loss
they have lost the weight
they have saved enough money for a down payment
they have updated their resume
their novel is written after ten serious drafts
they have the passport

But they have not:
joined the choir
accepted social invitations
engaged a real estate broker
interviewed
contacted a publisher
booked the trip

They are aware of this and regularly lament, "I don't know why I didn't do what I said I would last week!" "Why did I forget to make that phone call? Again?" "Why am I suddenly too exhausted to follow up?" "Why won't I edit my plays (which are written and have been performed to accolades) and submit them to the (interested) publisher?"

The final eighth is simultaneously concrete and ephemeral. It encompasses the execution of the ultimate series of actions necessary to complete a project, achieve a goal, and realize a dream, which is a transformational experience. The first seven eighths (which can take years) refer to all that went before. This can include emotional healing, discovering your passion and engaging in it, identifying resilient and destructive patterns of behavior, struggling with difficult habits, psycho-spiritual development, and self-exploration toward authenticity. The stall at the final eighth is usually a reflection of an enormous amount of hard work. Congratulations are in order.

Many People Stop In Sight of the Finish Line

Psychologists and scientists believe the imperative to strive toward higher levels of accomplishment has biological and developmental underpinnings. The final eighth is not dissimilar to the upper levels of Abraham Maslow's (1954) hierarchy of needs, which focuses on self-actualization by realizing one's potential through achievement and recognition as well as self-transcendence.

"The personal, intentional, planful, deliberate, goal-oriented, or striving component of motivation" (Baumeister, et al., 1998), which is integral to a commitment to making your dreams come true, incorporates self-reflection, self-regulation, self-concept, self-esteem, and self-determination. But which selves are primary in relation to the stated goal? Which selves support the dream? Which selves don't — and for good reasons? Are the Visionary Selves in synch with the Action Selves? And what is the unconscious relating through dreams? What vulnerabilities are being struck?

Growing and taking risks require enduring mistakes and failing, as it is inherent in the process of learning. In their early days, walkers spend considerable time crawling and falling! How do the Protector and Controller sub-personalities handle potential humiliation? People need to practice making choices, following through, tolerating the experience of things not working as envisioned, and maturing through the emergent problem solving. Whether it's playing the didgeridoo or investing in the stock market, extending your personal frontier takes courage as you voluntarily expose yourself to your brilliance, your inadequacies, and to public scrutiny. Progress is not linear. What selves are able to handle inevitable blunders? Hey, you never know — a series of missteps might syncopate into some kickin' choreography! Which sub-personalities step in when efforts are fulfilled beyond expectation? Who are positive role models for the final eighth? For example, how many people remember a politician who lost his bid for a seat in the U.S. House of Representatives in 2000 but won the more prestigious seat in the Senate in 2004? You will recognize him now as President Barack Obama.

198 The Voice Dialogue Anthology

The drive toward the final eighth is also influenced by the well-known condition that, despite how exceptional and intense an event, responses to complex or novel stimuli decrease after a certain point (Yerkes & Dodson, 1908). This is easy to see in the world of uber-sports. What do skiers who parachute from helicopters down to the mountaintop do for an encore? Don a wing suit, become a birdman, and do fly-bys at 140 miles an hour, I suppose. An important feature of culminating the final eighth is the certitude that it hurls you toward embarking on a first eighth again. Some writers start their next novel before figuring out the denouement of their nearly concluded book. This is an example of an effective technique to help people overcome their stalled state so they have somewhere to focus other than the abyss of a brand-new story. If the tool works, use it. However, this chapter explores the dynamics underneath the not-quite-culminated project that will not budge. Any behavior or attitude (like lollygagging or laziness) can indicate a variety of underlying possibilities on a continuum ranging from a legitimate timeout to gather your thoughts, to paralyzing anxiety and depression, to brain damage. The concept of the final eighth assumes that pathology is ruled out, and basic functioning (and beyond) is ruled in.

The final eighth is the dynamic phenomenon of thriving in your personal, uncharted territory of creative expression (which does not have to be artistic). Often, people do a tremendous amount of work and stop at the final eighth unable to continue, despite being highly dissatisfied with their status quo. They endorse myriad uncomfortable emotions whose source is not easily characterized. The client may feel dissatisfied, tense, unhappy, angry, anxious and irritable. Do these feelings reflect fear of acting on the final eighth, or are they the result of not acting on it? Either way the client feels stuck and perturbed.

Clients regularly blame themselves when their dream does not materialize. Inner Critics attack them for not doing visualizations "well enough." They use the lack of manifestation as evidence of failing at techniques that implore us to simply focus on positive imaging in order to attract what we want. The hidden secret to *The Secret* (Byrne, 2000) is that the agendas of all the relevant selves have not been explored and honored.

Every behavior serves a function. The factors that energize beginnings are often different from those that promote and sustain persistence.

Do Not Negate Negativity

As a practitioner, it is a privilege to work with these imaginative clients. It is important to not inadvertently get attached to their goal. When facilitating sub-personalities it is vital to also embrace ordinary, ignorant, inept selves. They have gifts to celebrate. There are Being Selves who may revolt and use any means necessary to slow down, such as activating fatigue and confusion. A self with this philosophy may subscribe to "don't just do something — sit there!" It is important not to negate Negative Selves.

Sometimes not executing the final eighth is a signal to relinquish the goal. It might be time to let it go. Not every plan is consummated, nor should it be. A powerful facilitation with a Disowned sub-personality who refused to support the ambitions of the Primary Self System exemplifies this. The uniquely talented sub-personality felt that the objective, toward which progress had been made, reflected the Pleaser's need to comply with social expectations. The disowned sub-personality wept as he acknowledged that his insurmountable resistance to completing the final eighth was enraging his Primary Self System. Still, he could not allow attainment, as he felt it would permanently bury any future opportunity for the client's larger gifts to come to fruition. Far from simply being "negative," this sub-personality was correct, which transformed the client's relationship with his goal. After separating from these selves, his Aware Ego Process incorporated refocusing and reprioritizing. There can always be surprises.

Tarrying at the final eighth may indicate the aspiration is unsuitable, misguided, or too small. Maybe the timing is off. Another client's disowned self admitted to being part of the force immobilizing her. This sub-personality reported: "Until she deals with her deficits, there is no chance she's going to flower." It is important to note that this was not a punitive Inner Critic; this was an accurate assessment of the client's inabilities in vital domains of her life including the physical and financial.

There are legitimate reasons for not completing the final eighth. Fears expressed by varying selves are validated, as for every gain there is a loss. Some sub-personalities worry that too much change in the status quo will obliterate them. Many sub-personalities enjoy privacy, anonymity, downtime, and low expectations. To these selves, capitalizing on opportunity is a nightmare of being on call and obligated to constantly invent encores superior to the previous undertaking. They prefer to avoid commitment, public exposure, strong emotions, dependence, independence, and change. For some, the mere sensation of acknowledging a need elicits anxiety, while other sub-personalities fear stoking their hopes and being unable to handle disappointment. Still others are terrified of evoking jealousy and rage and provoking an attack. Intransigent stuckness may lead to discovering Angry Selves who are furious over early childhood wounds. These selves won't allow success because they believe that will release the original caretakers of blame. Other selves consider it an act of betrayal to outdo their parents, or think it immoral to thrive while another languishes.

Inner Saboteurs

So-called saboteurs may astonish, especially when they do not look "obstructive." They take many forms including popular sub-personalities like the Hostess with the Mostess, the Nurturer (to everyone else), the Can-Do Guy, and the Peacemaker. One client, who identifies as a feminist, was stunned to find she *still* has a disowned Inner Snow White who is waiting for her prince and is stunting professional competence so as to preserve her chances for a relationship. Perfectionist Selves may purport to want a specific goal, but engage in effective, societally endorsed procrastination such as doing endless research (but never getting to the dissertation), or waiting for the right moment (that never arrives) as they protect against the direct experience of negative emotions.

Honoring prior agreements may not be feasible when one becomes serious about the final eighth, but the pressure to defer to familiar roles is immense. Using disapproval and rejection, the world may punish for the withholding of these energies. It's vital to process that some friends, family, and colleagues operate in the realm of deprivation and envy, are not willing to accept change, and will not share in the client's triumph. These Outer Saboteurs will do everything in their power to encourage the client's Inner Subversives. There can be far more foul-weather friends than fair-weather friends. Your diminished interest in meeting for coffee and complaining will not necessarily be met with a willingness to replace it with sharing java and joy.

The pressure is indeed on in the final eighth. What makes you strong can also make you vulnerable. There is the misperception that as we grow robust, wiser, and more conscious we need less protection. In fact we may need more. Hiding in the final eighth is a long-term comfort zone for many people. Since no actual calculations are ever made, as there is no final product to measure, the mortification of judgment is avoided.

Core Negative Beliefs

"I'm worthless.""I'm a victim.""I am unlovable." These are examples of core beliefs, the foundation on which many people unconsciously base their lives (Beck, 1995). Core negative beliefs often feel so intrinsic to who we are, that they have the essence of being asked to differentiate the "H2" from the "O" when drinking water. It can feel impossible to wrap one's mind around the fact that these beliefs are not only separate entities from oneself but are bald-faced lies that have fueled a lifetime's decision-making and behavior. Primary and disowned selves routinely maintain *unexplored* distorted internal schemata they deem *the obvious truth.* They include: "You will never measure up"; "Nothing works out"; "You are ugly, inferior, stupid, unlucky, etc."

Part of the confusion when beginning to explore these beliefs is the core negative belief that defines who we are (e.g., worthless) at the same time that we are desperate for it not to be true (e.g., I *am* worthwhile!) Our absolute conviction is also our worst fear. This conundrum is the organizing principle that motivates many self systems. For example, if we both believe and fear (and hope it's false) that we are worthless, different parts of ourselves react accordingly. Inner Perfectionists and Achievers bolt into action and are motivated to make it *not true* by trying to be the best at every endeavor. Automatic thoughts of Inner Critics and Pushers are mobilized in the form of constant rebukes to improve and mandates to comply with others' expectations and desires. One of the side effects is that accomplishments accrue and people often move toward the final eighth. To avoid feeling the vulnerability underneath the negative belief, an Inner Couch Potato triggers avoidance behaviors. An Inner Shopper impulsively hits the stores, maxing her credit cards. An Inner Philosopher may choose the intellectual route and deepen his commitment to nihilism. Some sub-personalities enforce negative paradigms so the Inner Critic may increase its toxicity through insults and other esteem-shattering mechanisms.

Perhaps the Inner Child is sad when a romantic date ends (just for the evening). She feels the separation as pain, and interprets the discomfort as verifying the "truth" of her core negative belief: I am unlovable. The fact that the couple has a date scheduled in two days does not quiet the intensification of unbearable emotions including shame, grief, despair, rage, depression, etc. Eventually her Inner Overeater, who feels helpless as a devotee of the core negative belief, takes action and picks up the tool she knows best — a spoon. She grabs the quarts of Coffee Heath Bar Crunch ice cream, nestles with her Inner Fantasizer (who hopes the negative belief is false), and picks up a romance novel to distract herself amidst the heaving corsets, Caribbean sunsets, and princely rescues.

Where do these core negative beliefs come from? They are the imprimatur of our original caretakers, metabolized by integrating parental and societal injunctions in order to protect vulnerability and ensure safety and acceptance by others. A few common regulations are "don't be self-ish," "be nice," "be loyal to your parents," "boys are strong," and "don't hurt people." Credos like "the punishment fits the crime," "you made your bed, now lie in it," "don't get too big for your britches," "a fool and his money are soon parted," paralyze initiative as many Inner Selves adopt these silent, powerful mantras. Under the banner of safekeeping, this advice is given to children, who internalize it and then perceive themselves as fundamentally flawed and irredeemably bad. The scar tissue around this primal wounding forms the core negative belief. People have only one or two core negative beliefs where everything fits, like a black hole in space pulling all matter inside, getting heavier and stronger. Although the variety of scenarios is endless, the foundation upon which they are played is the same.

Visualizing your one or two core negative beliefs as an invisible carpet is an effective metaphor. If your fundamental truth is "nothing works out," you will stand on that Inner Carpet unconsciously dedicated to your core negative beliefs, whether you are in a cave or on Capitol Hill. From that default vantage point, you can fail on a camping trip (by taking the rain personally) as easily as you can perceive failure while lobbying for clean water (even if your congressman actually met with you and agreed to bring it to the subcommittee the following month).

When sub-personalities no longer enforce ancestral schemata, grief and depression may be elicited as the separation from the family credos deepens. Sadness may accompany the realization of the final eighth due to any number of reasons including acknowledging that the feat does not measure up to the fantasy, or close relationships reconfigure, or a loved one is no longer alive to share the experience, or regret that thriving "took this long."

There's Gold in Them Thar Shadows

"I got off the rug yesterday!" is an expression often heard in my practice. The carpet of core negative beliefs is replaced by imagining a supportive base of vitality or presence. Most people assume their final eighth is the legacy of fear of failure, but the genuine resistance to transformation is far more often fear of success. Shadow work for many people has to do with welcoming their powerful, gifted, gorgeous Selves because, as Marianne Williamson states, "Our deepest fear is not that we are inadequate. Our deepest fear is that we are powerful beyond measure. It is our light, not our darkness that most frightens us"(Williamson, 1992, pp.190–191).

Separating selves from their endorsement of core negative beliefs can be revelatory. After a session, numerous clients experience vertigo that quickly resolves. This can be an indication of the clients' expanded perspective altering their center of gravity as the Aware Ego Process incorporates the gifts of the disowned selves and shifts the Primary Self System. Potential consequences of consummating the final eighth must include its transcendental nature, which can be disorienting.

The Final Eighth

Competencies are necessary to foster a dream. It's effective to instigate skills-building *in advance* when navigating the unplumbed terrain of achieving the final eighth. Illustrations include: take responsibility for your vulnerability and provide ongoing self-care; become less dependent on external validation; identify whether your physical/fiscal environs support your goal; nurture Inner Parents to navigate your altered status, strengthen your impersonal energy to set and maintain boundaries; know your work style and defend it; cultivate the ability to have peak experiences. Directly applicable is the work of Markus and Nurius (1986), who discuss the aspect of a "possible self" providing the bridge to action, as well as the contributions of Levenson (1978), who suggests that dreams and visions expand and define the "possible self." A metaphor for the process might be a relay race, with a team of sub-personalities passing the baton to the next series of Inner Selves. Clients investigate the possibility of cultivating additional selves to support the future goal as they live their current life.

The final eighth is not static, and once fulfilled cycles anew. The ability to manage the unknown and tolerate the doubt, uncertainty, chaos, and tentativeness accompanying the realm of the unfamiliar is required. While fear of failure, making mistakes and losing approval is part of the domain of the final eighth, I believe the stronger impediment is fear of success. Part of the journey of the final eighth is learning to relish oneself and one's accomplishments, recognitions and honors. Embracing opposite selves and letting go of core negative beliefs is basking in the joy and liberation of non-duality. Yes, that's transcendence. Voice Dialogue is an extremely effective tool to explore this terrain.

References

Baumeister, R., E. Bratslavsky, M. Muraven, and D. Tice. "Ego depletion: Is the active self a limited resource?" *Journal of Personality and Social Psychology*, 74(5), 1252–1265. In the online article: www.edpsycinteractive.org/topics/regsys/conation.html, 1998.

Beck, J. *Cognitive therapy: Basics and beyond.* New York: Guildford, 1995.

Byrne, R. *The secret.* New York: Simon & Schuster, 2006.

Levenson, D. *The seasons of a man's life.* New York: Ballantine, 1978.

Markus, H. & Nurius, P. Possible selves. *American Psychologist,* 41, 954–969, 1986.

Maslow, A. *Motivation and personality.* New York: Harper & Brothers, 1954.

Stone, H. and S. Stone. *Embracing our selves.* Novato, CA: Nataraj Publishing, 1989.

Williamson, M. *A return to love: Reflections on the principles of a course in miracles.* New York: Harper Collins, 1992.

Yerkes, R., and J. Dodson. "The relation of strength of stimulus to rapidity of habit formation." *Journal of Comparative Neurology and Psychology,* 18, 459–482, 1908.

Part II

Section I

*What Differentiates the Psychology
of the Aware Ego from Other Systems?*

Voice Dialogue: The Essential Difference

Miriam Dyak, BA, CC

The human brain is a collector. It gathers information, compares it to all the data it has previously compiled, and then files the new impression in a likely category. The brain is loath to go out on a limb and create an entirely new file for a completely unknown, unconnected classification. Some ancient alarm bell sounds alerting us we're going beyond the known, "off the deep end." Our primary selves, ever focused on safety and survival, assure us, "No, this concept isn't really new. See, here — it fits right in with what you've already learned. Relax, you're safe." This way of greeting the new also echoes our ancient tribal consciousness. There is a sense that what comes from a stranger outside the tribe may be dangerous, but, if one of our own — our shaman, our warrior — goes out and brings back this same new thing to the tribe, it is held sacred because we have won it and it now belongs to us.

Because of this, for all the years Voice Dialogue facilitators and teachers have sought to introduce this work to their professional and personal communities, we have been met with (in the early days) "Oh, I know what that is, it's just like Gestalt" or "That sounds a lot like Psychosynthesis." In more recent times we're more likely to hear, "I already do that — I'm trained in IFS (Internal Family Systems)" or "Yes, of course, I've done a workshop in Big Mind." All of these (most likely unconscious) responses have in common an effect of relaxation for the person hearing about

Voice Dialogue for the first time. When we're on the listening end of the communication about something new and different, our primary selves are relieved that we're already up on everything, i.e. we haven't missed something important, and there is no real challenge made to what we already know.

For the persons attempting to introduce Voice Dialogue there is a common frustration of trying to communicate what is essentially different about this work. With colleagues who work with a modality related to Voice Dialogue, I have often found the most benefit in exchanging sessions. Then we each "get it" and can go back to our respective communities and present the new ideas in a comfortable context. Certainly the colleague with whom I do the exchange will be better at communicating her/his impression of Voice Dialogue to colleagues and peers in Gestalt, Psychosynthesis, IFS, Big Mind, TA, etc., than I would be, because they are coming from within the "tribe" of that work.

At this point, however, in the evolution of Voice Dialogue as a method and the Psychology of the Aware Ego as a theory, it could be very helpful to articulate some of the essential qualities that are unique to this work and that make the Voice Dialogue method significantly different from other kinds of "parts work," personal growth modalities, and approaches to the development of consciousness. It could also be beneficial to have more understanding of where there is real overlap — what we share with other modalities. Then, whether or not we are able in any given situation to successfully communicate this difference to others, we would at least gain clarity for ourselves and establish a stronger ground and identity for our practice.

What follows is a *beginning* attempt to describe aspects of Voice Dialogue theory and practice that are essential and sometimes unique. I wish to state clearly from the outset that I do not have the necessary training and background to do a thorough side-by-side comparison of Voice Dialogue with other "similar" modalities (which might also require a much lengthier treatment), so I will place my primary emphasis on the qualities of the work I know and have practiced for over twenty-five years. I will try to make clear where these qualities are shared with other modalities that work with inner selves, and which ones are unique to Voice Dialogue. I will also try to point out where this work appears to overlap with these other modalities, but in actuality is distinctly different (references, 2).

Tracing the roots of Voice Dialogue and "parts work" would also be extremely valuable but lengthier than this exploration will allow. Suffice it to say that before the Stones developed Voice Dialogue as we know it, Gestalt had already pointed out "top dog" and "underdog" selves and used two-chair work to have selves talk with each other; Jung spoke in terms of complexes and archetypes, and revealed how the animus and anima were the masculine self inside the woman and the feminine inside the man; Assagioli created Psychosynthesis as a system for bringing parts of the personality into a more cohesive whole as well as accessing a higher, transpersonal Self; Satir worked with a "parts party" in family therapy; and Berne had created a way of working with parent and child selves in Transactional Analysis. In the same era, *The Three Faces Of Eve* and *Sybil* brought awareness of multiple personalities into the culture and helped us understand that selves were not merely mental constructs but have a profound physical and energetic impact as well. As of this writing (2010), several additional modalities have come along with new ways of working with parts and consciousness. In addition to IFS and Big Mind (the latter grew out of Voice Dialogue), there is also Ego State Therapy, focused mainly on trauma recovery, the DNMS (Developmental Needs Meeting Strategy) which, like TA, focuses on inner parent and child selves, ARC (A Return to Consciousness), which has some similarities to the Body Dialogue work developed by Tamar Stone, and perhaps more that I'm not yet aware of. People everywhere are waking up to the multifaceted nature of the psyche and devising new creative ways to work with parts or selves.

Doubtless we could also go back in time to earlier cultures and find a great awareness of human multidimensionality. Carl Jung, Joseph Campbell, the Stones, and others have all pointed out how the Greek pantheon of gods represented multiple aspects of human nature (as do other families of gods in Roman, Hindu, Celtic, and many indigenous religions). In fact, the earliest known written story, that of the goddess Inanna, dating back more than 5,000 years, is about "…what happens when we reject major powers in order to take on civilization," and "one of the major teachings of the myth is that all the things we sent away or killed wait for us to come and visit and reclaim them in the underworld" (Houston, J.). The concepts of primary and disowned selves, of the struggle of opposites, and that there is some core essence in our being that needs to be revealed and claimed, are as old as our oldest myths, fairytales, and folk legends, as well as the Old and New Testaments and the sacred stories of every culture. What is different and sometimes new is how we choose to work with these selves, archetypes, and opposites.

In that light it is also very important to mention that all these modalities, including Voice Dialogue, are in the hands of the facilitator. Something I might consider absolutely fundamental to my practice of Voice Dialogue might not even be included in the way certain other facilitators work with this process, and I imagine this is true for other modalities as well. Also, thankfully, there has been much exchange among colleagues, so that many of us are knowingly or unknowingly drawing on a blend of several approaches. What is possible to delineate, then, is the overall foundation, direction, and intention of the work rather than the unique qualities of each facilitator's practice.

Five Essential Elements Unique to Voice Dialogue

Let's begin then with five elements that are essential to Voice Dialogue and distinguish this process from other approaches. The first four are:

1. The physical/energetic separation of the selves/energies from each other;

2. The birth out of that separation of an Aware Ego Process;

3. The conscious regulation of energy both in the body and psyche of the individual and in relationship to others; and

4. The concept that identity and consciousness can be in the whole living process rather than the result of attainment or the realization of Self.

Fifth is the deliberate non-certification of the work, its development as an *open-source* process, and how that has not only determined how Voice Dialogue is practiced but also colored the experience of both facilitator and subject in pursuing the work.

1. Separation and embodiment of the selves: Dr. Betty Bosdell, who came to Voice Dialogue from a background in Psychosynthesis as well as Gestalt, TA, and Jungian psychology among other modalities, says that the "unique thing about Voice Dialogue is the separation of the energies. In almost all other methods, you have parts talking to parts. It's the major difference and also the genius of Voice Dialogue because it keeps all the energies of the parts really straight" (B. Bosdell, personal communication. December, 2009). This is the difference with Voice Dialogue that strikes people immediately. A colleague trained in ARC commented after her first Voice Dialogue session, "The clarity that separating the selves brings is really exciting. It's very real and very respectful."

Hal Stone, commenting on the difference between his experience of selves in Voice Dialogue from his experiences in Jungian analysis and Gestalt, says, "It is a very different experience to talk to a self in a visualization or in your journal than it is to become a self where the energy is held by someone else. Until I had the experience of becoming the self/complex they were not real to me. What is interesting is the fact that the same thing was true of my experience with Gestalt therapy. It was clear that [the selves] held different contents, but they just weren't real to me. This is why the beginning of Sidra's and my work was so very dramatic, even shocking for us. To know the child complex or self is one thing. To experience being the child was an entirely different experience, and we were in totally new territory" (H. Stone, personal communication, January 2010). Hearing this from Hal Stone makes perfect sense to me because it is through moving into a self that I discover its aliveness in my body and being. Until I move into the self's energy, I don't really have a clue how it changes me on physical, emotional, mental, or spiritual levels because the fullness of each self is revealed through embodiment. And, this is perhaps a significant reason why it's hard to grasp Voice Dialogue only on an intellectual level — it has to be experienced.

Involved in this literal physical and energetic separation is experiencing how each self lives in the body — how it moves, breathes, how it does or doesn't use the senses, its relationship to ground. Dramatically, physical symptoms may appear or disappear when one physically moves into or out of a self. The subject may become aware that a certain tension in the neck or shoulders is a sure sign that a particular self is present. Separating out the self through movement, and allowing its full embodiment, does not occur in the same way when the process of connecting to selves is internalized, experienced as an inner guided journey. Nor can one hear the nuanced voice tones or perceive the body language and gestures of each self in this way when the dialogue is purely internal.

2. The initiation and evolution of an Aware Ego Process: The Aware Ego Process differs from many other approaches to personal growth in that it is an ongoing process one cultivates rather than a result one strives for. The Stones, and many others, have described the Aware Ego as "more a verb than a noun." The nature of Aware Ego is in some ways very much like the "I" or "Self" in Psychosynthesis, and the process of Self leadership in IFS, especially as these are seen to have an ongoing evolving ability to function separately from all the selves, and at the same time be in relationship to them. However, Voice Dialogue and the Psychology of the Aware Ego hold a different perspective on the goal of separating from selves and creating an Aware Ego Process. There is not an explicit or implicit search for wholeness, unity, or integration in the sense of all the parts needing to in some way heal, transform, or reconcile with each other, though the process certainly leads to the selves being understood and embraced. The Aware Ego is just fine with ambiguity, lack of unity, unreconciled opposites — in fact from an Aware Ego perspective we expect them and have no judgment of them. *In Voice Dialogue you already have unity if you can become conscious of it,* so the only thing to strive for is separation ("disidentification," as Assagioli first put it), which results in conscious awareness, and the ability through the Aware Ego Process to exercise choice and create an ongoing dynamic balancing between opposites.

From a Voice Dialogue perspective, what we have before the Aware Ego begins to develop is an "operating ego," a group of primary selves that defines itself as the person, functions as the person. It is often some self or selves from this operating ego that go to therapy, enroll in workshops, or undertake a spiritual practice. Unless the personal growth process includes separation from these selves, it is possible for this self or group of selves to continue to pretend they are the person in question all through their exploration of the chosen modality. The Aware Ego Process, like the Self in Psychosynthesis and Self Leadership in IFS, gives us a completely different context in which to engage in therapy, and for that matter, in life. I believe that IFS, Psychosynthesis, and other forms of parts work definitely help us to shift out of the selves and into a consciousness that is beyond their realm. The Aware Ego Process in Voice Dialogue gives one a concrete, physical, and energetic place from which to choreograph the dance of one's inner selves. That separate place and the ability to recognize over time with practice when one has successfully arrived there, make a tangible difference in clarity, choice, and functioning beyond the world of the selves.

The Aware Ego is also fully both a psychological and spiritual process that activates a holographic connection between our personal history and archetypal, universal reality. The Aware Ego exists in relation to the selves from which separation has occurred, and Voice Dialogue is essentially a relational process, inside and out. Hal Stone comments, "The ignition of the Aware Ego Process is also the ignition of the Intelligence machinery that lies within us, and we begin to become open to information networks that were closed to us before. This Intelligence activation is related to what Jung called the Individuation process, but they are not the same. The Intelligence that is activated in our work leads to a relational process as well as our personal one. Individuation is a process that happens primarily within us" (H. Stone, personal communication, January 2010).

3. The conscious regulation of energy both in the body and psyche of the individual and in relationship to others: Working with inner selves on a purely energetic level apart from any content is an aspect of Voice Dialogue that is quite different from other approaches to parts work. For those who have not experienced this aspect of the work, an example would be separating from a very mental self and also from a very feeling self. After facilitating these selves, one would have the beginning of an Aware Ego Process in relation to them. From Aware Ego one could invite in their energy separately or together, find where each lives in the body, and create a workable balance between them purely on the level of energy and body experience. If the head and heart can function well in the same body, then the *energies* of a mental self and a feeling self can work together just as well even if they are not in agreement on a content level at all.

Many other therapeutic modalities focus on tracking a felt sense of energy in the body and also on energetic, nonverbal communication between people. IFS, for example, will help the client notice how a particular self feels in the body. I do not, however, know of another approach to parts work that works with consciously calling in the *energy* of a particular self, locating that energy in the body, being able in Aware Ego to have choice about how that energy affects the physical body, using intention to increase or decrease the intensity of the energy (dialing up and dialing down), and then learning how to do the same with the energy of an opposite self in order to bring the opposite selves into a new dynamic balance. All these things are done purely on the level of energy through the Aware Ego Process.

Regulating the energies of the selves in this way is a direct outgrowth of the *physical* separation of selves and the development of an Aware Ego Process out of that separation. Having an ability to rebalance the selves purely on the level of energy can be life changing because it makes it possible for us to immediately get beyond the entrenched issues, attitudes, oppositions, and histories of the individual selves, and find a way through Aware Ego to have the *energies* of the selves work together on the level of body, felt sense, and nonverbal communication *without trying to get the selves to change.* Making changes in the self system purely through shifts in energy and learning in Aware Ego to regulate these energies can have very positive consequences for the selves, especially since they don't have to change in order to make that happen.

In addition, Voice Dialogue carries an awareness of energy a step further by focusing on the recognition and regulation of energy in outer as well as inner relationships. Through the facilitation of selves, the subject learns to identify when there is/isn't "linkage," the Voice Dialogue term for a felt energetic connection between people. It is also out of the full physical embodiment of each self that we become aware of the degree to which any particular self can "link" energetically with others. This ability to create a felt energetic connection between ourselves and other people is key to Voice Dialogue relationship work. And when this is further developed into the ability to link energetically through an Aware Ego Process, it is unique to Voice Dialogue.

What also is different in and possibly unique to Voice Dialogue is that the facilitator is in direct verbal and energetic communication with the selves, rather than guiding the subject to communicate on an inner level with each individual self. This means the facilitator must match or resonate with the energy of the self being facilitated as well as hold an energetic connection to its opposite. In other words, the facilitator has to be in the Aware Ego Process, hold an energetic balance between opposites, and model a conscious energy management so that the subject will gradually be able to grow into these abilities as well.

4. Identity and consciousness in the whole living process: Voice Dialogue offers a radically new approach to consciousness. *You are already conscious* whenever you can achieve three elements: experiencing the selves; awareness of the selves; and holding balance between the opposites of the selves through an Aware Ego Process. Within the Psychology of the Aware Ego there is no hierarchy created within the psyche — no Self is made higher or better or beyond other selves to strive toward, and at the same time there are no selves that need to be rejected as less than, inauthentic, false, etc. There is nothing that needs to be changed in the personality in order to reach consciousness, and identity resides in the whole process rather than in any self or Self, or in any attainment of either a psychological or spiritual kind.

Among other results, this has a profound effect on the way our inner selves perceive the Voice Dialogue process. Even though all the modalities I have mentioned hold inner selves with (varying degrees of) respect and certainly treat them with compassion and kindness, there is a profound relaxation that occurs when selves understand they are being appreciated *as they are* and are not expected to integrate, unburden, change, evolve, or do anything other than be themselves. To be sure, integration, unburdening, change, and evolution all occur, but instead of expecting the selves to change, Voice Dialogue changes the context within which they operate. In a sense Voice Dialogue facilitation invites the selves into a new home where each can have its own room — room to breathe, room to live, room to be itself free from attack and interference. Quite naturally the more the self lives in that place, the more it does relax and to a certain extent evolves, but at its own pace.

5. The open-source nature of Voice Dialogue as an approach to consciousness: I'm coming to understand that everything in Voice Dialogue happens within the context of the Stones' decision not to certify this work; this in itself not only colors the entire practice and experience of the work but also makes Voice Dialogue really a hybrid between a personal growth or therapy modality and a spiritual practice, which of course is ongoing and cannot really be certified. When the Stones talk about surrendering to the consciousness process, it's a bit like taking vows in Buddhist practices, which are seen as "taking refuge in our own intrinsic enlightenment" (Mipham, S. 2000), and where no one on the outside can really certify that one is keeping those vows.

Keeping the work as an open-source process means that the ways in which Voice Dialogue can be implemented are open-ended, and are increasing as more and more people adapt this approach to their own areas of expertise. It flattens the hierarchy on all levels (inner and outer), and means the process is available for creative use in everything from clinical work to executive coaching to peer facilitation to use in the arts. On their website, Hal and Sidra Stone assert that their "work belongs to everyone; it is a gift to us that we are passing on," and their hope is that people will build on it with their own creativity and in turn pass it on to others. They continue with a statement that it is impossible to certify an Aware Ego Process, and that the best facilitators are always growing and learning and continuing their own process with the work. They do not support certification by themselves or anyone else. In other words the work is and remains an open, ongoing, evolutionary process for both facilitator and subject that cannot be pinned down to a set of practices, rules, theories, or ways of working that everyone can and should do alike (www.voicedialogue.org).

These five elements together result in a singular personality and energy profile of Voice Dialogue as a method, so that even when one finds parallels with each of the five elements in other approaches to healing and consciousness, the combination of all five is unique and can have profound effects on the person experiencing it as either facilitator or subject. Let's now explore further the foundational elements of the work and their similarities to and differences from other modalities. Then, at the end of our journey, we will come to an expanded understanding of the overall qualities that add up to the essential nature of Voice Dialogue.

Underlying Premises Shared by Voice Dialogue and Other Forms of Parts Work

In addition to the five elements unique to Voice Dialogue and the Psychology of the Aware Ego, there are also a number of other fundamental suppositions and characteristics of the work that are shared in part with other forms of therapy, personal growth work, and spiritual practice.

Voice Dialogue shares with all the other forms of parts work the concept that the psyche is by its nature multidimensional, though the perception of these selves as fully embodied individual entities varies. IFS sees the selves as very real and embodied, while on the other end of the spectrum, Jungian psychology views them as more intellectualized complexes. IFS,

Ego State Therapy, and the DNMS are all trauma-based clinical models, and as such are concerned more with wounded selves (especially those that have been injured in childhood and are consequently stuck in reaction to that wounding) and their relationship to parent selves. In IFS "Parts... carry... burdens which are extreme emotions and beliefs that they accumulated through experiences in their lives. And those burdens are what drive those extremes. Once they feel really witnessed in terms of where they got the burdens and retrieved from where they are stuck in the past, they can actually unload these extreme beliefs and emotions, and then they transform into their naturally valuable state" (Schwartz, February, 2010, USABP).

The primary purpose of these more clinical approaches is healing, whereas the primary purpose of Voice Dialogue is consciousness. In the end, both kinds of approaches will achieve both of these results, but the contrasting emphasis changes the feel of the work, and people then are attracted to using these methods for different reasons. For example, clients commonly enter into Voice Dialogue looking to resolve inner or outer conflict, and end up discovering that the cultivation of an Aware Ego Process can actually become a lifelong spiritual practice. I believe this also occurs with Jungian dream work and the pursuit of a transpersonal Self in Psychosynthesis. I would think that the cultivation of Self leadership in IFS can also evolve into a life practice in consciousness, even if the beginning of the process is focused on healing from trauma.

While all these modalities recognize the reality of parts or selves, they vary greatly in how open-ended they are in viewing the inner world of the psyche. For the trauma-based models, the wounded selves and their protectors, defenses, managers, and firefighters seem very real. There is not, however, perhaps the emphasis shared by Voice Dialogue, Jungian psychology, Gestalt, and Psychosynthesis on selves that are found in dreams, guided imagery, and through connection with the archetypes. Archetypal and dream selves may be entirely new and not necessarily directly related to trauma or early life experience.

However, the viewpoint that inner process and becoming aware of one's selves are intrinsically valuable is shared in all these modalities, and also by Big Mind (and some forms of Buddhist practice), though perhaps from a different perspective. Voice Dialogue also holds the view that there is a force within us and in the universe that seeks wholeness and balance. This is most clearly evident in the realm of relationships, where either we come to a place of self-knowledge and take responsibility for our own internal dynamics, or we project outward and get other people to fill in for the parts of our personality we refuse to claim as our own. There is a recognition that every aspect of human nature is within us, and an assumption that whenever we refuse to own or fail to regulate some aspect of our personality, we will be subject to someone else who will. This perspective is shared to one degree or another with all the approaches I have mentioned, but again with much variation regarding how much emphasis is placed on relationships. At one end of the continuum is TA, which is all about transactions between people. At the other end might be Jungian analysis, where one may discover one's shadow material through relationship to others, but emphasis might be placed first on one's own internal process and secondarily on working out the relationship.

It is not surprising that Voice Dialogue has a great deal in common with other forms of therapy and personal growth work, because its roots are definitely intertwined with Jungian therapy, Gestalt, and Psychosynthesis. However, the realization that not only certain individual elements of Voice Dialogue but really the combination of all of them that gives the work its particular potency and effectiveness is also of key importance. Let's take a deeper look at how Voice Dialogue works with selves, how the Aware Ego and Awareness figure into the story, the implications of conscious regulation of energies, the role of the facilitator, and Voice Dialogue as an evolutionary process.

Selves in Voice Dialogue

In Voice Dialogue the selves are real, live energetic beings, each with its own history, viewpoint, beliefs, physical reality, and expression, desires, attachments, skills, talents/gifts. Each self has its own reason for being, its own internal logic, which we can come to understand no matter how different or unusual it may be. We often notice a self because it shows up in an attitude, a habit, or a sort of default behavior. As in IFS, an important part of Voice Dialogue is really letting each self we work with have full expression so that we are able to unwrap the package of the self enough to see its dimensionality, and get away from the habit of defining it by the behavior that has been evident. This in itself is healing. Other selves may dislike this self, may even bring the person into therapy to get rid of it, but the facilitator encounters each self with open curiosity and true honoring. This is often met with great relief on the part of the self as it becomes separated out from the others, receives genuine interest in what it is trying to accomplish, and is truly appreciated for the ways in which it has served in the person's life.

Selves in the Voice Dialogue process do not interact with other selves, nor are they expected to evolve or alter their behavior of their own accord as they are in some other modalities. This is quite different from the negotiations with parts in IFS or in Gestalt. Richard Schwartz developed IFS as a "way of working with parts of people, sub-personalities, but using systems thinking to understand how they relate to each other..." hence the name Internal Family Systems (Schwartz, February 2010). In contrast, Voice Dialogue acknowledges the inner dynamics between selves, but it does not necessarily address them or attempt to change them directly. Instead the focus is on separation, creation of an Aware Ego Process between opposite selves, and developing the capacity to relate to the selves and the dynamics between them through the Aware Ego Process. One image of this is the Aware Ego grabbing hold of the rope between two selves who are in a tug of war, so that there is slack in the line and they are no longer pulling against each other. Before a person comes for her first Voice Dialogue session, her selves have already had considerable experience with being manipulated, bullied, and cajoled, etc., by other parts of the personality (often this mirrors exactly experiences the individual had in early life with parents, siblings, and playmates). In the facilitation process, selves interact first with the facilitator, who energetically matches and holds the self, and then with the Aware Ego as it grows in its ability to take the facilitator's place. This principle, along with the physical separation of selves, results in a unique experience of safety for selves in the facilitation process.

Selves, no matter what their behavior or emotional experience, are not seen as problems and are not pathologized in this work. Voice Dialogue gives great consideration to how the selves feel about the process, whether they like being facilitated or not. They are treated with respect — period. Other modalities also hold respect for selves, and at the same time the therapist is often focused on an idea of what selves might need in order to move them toward some end, get them to integrate, as in Gestalt and Psychosynthesis, or unburden them as in IFS. Even though evolution, integration, and something quite similar to "unburdening" may occur in the Voice Dialogue process, these changes come about organically, not as a result of any intention on the part of the facilitator, and it's fine if they don't. Voice Dialogue uncovers these various dynamics among selves, and then that awareness is given over to the Aware Ego, which will use it in its experiments with how to live life. In this way Voice Dialogue work is often the opposite of many clinical approaches in almost everything from analysis to manners. As I often teach in Voice Dialogue facilitator trainings, the selves are not people who have agreed to do therapy, and cannot be treated as such.

Where and when do selves originate? Like IFS, the DNMS, Ego State Therapy, and other modalities, selves may be seen in Voice Dialogue to originate in early childhood (including infancy) and even in the womb, often as a response to traumatic situations. However, Voice Dialogue accepts and honors each self's description of its own history, including those selves that say, "I'm ancient. I'm way older than this lifetime" and those that say, "I've never been here before — I'm getting born right now out of this process." The times in a person's life that typically tend to generate the most new selves (new ways of coping with reality) are birth and infancy, early childhood, the birth of a sibling, parents' divorce or loss of a parent, any major injury or disease process, the beginning of school, going away from home for the first time, first sexual experiences, marriage, birth of a child, entering into a career, any major change or loss in relationship or career, moving to a new place, or embarking on a spiritual path.

As in Jungian therapy and Gestalt, Voice Dialogue embraces all energies as potential selves, with the caveat that in facilitation one first honors the primary selves that have "seniority" in the person's life. The facilitator and client can together creatively use imagination to explore the psyche. It's just as easy and just as fruitful to talk to a tree or an animal from a dream, or have the subject move over into the energy of a friend or family member, as it is to explore more familiar inner selves such as a Pleaser or the Voice of Responsibility. The point is that any energy a human being can express or own is fair game, not just historical psychological ones. This is the nature of psycho-spiritual work, and it can go beyond problem solving and trauma healing into other dimensions of realization and creativity.

Voice Dialogue recognizes that the number of selves may be infinite, and does not attempt to place them into categories other than primary and disowned. With other forms of parts work there is often a framework into which every part of a person must fit; i.e. we are looking at the personality through the lens of parent, adult, child in TA, or looking at them in terms of managers, firefighters, or exiles in IFS. In Voice Dialogue, the designation of primary self means simply that the self is an integral part of who *this person* thinks he is and/or how he functions in the world. *Primary* selves include those that have developed defensive strategies early in life (controlling, pleasing, caretaking, rational thinking); they also include selves that possess certain talents and abilities that are accepted parts of the personality (organizing, creativity, athleticism). *Disowned* simply means this particular energy/self is not allowed in *this person's* self system. Primary and disowned are not roles that the selves have to fill, and can be quite fluid. A self may be situationally disowned or primary. For example, it might be okay to be wild and crazy on vacation, but not at home. Also one person's primary self is another's disowned self and vice versa — hence the outbreak of wars on both an intimate and global level.

Voice Dialogue allows for greater dimensionality in its view of primary selves. A person might try out a variety of modalities and experience the same inner self from differing perspectives. The self might get labeled a defense in one system, a manager in another, but if it is seen as a primary self in Voice Dialogue, it will be met with inquiry about how it is unique rather than how it fits into a predetermined category. Often the facilitation helps the self to remember or discover a much greater range of interests than its most recent experience would imply. As in most parts work, primary selves are often seen to develop out of our vulnerability in childhood, when they arise to devise strategies to protect the vulnerable parts of us from pain and harm. It's clear, however, that primary selves also hold many of our gifts and innate talents. One child who is gifted intellectually may develop a primary self that has this gift and uses it to get good grades, to win approval, or perhaps to retreat into books as form of protection. Another child with a different talent uses her sports ability to get rewards and avoid other areas that are challenging. In this way primary selves are both expressive of each person's strengths as well as protective of his/her vulnerabilities.

Often, by the time people reach adulthood, many of their primary selves are overfunctioning and they go into counseling or coaching or a spiritual practice in order to try to get away, for example, from being "too in my head" or "too controlling." Typically, in many therapeutic modalities and spiritual teachings, one finds a great level of respect *for individuals*, but the selves are, at worst, seen as "inauthentic," "codependent," "wounded," and, at best, found to be subtly "less than," in need of integrating or returning to a healthy state. While the client/participant/ student may for the first time experience a recognition of her/his deeper essence, this acknowledgment and honoring of the individual's essence often comes at the expense of dishonoring the selves. In some cases this is expressed as "You are powerful, creative, a real soul, etc. These other parts of you are not the real you, are not authentic, are only ego." The implication is that when you get beyond these unreal, inauthentic parts of yourself, you'll be able to shine forth as the exquisite, enlightened being you are. There are two very large problems with this. One is that it gives the person one more, and indeed impossible, task to accomplish before she/he can be validated as a fully realized and worthy human being. The other is that these primary selves have been doing most of the hard work of living this person's life, and once again they get little or no credit for their efforts. Thankfully, this is truer of other forms of therapy and personal growth than it is of most kinds of parts work. IFS, for example, is very sympathetic to these kinds of overfunctioning protective selves, and creates real relationships with them even as it asks them to step aside and allow for change.

There is no concept in Voice Dialogue of aiming toward or looking to create (an often elusive) Self that is more valuable than the rest. Certainly there are some selves that seem to be closer to the core and hold more of that "psychic fingerprint." Actually, most often the rest of the selves each have a bit of that essence too, a bit of talent, natural inclination, temperament, etc., that has been appropriated and developed toward a particular purpose or use. A great deal of work in the Aware Ego Process is discovering how to regulate the energy of any particular self at a level where it can contribute the best of what it does naturally (e.g., discernment rather than being judgmental, exercising control rather than being controlling, self-care instead of selfishness), and not viewing the self as in any way limited to the negative end of its expression.

Understanding the selves in a context of relationship is central to Voice Dialogue and the Psychology of the Aware Ego. Experience in facilitation has taught me that in every individual session the issues are connected to relationship, and in every relationship session the issues reflect back to the individuals involved and affect the internal relationship dynamics among each person's inner selves. Because the earliest most primary (and most disowned) selves are formed in relationship at the beginning of our lives, it is really impossible to understand them out of the context of relationship. We form our personalities as a collection of selves that come out of our family of origin experience, our community, our culture, and our country. When we encounter someone new — a friend, a teacher, a lover, a boss, a coworker — our selves interact with theirs. Whatever happens in the relationship reflects back to us a mirror of the energies we carry that are opposite to the ones the other person carries. At that point, we have the choice to learn from the relationship, integrate the other person's qualities/energies, or continue a pattern of projection and blame that may ultimately destroy the relationship.

That loop — the individual affecting the relationship and the relationship affecting the individual — along with the dance of how we hold the opposites for each other, is what makes relationship of all kinds such a profound psycho-spiritual teacher. The other modalities to which we have been comparing the Voice Dialogue process all recognize the concept of projecting our shadow or disowned selves onto others, but the discovery of positive and negative bonding patterns as a way of unraveling the complex interpersonal interactions of selves and the understanding of energetic linkage as key to the success of relationships are both unique contributions of the Stones' work.

Beyond simply identifying shadow projection, positive and negative bonding patterns clearly show how one person's selves interact with another person's based on automatic, or instinctual, parent-child interactions (bonding). The Stones speak of these as "hard-wired" or "archetypal." Bonding patterns are never general — they are always rooted in actual relational events between people. Identifying them and diagramming these patterns of interaction between selves enhances separation from these same selves and helps to build the Aware Ego Process. The closest comparison I can find to the Stones' work with bonding patterns are the diagrams used in TA to illustrate interactions between people from parent, adult, or child realities. "Crossed transactions" from a parent energy in one person to the child in the other, and vice versa, are seen to be rooted in the past and result in putting a stop to communication, whereas adult-to-adult (somewhat like Aware Ego to Aware Ego) transactions are in the moment, and communication continues. Even though TA also focuses on the total communication package of words, voice tone, expression, and gesture, and also recognizes the difference between positive and negative parent modes, the descriptions of parent-child transactions seem to me to be more clinical because the selves are so generalized into three categories. TA also does not appear to have the same concept of energetic linkage as key to determining the nature and feel of the interactions (transactions). As a result (to someone coming from Voice Dialogue), the parents and children in TA seem a bit lacking in personality, somehow less alive (Berne, E.).

The Role of the Aware Ego Process

The Aware Ego Process is the most mysterious and revolutionary aspect of Voice Dialogue, as is Self Leadership in IFS, which perhaps comes the closest to the Aware Ego Process in terms of its internal function. We talked earlier about the brain's reluctance to add entirely new categories to its filing system, and the Aware Ego is definitely a new concept that doesn't quite fit anywhere in our preexisting organization of reality. Once the Aware Ego Process has been initiated, it's quite clear to the person experiencing it but still hard to explain adequately to others.

It's perhaps most effective, then, to describe the Aware Ego Process in terms of how it is experienced, and, in fact, Richard Schwartz does the same in his description of Self Leadership: "After twenty years of helping people toward Self leadership, I can describe what my clients exhibit as they increasingly embody self" (Schwartz, R., 2001). Schwartz continues with eight words beginning with "C" that capture the essence of the Self-led experience: "calmness, clarity, curiosity, compassion, confidence, courage, creativity, connectedness" (Schwartz, R., 2001, pp. 44–57). All of these are definitely qualities one also finds in the Aware Ego Process, with perhaps some differences in the ways in which these qualities are experienced. I'll comment on some of them and discuss other elements of the Aware Ego Process that I have not found described in IFS or other parts work.

Calmness in the Aware Ego process is a sense of neutrality, of in-betweenness (in some ways comparable to neutral gear in a car) where there is the potential at any moment to shift into any particular self/ energy, and at the same time a clear sense of not having to do anything or go anywhere. This sense may be reported as a sort of ordinary calm in the body (vs. a deeper calm that might come in meditation); a feeling of spaciousness as well as literally more breathing space, and a sense of

"I feel fine." Sometimes there is a slight deflation or flatness of affect because the self that was separated is pumped up full of energy, and Aware Ego just feels very simple and "personality-less" by comparison.

Definitely a natural, organic, and effortless experience of compassion develops in Aware Ego, and while it extends into our outer relationships, it is first and foremost experienced in relation to the selves. Though the Aware Ego is not caught up in being any self, it definitely feels the reality of each self and can often discover new alternative solutions to problems the selves experience, which they might never think of on their own. However, some decisions by their nature leave one side or the other disappointed: one cannot, for example, both buy a new computer and not buy it, or both go on a trip and not go on it. In these situations the person in her/his Aware Ego Process fully experiences the loss of a self that does not get its way. This nature of the AEP then organically translates into an experience of compassion, with both the person in Aware Ego experiencing being compassionate, and the selves feeling themselves the recipients of compassion. I believe this can be also very similar to the Buddhist practice of directing loving-kindness toward oneself.

Curiosity is a quality many of the selves lack because of their single-minded focus on a particular belief or agenda. Separating from a self automatically opens the possibility of embracing its opposite and balancing between the two, and since people in the Aware Ego Process are now connected to both sides, they become naturally curious about what's going on inside themselves and in others. When it's only selves present in a relationship, there will be lots of judgments (both negative and positive). The person in Aware Ego and the Self-led person won't have these same preconceived ideas to defend, and as a result will be more able to open up and learn about the other person.

Connectedness in Voice Dialogue is based in energetic linkage through the Aware Ego, and it is the Aware Ego's ability to manage one's energetic expression that radically enhances our ability to sustain intimate relationship, and to have much deeper connections with people. To the degree we are able to access the AEP in our lives, we are also able to relate to others through an Aware Ego Process. This utterly transforms any relationship in which it occurs, because it is the selves that create the polarizations we experience between others and ourselves. The more we can be in relationship from this center of holding opposites in balance the less we depend on our spouses, children, work partners, employees, etc., to hold our disowned selves for us. It becomes possible to relate in wholeness to others on the outside and to our own selves on the inside. Because Aware Ego is an ongoing, evolving process, so is our ability to connect with others through Aware Ego. On the bright side, though, even if only one person in the relationship has begun to separate from selves, the balance of the energies will shift. Gradually even the person who has not begun this work will either find less "matching Velcro" to get the bonding pattern going or will move on to a different relationship where he/she can continue to make the old patterns stick.

Of all the modalities with which we're comparing Voice Dialogue, IFS really seems to be the most similar in regard to this view of what happens between people when there is more Self Leadership or more Aware Ego in the mix. The differences, though, are subtle but important. Schwartz sees Self as innate, that it's always there and has always been there. When his clients discover it they say, "that's not a part, that's who I really am." According to Schwartz, what he is calling Self "spontaneously emerges in everybody," once parts have stepped aside, separated (Schwartz, February 2010). Applying that concept to relationship, IFS also has the perception that "Self in one person is a magnet for Self in another" (Schwartz, 2001, p. 56). Voice Dialogue, on the other hand, definitely does not see the Aware Ego Process as innate or preexisting as some essential core of the personality ready to emerge, although Aware Ego does also spontaneously come into being out of the process of separating from selves. And, yes, the Voice Dialogue perspective sees that holding balance between primary and disowned selves internally frees us from polarizing against someone who holds our disowned energy, and in turn frees them to find their own balance. The other person might go on to separate from selves and develop her own Aware Ego process, or she might simply find someone else with whom to do the dance of polarization. Her Aware Ego process would not necessarily be magnetized by the presence of another.

Like Schwartz, I have collected observations of what seems to happen with people (clients, myself, etc.) in the Aware Ego Process. In addition to his eight C's, I have also noticed the following qualities of the Aware Ego experience:

Our relationship to time changes — in the Aware Ego, urgency disappears, as the urgency belongs to the selves, and correspondingly inertia disappears as well. A person experiencing the Aware Ego Process (even if it's only for a few moments) is not pushed by her past or pulled by her future — that push/pull belongs to the selves.

We are aware of more options than we can normally perceive from the perspective of any one of the selves — it's as if we put on new glasses that somehow widened as well as lengthened our vision. Aware Ego exercises choice based both on the complete story of what the opposite selves want (not just one side or the other) and an awareness that goes beyond what either side can see. It's a common experience in the Aware Ego Process to think of completely new possibilities that just did not occur to us before we separated from the selves.

The Aware Ego showing up and being present with a vulnerable self (or any self) is in itself stabilizing and comforting. In a way, the Aware Ego does with the selves what most of our parents never did for us as children: it listens to the selves and takes each of them seriously. It acknowledges, for example, an inner child's feelings and desires *as real feelings and desires*. Whether or not we can give this inner child what it wants, in Aware Ego we deeply acknowledge what it means to that self, how much it matters. At the same time, however, there is no agenda on the part of the Aware Ego, no attempt to comfort, placate, protect, cajole, etc., because again these behaviors/attitudes belong to the selves.

In Aware Ego there is not only movement out to the selves, but once we have separation we can also, from Aware Ego, invite the energies of the selves into the body. We can titrate these energies and shift them. We can choose to bring in only a small amount of an energy that may otherwise be overwhelming, or adjust where and how a particular self functions in the body. A self that is very tender and open, for example, may seem diametrically opposed to a judgmental protector that is all about holding strong to certain principles. Once we discover, though, that the energy of the first self lives in the heart area, and the second self would work really well "dialed down" and situated in the spine to give us strength and "backbone," then we find that they can work together as wonderfully as heart and bone work together. Other modalities such as IFS, ARC, and Focusing definitely pay attention to the felt sense of the selves or energies in the physical body. I don't believe, however, that these approaches work toward discovering and changing how these selves live in the body, nor do they create a way to hold two or more disparate energies together, and find a way to balance them energetically and physically even when, on a content/cognitive level, the selves do not agree with or like each other. This aspect of Voice Dialogue work is always done through the Aware Ego Process and can only be accomplished to the degree that Aware Ego is present. The Aware Ego Process is a radical transformation from an *either/or* consciousness to a *both/and* type of reality all the way through one's whole being, including the physical body.

Self leadership in IFS and Self in Psychosynthesis seem to be so close to the Aware Ego because they are also seen as dynamic and evolving and not exactly another of the inner selves. In contrast, many other forms of therapy and personal growth encourage the idea of an adult self, nurturing self, parental self, etc., to take care of inner children. The Developmental Needs Meeting Strategy, for example, works to "guide clients to establish three internal Resources: a Nurturing Adult Self, a Protective Adult Self, and a Spiritual Core Self" (DNMS Institute website). From a Voice Dialogue perspective, this might be seen as theoretically a good idea but very difficult to bring about. I suspect if it were likely that selves would be able to take care of each other *consistently* in this way, it might have become a more organic process of human development.

From a Voice Dialogue point of view, we perceive that the reasons this does not work well is because of the way in which the selves occupy the body and appropriate a larger or smaller share of the available energy. Just think of the last time you got really upset. What happened in your body? Did feelings well up and overflow in tears or burst through in a hot explosion of anger? Was there energy available in that moment for a Nurturing Parent self to come through and take action? From a Voice Dialogue perspective, we see all selves as unreliable in that they don't have staying power; life happens, other selves are triggered, and the self we were counting on gets pushed out of the picture. Also, each of the selves has its own agenda and is likely to take a direction based on its own point of view. The Aware Ego Process, on the other hand, in part because it's not a self and not subject to the same dynamics, has the capacity to remain present. Through Aware Ego we feel the emotional tidal pull of the selves without getting sucked out to sea. From the place of the Aware Ego there is the potential to develop, over time, more and more direct connection with vulnerable selves, creating a mature presence that can truly be relied on, in contrast to an "adult self" that might come and go.

Since the Aware Ego is always a process occurring between opposites, it has to deal with the fact that in trying to connect, perhaps with a vulnerable child, it's likely that other selves will interrupt and try to short-circuit that connection. In an Aware Ego Process one connects with the selves that interrupt in the same way one connects with the inner child. From the Aware Ego's place of separation from the selves, one can acknowledge their concerns — "the child will be too emotional, you'll get lost in the child, the child will take too much time, it's weak and unacceptable to feel emotion, etc. — and hold a balance/center between these selves. That is what the Aware Ego is all about — holding balance/ center between opposites. Gradually the person evolves through practice to more and more ability to function and exercise choice at center in an Aware Ego process. From this place, the vulnerable selves finally experience a consistent "adult" presence, and they begin to count on that relationship. The other protective selves begin to relax a bit and gradually start to trust the person in the Aware Ego Process for support, i.e. begin to count on it to take care of the vulnerability in a different way than has happened in the past.

One process used a great deal in Voice Dialogue work is very similar to Psychosynthesis and to IFS — guiding a person sitting at center in the Aware Ego Process to connect with a particular young/vulnerable self (one encountered in the session). How they make that connection doesn't matter; it could be anything from simply imagining extending energy toward the self, on one end of the spectrum, to seeing/feeling a literal child and experiencing an inner physical connection with that child on the other end. Whatever works — and what works can change during the guided process and in future attempts to connect with this self. It is a relationship between the person in her/his Aware Ego Process and the vulnerable child, and that relationship evolves. Many other forms of therapy use a similar process to take care of a vulnerable child "from an adult self." Again, the difference is not the intent or even the way of connecting with the vulnerable inner child. The difference is that in Voice Dialogue we separate from the selves first, and do not attempt this kind of relationship with the child until there is enough Aware Ego Process available to do it.

This last comment about the Aware Ego process brings us right back around to our beginning observation that the natural tendency is to try and fit the unknown into the known. It is often an ongoing discomfort for people that Aware Ego is a process and not a self and that we are not in Voice Dialogue facilitation being encouraged to become it or identify with it. Unlike Schwartz's clients, who claim that the "Self is who I really am," Aware Ego remains an equal part of the consciousness process along with the selves and with awareness. The often-used analogy of Aware Ego functioning in a similar manner to an orchestra conductor is aptly applied. Without the many instruments of the selves, there would be no music regardless of how wonderfully the Aware Ego might be able to conduct. And without the audience of awareness, the performance of life would be unwitnessed and incomplete. Let's look at both awareness and the conscious management of energies through the Aware Ego next.

Awareness as a Part of the Process

Under one name or another, Awareness, the ability to step outside oneself and simply notice what is going on from a nonattached place, is a key aspect of almost every personal growth and therapeutic modality, and certainly a part of spiritual practice as well. Voice Dialogue, however, gives Awareness its own physical place to stand (or sit) apart from both the selves and the Aware Ego/operating ego place at center. Moving into a separate place makes the experience of Awareness more real, just as moving into the selves makes them more real and embodied, and it also draws a very clear distinction between Awareness and Aware Ego. I do not believe this distinction is made clear in other modalities, which can lead to the confusion of thinking one has achieved separation from the selves because one has become aware of having these selves. Both Voice Dialogue and IFS realize that communication and inner relationship are needed to accomplish that separation, and Voice Dialogue would add the essential element of movement.

In Voice Dialogue, the Aware Ego draws on the perceptions that come through Awareness as well as on the experience of the selves in considering action and exercising choice, and it's the combination of these three elements that comprise the consciousness model in the Psychology of the Aware Ego. It's important to note that awareness in Voice Dialogue is a part of the consciousness process and not a goal of consciousness. To be aware and to be conscious are not the same thing, and Awareness is not made special or set up above the selves or the Aware Ego in value. In Voice Dialogue this leads to a fairly easy and consistent ability to access the Awareness level — easier because there is no attempt to stay there — and to not make oneself wrong or unenlightened when one is not aware.

Conscious Regulation of Energies

The ability to regulate and balance the energetic experience of the selves, as well as the exploration and balancing of personal and impersonal energies, is enormously helpful in successfully creating and holding boundaries. Other modalities also acknowledge the reality of the energetic nature of boundaries, but most do not teach the subject how to make these boundaries more effective by intentionally bringing in the energy that is missing and learning to hold it at a level that works well in both general and specific situations. This holding and blending of energies is perhaps more readily found in various approaches to working with subtle energies and energy medicine, not necessarily in any forms of therapy or specifically parts work (International Society for the Study of Subtle Energies and Energy Medicine website).

Voice Dialogue, we have already noted, pays special attention to the recognition of linkage as a palpable energetic connection between people. While other approaches definitely talk about "felt connection" on both an inner and outer level, Voice Dialogue helps us to recognize which selves naturally create an energetic link with other people, and which are completely lacking in that ability. There is no attempt to get non-linking selves to be more connected. Instead they are honored for their contribution in other areas. Overly linking selves are also not shamed for becoming enmeshed or "codependent." It is the job of the person in the Aware Ego Process to create a living balance that will allow for both connection and boundaries.

This has considerable consequences for human relationships, which often founder on unconscious nonverbal energetic communication. If one person is communicating ideas without any linkage, just the mind in gear, it might not feel very good to the person receiving this communication. Without linkage, the listener might ignore the content of the communication because he just doesn't want to receive the gift of information wrapped in an uncomfortable or disconnected energetic package. Learning to hold in the Aware Ego Process a combination of an unlinked mental self focused on content and another self whose focus is linkage with the other person changes all that. The result is quite different from the kind of communication we're too often used to, which either delivers a download of information without any felt connection, or avoids talking about information for fear that would be too heady and might break linkage with the other person. In the Aware Ego Process, holding both sides, one may speak more slowly, listen more, feel the other person and how they are receiving the communication, and still be able to address issues and get the verbal message across.

Voice Dialogue also goes one step further in opening energetically to people who hold our disowned selves, i.e. people whose behavior we judge negatively or overvalue. Instead of remaining a victim to someone else's aggressive behavior, for example, I can use imagination to bring in a tiny amount of their aggressive energy, just enough to give me more backbone and help me hold my ground in their presence. This approach of bringing energy into the body in order to claim it and hold a balance is unique to Voice Dialogue. It bypasses issues of judging the opposites and gives us a creative way to deal with difficult disowned energies.

The Role of the Facilitator in Voice Dialogue Work

The Voice Dialogue facilitator essentially shepherds a process that is not under her control, and she does not hold preconceived ideas of the selves or try to fit them into predetermined categories. This requires both genuine curiosity and a certain humility, as well as openness, imagination, and intuition. In addition, the work is open-ended, improvisational, and depends on the ongoing dedication of the facilitator to surrender to the process and do her own personal work. Because Aware Ego is an ongoing process, neither facilitator nor client can say that she has achieved an Aware Ego. It can become an interesting challenge then to work in a field where in a sense you cannot truly arrive, cannot become degreed or certified. Instead of completing certain requirements for certification, the key requirement for all facilitators in Voice Dialogue work is *to be facilitated* on an ongoing basis.

The facilitator in Voice Dialogue has to be adept at energy shifts inside him-/herself and at recognizing them when they happen in the subject. One cannot rely on the subject at center to report back to the facilitator what is happening with the selves as in IFS, Psychosynthesis, and other ways of working internally, because here the facilitator is in direct relationship to the selves. It is a bit like entering a foreign country, minding your manners, finding out what is/isn't acceptable in relating to the inhabitants, getting an understanding of the politics there (the dynamics between selves), and building enough of a relationship so that they will want to talk with you. One cannot come in with an attitude of

"I know what you people need." In Voice Dialogue, unlike IFS, one has to observe the protocol in each person's self system, so one cannot ask a self to "step back." My sense is this works well in IFS because the request is coming from the subject to one of their selves, and not directly from the therapist/facilitator. Where IFS would ask a self to step back so it's possible to hear from and get to know another self, Voice Dialogue would separate first from whatever self is present, and wait for there to be an organic way to move to the next self.

It's small wonder that working in this way with selves comprises a very small part of the general fields of personal growth and clinical therapeutic work. It takes more effort on the part of the facilitator/therapist to: 1) develop many relationships with different selves and not just with the client; 2) step out of the therapeutic relationship when working with selves, with a resulting loss of position of expert (person who has it all together); and 3) realize that this kind of work necessitates the facilitator doing his own separating from selves in order to be able to be present in the Aware Ego Process (or Self leadership process).

The facilitator must not only hold unqualified honoring of all selves without any negative or positive judgments but must also be able to meet each self in its own world and match its energy. The same deep respect that is given to the client in all modalities is given as well to the selves in Voice Dialogue work. This is quite different from most therapeutic models. The Voice Dialogue facilitator has no expectation or goal of changing any self, no problems to solve or resolve. The work is essentially practical as well as profound, and is more about skills, practice, and awareness than about problem solving. The goal for the facilitator is to help clients develop an Aware Ego Process to the point where they no longer need a facilitator to hold that process for them. Because of this, many facilitators market themselves as teachers or coaches rather than as therapists.

Hal and Sidra Stone comment: "The facilitator is an explorer, an interested observer who is trying to discover as much as possible about each self. The selves are extremely sensitive to the feelings and judgments of the facilitator, and they will not respond if they sense disapproval or manipulation. This is a method that will not work effectively unless it is used with a proper attitude. When it is used properly, however, it provides quick and easy access to much of the psyche" (Stone, H. and S., 1994).

There is, of course, an art to facilitation, and some people do truly have a natural talent for it — sensitivity to energies, and a mind given to piecing these particular kinds of puzzles together. Without this natural ability, learning all the moves, going through the programs, or even being regularly facilitated might not lead to inspired work. This is true, of course, of every modality, but for Voice Dialogue, without any stamp of approval through certification, each facilitator is in the same boat with the people he facilitates — all working day by day, bit by bit, to develop an Aware Ego Process.

Voice Dialogue as an Evolutionary, Improvisational Process

If I do my work well as a Voice Dialogue facilitator, my clients will feel it is they who created the changes in their lives, and Voice Dialogue was just a tool they used to accomplish that. What each person uses Voice Dialogue for is different (part of what keeps the work so exciting for me). It could be a shift in decision-making, relationship improvement, or a boost to creativity. One client rebalances the energies of the selves and finally completes a dissertation ten years in the making; another reconciles age-old differences in the family, and then moves into better self-care and better physical health. A third stops being taken for a ride over and over again by Aphrodite, and learns to contain that divine energy and focus it within the context of a deep relationship. For each and every one, facilitator and subject, it's an individual journey.

Like many of the approaches we have been discussing, Voice Dialogue is a psycho-spiritual process for the development of consciousness. Dreams and connection to the unconscious and to the "deeper intelligence of the universe" are fundamental to this work. Unlike many spiritual practices that aim toward developing consciousness, in this process there is no relinquishing of selves (ego) in order to become conscious, and there is no abandoning of the psychological in order to become spiritual. Consciousness is a different kind of goal from problem solving, functionality, even integration. Consciousness may result in some of the same things, such as better balance, more peace of mind, freedom, choice, etc., but because the path to these is different (without judgment or the placing of values), the result feels different and is lived differently.

In summary we might say that Voice Dialogue is more like jazz — the basic riffs are present as principles of the work, but everyone will invent her own take on it. It remains an uncontainable and open-source method. If it were certified, it might be more like classical music, and all facilitators would be trained to play the same standardized notes. Instead, Voice Dialogue is a process that complicates rather than simplifies; i.e. it allows for the natural complexity to unfold, so that selves that may have formerly manifested only as vague yearnings or perhaps repeated phrases or annoying habits can now unfold into story, history, and meaning. It makes me think of the beauty, rich taste, vibrancy, and health of the environment that comes with organic farming. Each plant/self has its own intrinsic way to grow, and if we limit it, declare how it has to grow, then the biggest loss is never finding out what it would have done on its own. At a time when we are losing diversity everywhere, it feels so precious that this work honors and preserves an inner diversity of the soul.

Finally, although Voice Dialogue shares many of its characteristics with other modalities (with the exception of the physical separation of selves, aspects of the Aware Ego process, and through that process the regulation of energies), what ultimately differentiates it from all of them is the unique package of all these elements together. Like each of the approaches to which we have been comparing Voice Dialogue, the work itself has a personality that is the sum and more of all the qualities we have been discussing, and it is this personality that attracts certain kinds of selves and discourages others. Perhaps next time you encounter someone who thinks Voice Dialogue must be just like something they already know, you might say simply that it is related to other work, in the same family, but it has an energy and life all it's own. "Perhaps if you are interested, I can introduce you in person."

References

1. Since it is the most commonly used term in Voice Dialogue, I have chosen to use the word "self" (or "selves") to represent inner selves, parts, sub-personalities, energies, complexes, etc. I have also deliberately not capitalized self or selves so as to keep a clear distinction between this term and the word "Self" that is used in Psychosynthesis and IFS to mean something quite different from parts, selves, and sub-personalities.

2. My understanding of and references to other modalities are based on conversations with practitioners, publicly available writings about the work from printed sources, official websites, recorded interviews, and some experiences in being facilitated in IFS, Psychosynthesis, Gestalt, and ARC. With IFS and ARC, I have traded sessions so that I could both experience these modalities and hear from my colleagues their comparison of their experience of Voice Dialogue with their own work.

3. One could also make comparisons to many other forms of therapy, personal growth, and consciousness work: body-centered modalities such as Hakomi and Focusing come to mind.

Berne, Eric. I've drawn my information on Transactional Analysis theory and diagrams from the following websites: <www.itaa-net. org/> <www.ericberne.com/transactional_analysis_description. htm>, <www.businessballs.com/transactionalanalysis.htm>

Voice Dialogue International website: <www.voicedialogue.org>

Houston, Jean. Recorded telling of the Myth of Inanna, <www.jeanhouston.org>, audiovisual room, April 23, 2007

International Society for the Study of Subtle Energies and Energy Medicine. The work of the ISSSEEM is founded on the work of Elmer and Alyce Green, pioneers in "understanding and facilitating the use of subtle energies, both for therapeutic purposes and for the study of human potential...." <www.issseem.org/about.cfm>.

Mipham, Sakyong. "Becoming a Buddhist." *Shambhala Sun*, <http://tinyurl.com/yd2l2tv, 2000.

Schwartz, R. *Introduction to the Internal Family Systems Model*. Oak Park, Illinois: Trailheads Publications, pp. 44–57, 2001.

Schwartz, R. "Conversations." In Prengel, S. (ed.), Somatics Perspectives Series. United States Association for Body Psychotherapy, 2010.

Stone, H. and S. Stone. "The Psychology of the Aware Ego." *Psychotherapy in Australia*, Voice Dialogue International, 1994.

The Developmental Needs Meeting Strategy Institute, www.dnmsinstitute.com/index.html#brief>

SECTION II

Voice Dialogue and Other Theoretical Systems

Integrating Voice Dialogue and Chinese Five-Element Theory

Paul Abell, PhD

Background and Introduction

In the early seventies, with fate truly as her muse, a stately elderly friend in Brentwood, California, introduced her "Jungian analyst," Dr. Harold Stone, to me. She did so with great enthusiasm, citing that the two of us might "get on well," as we both harbored a similar interest in the subtle body energies known to the ancient Chinese and Hindus. Though my own professional background had also been in psychology, a few years earlier I had left the challenging world of treating emotionally disturbed adolescents to explore various forms of Asian healing such as acupuncture, acupressure, herbs, Do-In, Tui Na, and Jin Shin Do.

Our erstwhile old friend must have had great intuition. Within weeks, Dr. Stone not only invited me to share his professional office space but also asked if I might teach at his newly formed Center for the Healing Arts — a melting pot of intellectuals, teachers, professionals, lay healers, and individuals looking for alternative pathways to health. The atmosphere was ripe for the exploration of innovative thought and the rediscovery of ancient truths. It was a wonderful place to be in a time of unbridled creativity. Certainly I didn't fathom the full significance of the moment, but the synchronous forces of the universe had landed me in a ringside seat to view the birthing of Voice Dialogue and the development of the Psychology of the Selves. I should have brought my camera!

From its very inception, the Voice Dialogue technique had extremely practical and diverse applications to my own emerging work. My goal back then was to discover/develop some eclectic and effective healing methods through which a practitioner might promote balance, aware-ness, and optimum health. Perhaps the most intriguing aspect of the Voice Dialogue process was revealed during the early Summer Kamp seminars. The various component selves are, in essence, "energy systems," vibrant internal vortices within the greater dynamic whole of the human personality. At times, these selves emerged in sessions as if they were virtual energetic beings, intimate and actual, complex and interactive. Often, during a facilitation exchange, we would watch in astonishment as the phenomenon of operant energy systems became tangible and profoundly salient.

For me, the experience was catalytic. Conceptualizing those liber-ated inner selves as energetic systems seemed to uniquely parallel the ancient Chinese view of the physical body in terms of energy networks (Matsumoto & Birch, 1983. p. 1). In practical terms, both models involved working with subtle yet powerful energy dynamics to ignite transforma-tion that might activate healing and growth. Of course myriad questions immediately arose as to how those two systems simultaneously function in an individual. Are they one and the same? Is there some predictable and manageable way in which they can be integrated and altered for the betterment of someone seeking help?

Over several decades, I have come to appreciate and understand, in part, how these energetic matrices, ancient and modern, overlap and coexist. First, I am struck by how the time-honored laws of energy that regulate the ancient Chinese system are directly applicable to the way the energy systems of the internal voices function and interact. Having used the Voice Dialogue tool as an adjunct in my own holistic healthcare work for more than thirty years now, I am especially impressed with how well it fills a great gap in the way traditional Oriental medicine is used to treat

disease. Although the ancient masters understood well how personality and emotions affect health, they had no real psychological tools to
intervene with emotional variables that were (in that culture and time)
considered somewhat socially taboo. The Voice Dialogue technique is
the perfect consciousness tool to use toward those ends.

The aim of this article is to present more specific information about
how one can integrate Voice Dialogue and the Asian systems and use
them together. I will also provide two case summaries to demonstrate
how well this approach has worked in practice. In order to discuss, compare, and meld East and West, the uninitiated reader must first become
familiar with the more detailed aspects of the Meridian Energy models
and the Chinese Five Element Theory.

The Asian System and the Psychology of Selves

Most Westerners think of Asian healthcare as merely acupuncture and
herbs; however, it involves much more than that. Traditional Oriental
Medicine is a highly complex system of diagnostic procedures and treatment modalities with a comprehensive philosophical superstructure. The
roots of healthcare in the Far East predate recorded history, and are as
old as the Chinese culture itself, with the earliest treatises dating back
to the 28th century BC (Veith, 1972. p. 7).

Though the origin of the Asian healing model actually begins before
the ancient Taoist writings of Lao Tzu, one of his poems best describes
the origins of the energetic philosophy:

> The Tao begot the One,
> The One begot the Two,
> The Two begot the Three,
> And the Three begot the Ten-thousand things.
> — Feng and English

In essence, this poem describes what Einstein postulated in modern
times through his $E=mc^2$ formula. In simpler terms the One refers to

the primordial energy of the universe (some refer to this as God or the force behind the Big Bang). The Two is the Yin/Yang energetic interactive duality constituting the flux or dynamic polarities of the opposites. The flux/tension between the Yin/Yang opposites is the actual generative source of energy, and that force creates the Three, or the matter manifested from that energy. That matter/energy continuum (Three) then provides the building blocks for the "Ten-thousand things," literally all those things that can be described. The ancients were inferring that everything constituting the world in which we live is nothing more than some thing created by Chi, or in the terms of modern physics, energy. Move over, Einstein!

That very same universal Chi energy is the core force maintaining wellness in the Chinese healthcare system. That entire system is based on a pulsing/life-giving/biological Chi energy that flows through the body in a well-defined circulation network of pathways called meridians. In that regard, the body is actually nothing more than one more of the things amongst the Ten-thousand things.

The energy meridians in our bodies transfer energy, infusing the visceral organs, the bones, the bodily tissues, and fluids with aliveness and vitality. On the flipside, the lack of normally flowing Chi in the meridians leads to what most Westerners label *disease*.

Because Chi energy comes from dynamic duality, it also follows certain basic laws governing that duality as it functions in nature and the human species. The diagram of the T'ai Chi T'u below symbolically represents those laws.

Figure 1. Yin/Yang Symbol

Although most people appreciate this familiar graphic as a beautiful piece of art emblematic of Asia itself, the symbol is much, much more. Within it one can discern all the Yin/Yang laws of duality; it is a symmetrical arrangement of the dark, Yin, and the bright, Yang. Literally translated, the words Yin and Yang describe a river cast half in shadow and half in sunlight (Franke. p. 197). Ultimately, the flow of the Tao (the stream of life energy) is defined by two changing aspects of one variable, light/energy. The Chinese viewed all things in terms of their relative polarities, following the principles represented by the T'ai Chi symbol:

♦ Yin and Yang are always relative; their energy is never neutral.

♦ Within Yang one finds Yin, and within Yin there is always Yang.

♦ Yin attracts (generates or leads to) Yang, and Yang attracts (generates or leads to) Yin.

♦ As Yang develops to fullness, it creates the beginnings of its opposite, Yin.

♦ When Yin changes to Yang or vice versa, one will be temporarily dominant in energy. In time, however, each extreme will always be supplanted by its opposite.

♦ Too much of any one polarity creates movement toward its opposite.

♦ Yin and Yang are always proportionately perfect within the whole.

Balance is not a static point, but is found in the flow of opposites embracing. Balance is a temporal phenomenon that can only be seen in the context of the whole pattern and not just as a position within that pattern.

I have listed below just a few of the typical Yin/Yang polarities (Porkert, 1978, p. 24).

Yin — Yang
Earth — Heaven
Light — Dark
Female — Male
Night — Day
Internal — External
Earthly — Heavenly
Cool — Hot
Soft — Hard
Receptive — Giving
Negative — Positive
Passive — Dynamic
Contractive — Expansive

Putting Asian medicine aside momentarily, those readers familiar with the facilitation technique will quickly understand some of the immediate applications of these dualities. From the vernacular of the Psychology of Selves, one can see that each Yang or dominant strong voice (identified self) has a weaker/passive Yin counterpart (disowned self). As a sub-personality gets to the peak of its strength, it initiates or triggers the emergence of its counterpart. As one can see in figure 1, the two adjacent black/white alternating color swirls graphically represent this concept. When the Yang aspect of the graphic reaches it largest size, the smallest leading edge of the opposite (Yin) graphic begins. Within each dominant voice (Yang, light side of the circle), we can see elements/seeds (a small black dot) of its disowned self (Yin), and vice versa. In looking at the diagram of the principles of Yin and Yang in figure 1, the reader can begin to see how the language of the voice dialogue facilitator parallels the energy ideology of the ancient masters. Once the complete model is known, I will show how the Yin/Yang theory can be more practically applied to the Voice Dialogue process.

Before delving more deeply into the integration of the two models, the reader needs to know a little more about the Asian system. The dynamic interplay of the fluctuating Yin/Yang forces determines and defines how

Chi works in a human being's body, mind, and spirit (Porkert, 1974, p. 9). The Chi energy of the previously mentioned meridian system was also seen in terms of its Yin/Yang duality relating to the internal organs and physiological processes. The energy in the Yin/Yang pairs of meridians ran in complete circuits both internally and externally (McGarey, 1974. p. 27). The meridians were bilateral, even those influencing organs that are solitary, such as the heart or spleen or liver. The meridians paired up in the following manner:

Yin — Yang
Lung — Large Intestine
Spleen — Stomach
Heart — Small Intestine
Kidney — Bladder
Heart Governor — Triple Warmer
(circulation) — (metabolism)
Liver — Gall Bladder

To assess the quality of the Chi energy in each of the twelve meridians the ancient masters developed a sophisticated form of pulse reading along the radial artery at the wrist (Amber, Babey-Brooke, 1966, p. 16). Whereas Western doctors measure blood pressure and the beat rate of the heart, the traditional Asian practitioner had to master the art of sensing scores of unique pulse qualities and nuances for each of the twelve meridians to evaluate how they were functioning — truly an enormous amount of information.

When energy does not move in a proper way through the meridians, Asian intervention involves techniques aimed at restoring the energy flow. For the traditional Chinese doctor, the treatment protocol would involve more than concocting herbal formulas and physically manipulating the energy at specialized loci (acupuncture points) with heat, needles, finger pressure, or his own Chi, through what Westerners would call hands-on healing. In the Royal Courts of the Emperor, it was a lower-level doctor who would need to resort to treating a disease that had already become manifest (Hsu, 1976, p. 67). The top physician could read the body signs, feel the pulse, analyze the energy in the body, and understand how external influences might be affecting the energy system.

To understand how a multitude of parameters might affect that system, the ancient Asian practitioners began watching and classifying how external and internal variables correlated. The Chinese doctors developed a more comprehensive treatment model as they observed how the human organism was, in fact, an inseparable part of nature. One must remember that system evolved at a time thousands of years ago when, out of necessity, man lived closer to and in harmony with his environment. For his very survival, early man depended on an awareness of the cycles and changes in the seasons and the surrounding elements. The phenomenon of adaptation creates an internalization process reflecting the way those outer forces function. Consequently, traditional Chinese doctors used nature itself as a metaphor to explain energetic relationships of the organs within the human being. They saw that, just as spring moves to summer; summer moves to Indian summer; Indian summer moves to fall; fall moves to winter; and then winter back to spring in a continuous cycle, so does the elemental energy within the human metaphorically move through a similar five-phase cycle. Specific elements in nature seemed to resonate with each of the seasons: spring was Wood; summer was Fire; Indian summer was Earth; fall was Metal (air); winter was Water (Birch & Matsumoto, 1983 p. 50). The doctors of ancient China then associated Yin/Yang pairs of body organs with those elements. Keen observers, they saw that the function of those organs in the body correlated with other variables such as food qualities, sounds, colors, body parts, spiritual dynamics, and specific emotional/psychological states. Most interestingly, the ideographic character used in the Chinese writing system for the concept of "element" within the Five Elements system is actually more broadly translated as "crossroads, phases, or movements." In the words of Matsumoto and Birch, "This more literal meaning had the symbolic advantage of implying the energetic coordinates of a larger cosmological system" (Matsumoto & Birch, 1983, p 1). The complete list of Five Elements relationships is extremely long and complex; the following is a brief summary of some of the basic relationships (Veith, 1972, p 21).

Table 1. Five Element Relationships.

Variable	Wood	Fire	Earth	Metal	Water
Season	Spring	Summer	Indian Summer	Fall	Winter
Yin body organ	Liver	Heart	Spleen	Lungs	Kidney
Yang body organ	Small Intestine	Stomach	Large Intestine	Gall Bladder	Bladder
Direction	East	South	Center	West	North
Adverse Climate	Windy	Hot	Damp	Dry	Cold
Energy Process	New Vigorous	Peak Power	Exacting, Perfecting	Collecting, Storing	Resting
Sense Organ	Eyes	Mouth	Tongue	Nose	Ears
Body Tissue	Brain & Tendons	Vascular System	Muscles	Skin & Hair	Bones
Body Fluid	Tears	Sweat	Saliva	Mucus	Urine
Voice Quality	Shouting	Loquacious	Singing	Whining	Groaning
Feeling	Rebirth	Expanding, Generous	Calmness	Quietness, Mellowness	Orderliness
Food Flavor	Sour	Bitter	Sweet	Spicy	Salt
Color	Green	Red	Yellow	White	Blue
Balanced Emotion	Will Power	Joy, Sympathy	Reflection	Normal grief	Courage
Deficient Emotion	Placid, Indecisive	Overly sad	Scattered, spaced out	Excessive sorrow	Fear and anxiety
Excessive Emotion	Rage	Hysteria	Obsession	Holding grief	Foolishness

The correlations within the Five Element system were made over many centuries of observation by traditional Chinese doctors, and to the Western mind may seem somewhat mythological, arbitrary, and rigid. At the very least, the correlates most certainly have some cultural bias. The logic of how this system interrelates can seem perplexing until one understands that in some ways the symbolic pictographic nature of Asian language comes into play. The biggest criticism I hear is that the chart is too archaic to be applied to modern times; however, a simple acceptance of this system at face value, and its use as such, can in fact work quite well in practice. As an organizational model it has proven helpful. In truth, the Five Element (phases) chart should be updated to encompass current developments and our present-day lifestyle. To that end, Dr. Lisa Hughes (a psychologist colleague who is knowledgeable about Voice Dialogue and Chinese medicine) and I developed an addendum to the traditional Five Element chart during our early years using the two systems in concert. As seen in the following chart, we noted and classified some of the sub-personalities that seem to directly influence and relate specifically to each of the elements. Certainly, the choice of element and associated "self/energy system" is neither absolute nor complete. Without a doubt, the classifications are subjective, but they are only offered as a guideline gleaned from experience.

Table 2: Five Element Sub-personalities/Selves/Voices.*

Wood	Fire	Earth	Metal	Water
Critic/victim	The lover	Whimsical	Griever/Stoic	Vulnerable
Pusher	Spiritual seeker	Nurturer	Tearful one	Foolish
Success/failure	The good person	Smothering	Guarded	Adventurer
Driving ambition	Playful	Dependent	Denial	Coward
Planner/quitter	Hysterical	Caretaker	Letting go	Soldier/warrior
Ambitious/bum	Overactive	Super-parent	Protector	Anxious

Wood	Fire	Earth	Metal	Water
The special one	Playboy/girl	Pleaser	Death	Fearful one
Superstar	Devotee	Obsessive	Oblivion	Serene
Growth	Outgoing	Grounded	Attached	Changeable

*Note that each of these voices/selves exists on a Yin/Yang continuum of degree and severity. One self/energy system may have numerous facets and nuances. This is just a small sample of voices that may impact the Five Element phases.

Before discussing the specific ways in which the Five Element system and Voice Dialogue process can be integrated, the reader must become further acquainted with two more aspects of the Asian system. These are highly relevant to the way the energies of the Five Element system influence each other and, more important, how the energy systems of the selves interact in a parallel manner. Herein lie the true gems adorning a multicultural approach.

There were two additional cycles or spheres of energetic influence within the Five Element system that helped the Oriental doctor understand how bio-energy maintained flow or, conversely, became imbalanced within an individual. Those cycles are known as the "*Sheng* and Ko relationships." The Sheng and Ko are also known as the creation and control cycles. These Sheng and Ko relationships of influence are depicted by the chart in figure 6 (Matsumoto & Birch, 1983, p. 41).

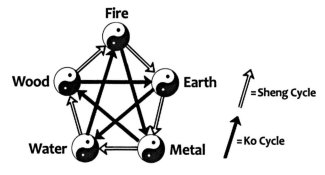

Figure 2. Sheng and Ko relationships of influence.

258 The Voice Dialogue Anthology

In the Sheng cycle, the elements are seen to generate (parent or create) each other. Wood creates Fire, Fire creates Earth, Earth creates Metal, Metal creates Water, and Water creates Wood. In a more familiar sense, the Sheng relationship is truly parental; the female (Yin) aspects of the wood element would be considered the mother of fire, and the Yang aspects of wood would be the father of fire.

Perhaps the most interesting and complex aspect of the energetic influences seen in figure 6 is that the Sheng relationships can be overlaid and applied to the entire Five Element chart of correlated variables seen in table 1. As seen in figure 2, not only does Wood create Fire, but all those elemental factors associated with Wood in the body (i.e. those items on the elemental chart under Wood in table 1) also generate energy for all the respective variables in the chart under Fire. So, when wood creates fire, spring creates summer, vigorous energy creates power, and so forth for every variable associated with Wood and Fire. This Sheng generating relationship becomes particularly fascinating when one looks at psychological parameters. For example, if the Sheng energy-generating system is functioning as it should in a healthy, balanced individual, then the normal Wood element psychological dynamic of the "will-to-become" will effortlessly generate the balanced Fire element psychological dynamic: the realization of Joy. In another scenario, if the Water element (bladder/ kidney) psychological aspect of "courage" gets out of balance and displays the Yin-deficient condition tendency for fear, then that emotion would "create" or sow the seeds of depression. This Sheng cycle is not only somewhat of a predictive tool as to how disease will develop but also how certain inner selves will relate to or even "create" each other. Again, the more significant implications of this generating or "parenting" effect will become more apparent in the case study section of this chapter.

In addition to the Sheng cycle, the Ko cycle represents the manner in which energy in one element regulates or controls that of another. In this cycle, Wood controls Earth, Fire controls Metal, Earth controls Water, Metal controls Wood and Water controls Fire. In the oldest books of Chinese medicine such relationships were of great concern and poetically described:

Wood brought in contact with metal is felled; fire brought in contact with water is extinguished; earth brought in contact with wood is penetrated; metal brought in contact with fire is dissolved; water brought in contact with earth is halted.

— Veith, 1972, p. 19

Just as there is a familial relationship, mother to child, in the Sheng cycle, the Ko cycle can be seen as grandparental. In the Ko relationship, Wood is the grandparent of Earth, having the role of disciplinarian (controlling), as paralleled in the traditional role of the elder in Chinese society. In this relationship, for example, an over-regulating Fire-element desire for Joy at any cost might repress the Metal-element appropriate expression of grief. This Ko-cycle system provides yet one more layer of information as to how energies might interact.

Of course, the psychological implications of the Sheng and Ko cycles, with respect to the voices, are perhaps more significant than most therapists might realize. If indeed the energetic relationships pertaining to the Chinese system hold true, even in part, for people around the world regardless of culture, that equivalence would mean that the selves that relate to them not only generate/parent one another but can also can control each other in a *predictable* manner. Those who have facilitated the various selves surely have seen how the struggles among the parts create psychological havoc. Imagine the advantage for the therapist to have a hint from the Asian model as to where the voices might appear, or have the most impact on each other, or how they might influence a person's health. In the Asian energy system, imbalance is a two-way street where the physical manifestation of "dis-ease" can actually energize the various destructive selves. To comprehend how voices give rise to each other and control each other, as described by the Sheng and Ko cycles, has truly proven to be of immense value for those helping the ill to understand psychological aspects of the disease process.

In conclusion, if one overlays the meridian energy system, the Sheng and Ko process, and the Five Elements variables, the combination of influences is like an extremely complex array of forces akin to those of the universe itself. The cosmic energy expanding in the galaxies of stars is complex, orbital, interacting, creating, nurturing, controlling, and destroying. Metaphorically, the immensely intricate and very same universal energy in the Asian matrix gives a wealth of valuable information in a blueprint for building health. Furthermore, the Chi system of energy, as viewed by the Chinese, does indeed lend itself to integration with the concept that the voices within the Psychology of Selves are systems of the same energy.

Case Histories

Number One

Sara booked an appointment to see if she could find a non-medical, noninvasive solution to her severe lower lumbar pain. She complained there was an alien monster living in her spine that was quite adept at torture. She had a flair for the dramatic that must have served her goal to become an actress/dancer. Unfortunately, Sara was facing back surgery because the disk between L3 and L4 was bulging and pressing on the nerve, so much so that she could hardly walk. The moment she limped into my office, I became quite concerned.

Though attractive, Sara was too much in agony to be engaging. The black circles under her eyes told me her kidney Chi was exhausted. Her weight, especially for a dancer, was subnormal (Yin) by at least ten pounds. She had a very difficult time even getting up on the treatment table because the muscles in her back were in such spasms. The acupuncture points at that position in the lumbar area are the Water element (kidney) and alarm (Yu), diagnostic points in the Asian system that were screaming for help. After feeling her pulses, I became even more concerned. All the Five Element pulses were very faint, shallow, thready (hard to find), and sometimes floating like a stick on the water. Sara was more Yin deficient in her Water element than anyone I had ever seen, and her whole system was simply lacking in Chi. Clearly, her body had more at issue than just a bad back. She looked anemic, and I suspected that she, like many other female actors, had an eating disorder. Upon further questioning I found that, indeed, she was under psychiatric care for both anorexia and an anxiety disorder. Sara was rather shocked when I said that I wouldn't work on her back until we first contacted her psychiatrist and physician. We phoned them immediately. Sara stayed prone on the treatment table while waiting for the Western-trained doctors to get back to us.

During that time, Sara filled me in on her personal history. She had arrived in Hollywood three years earlier to become "a star." Basically, she worked two jobs and spent most of her money on dancing and acting lessons. What little food she would eat, she would purge so she would "look good on camera." Toward that end she would only consume red meat for the protein. Most probably, she was in ketosis. Being in that toxic state even part of the time is very hard on the Water-element organs, the kidneys and adrenal glands. Plus, those adrenal glands were already exhausted from Sara's overworking and studying so hard and her anxiety disorder. Release of adrenaline in the fear/fight/flight response must have been nearly constant. She said she had a plethora of phobias, such as bags, snakes, trains, high places, and dark rooms. Most of all, she feared that she might not win an Oscar someday. I told her that if she didn't take care of herself, body and mind, her biggest fear might become reality. Just entertaining the thought of failure brought tears to her eyes. She said she knew what I was saying might be a real possibility.

In that moment of vulnerability, Sara also shared her fears over the quantity of medications she had been ingesting. She was hooked on the strong analgesic Vicodin, and continued to take her mood-stabilizing psych meds. Ashamedly she admitted to doing some "party drugs" as well. That cocktail of dangerous substances could kill, as Sara was well aware!

The psychiatrist called us back right at the end of the hour and gave his full approval for Sara to work with me. He confided that he was quite worried about her "not making it" — and he wasn't referring to her career as an actor. The back specialist didn't return our call for two days. He seemed less than enthusiastic about holistic alternatives, primarily because traditional Asian treatment modalities were new on the scene and he knew little about them. With some reservations he agreed to allow a trial run of a few weeks, but said if Sara didn't get better in that time, he would recommend the surgery.

Sara was clearly in very precarious health, and there was little time to waste. Given the green light by her Western doctors, we began the work of addressing the muscle spasms in her back. I also suggested that we do some "consciousness" work to see what forces might be contributing to the elemental imbalances.

We spent the better part of an hour talking about nutrition, fatigue, special exercises, drugs, and the obvious holistic guidelines to promote back wellness, but I sensed the real key was with the psychological/consciousness work.

As is true with many actors, Sara had a difficult time accessing the parts without trying to *act* them out. In time she finally dropped into the true voice of the Pusher, driving her Will to Become (Wood element) superstar self. It turns out both her parents were "B" theater actors, somewhere in mid-America. Ever since Sara was ten, they had been "guiding" her to make it big where they had not. In essence, that programmed agenda was at the core of the Earth element Pleaser sub-personality, whose pressures had caused the eating disorder. The Ko energy of that overdriving Wood element Pusher/Pleaser duo was hyper-regulating all the other elements to such an extent that Sara's entire system of energy was not flowing or functioning.

Fortunately, through some nutritional changes, sheer physical work on the acupuncture points, and some well-placed gentle Feldenkreis body movements, we managed to relieve the muscles spasms and pain enough in the first two weeks so that the back surgeon agreed to wait before operating.

Knowing that in Chinese medicine the lumbar spine area is ruled by the Water element and that Sara had a history of fear-related issues, I was eager to speak with the voices in that area. After all, she had stated that there was an alien living in that region. Treading on that soil was a delicate proposition, as the energy vortex protecting the parts living there was quite guarded. Pressing the issue would only make the hidden fearful selves more hesitant to speak, so it took nearly three weeks before the first breakthrough allowed the protective gate to crack open and allow some entry.

The key was to give the Yang side of the Water element emotional structure, the Foolish voice that had been relentlessly driving Sara without any sense of personal safety. She spent a lot of time revealing life in the industry fast lane, the parties, the cool people, the lure of Hollywood, and the dream of walking the red carpet on Oscar night. She also began to express some deeper concerns over the risky behavior of studying too hard, overworking, eating poorly, taking all kinds of drugs, and being all alone in the big city. Within the Yang field of the Water-element's *groaning* voice quality of Sara's comment about being "all alone in the big city" lay the dot of Yin, signaling the seeds of vulnerability to deal with the energies that were so imbalanced as to create her back issues. When I asked Sara to elaborate on what it was like to be so alone in the big city, she let her guard down enough to speak of her fears. She then dropped quite naturally into the Water-element constellation of voices dealing with her vulnerability. The darkness of the landscape they lived in was like a black hole in space, sucking in all light and matter. In time she began to understand the relationship of those voices to her continually contracting lower back muscles, which had become her wall of defense. She grew to become friendly with the alien monster that lived behind that wall, and to understand the lessons he had to teach about being safe. All along, the Water Yu point had been screaming a warning that Sara didn't comprehend. She finally discovered that the monster actually was trying to save her life, for without the back pain she was on a road to utter self-destruction.

Over the next six months Sara's back slowly improved. Of course, it's hard to say if it was the exercises or changes in life style or body treatments or the conscious shift in her awareness that made the difference. It really didn't matter, as long as she got better.

The voices in the Wood element seemed to change the most. The "wanna-be-a- star" voice saw that to "lighten up" a bit was essential lest it kill Sara. The Wood-element "good daughter," who had internalized her parents' dreams to the point of obsession, had a lot of hidden anger buried there. There were some great "aha" moments as to the deep motivation for, and the extreme costs of, earning an Oscar. When these driving forces in the Ko cycle released some of their hold on the system, Sara's pulse energy actually came back quite dramatically, and those deficient weak pulses returned to nearly normal levels.

Sara started eating a balanced diet, stopped purging, and regained the ten pounds she needed. She still thought she was fat, but understood that health is more valuable than some industry-imposed standard of beauty or distorted perception of success. Within a year, she had greatly reduced her reliance on pain medication, and never did have the surgery. She also never made it in Hollywood, but instead got married, had two kids, and enjoyed life with a great husband. Over the years, Sara's back did flare up occasionally (during pregnancy), but those episodes passed with some gentle bodywork. In the end, she bragged that giving birth to her wonderful children was much more meaningful than winning a gold-plated statuette.

Number Two

Roger was a forty-three-year-old businessman who had asthma attacks so severe they would put him in the hospital for days at a time. Though doctors had him on every medication imaginable, Roger knew that the disease was getting progressively worse. Attacks came more frequently, breathing was more difficult, and the medications seem to be less and less effective. Roger feared that someday he wouldn't make it to the hospital in time and would die. He was desperate to find a solution.

His pulse readings revealed energy patterns that were what a practitioner of Asian medicine would often find with someone suffering such a condition as his. There was a very Yang and also full (like a sumo wrestler's backside) i.e. excessive, quality in the Metal element of the Lung and Large Intestine. There was also a heavy, choppy, over-controlling quality in the Fire element (Heart), and a weak/thin/dampness/skimpy pulse in the Earth element (Spleen) energies. In terms of the Sheng/Ko cycle, the Grandparent Fire was over-controlling Metal, and Metal (the child of Earth) was draining its parent of energy. The Water element, in general, was extremely deficient as well, because Metal was not nurturing Water.

In Western medical terminology, Roger had a huge overproduction of mucus and was highly allergic to everything floating in the air. His immune system was deficient and worn out from attacking every foreign protein and antigen entering his body with each breath. The muscle system around his trachea had a hair trigger, and would close down so he couldn't breathe at the first sign of any stress, pollutant, allergen, emotional upset, bad dream, or chemical toxin. In the final analysis, Roger was suffocating himself to death.

For Westerners who do not understand the significance of the Asian diagnostic description, let's take a look at a few variables in the Five Element chart under the Metal element. There we find mucus is the fluid, hence the poor man blew his nose every two minutes. The process of the muscles contracting down on the windpipe was as if the Fire grandparent was over-controlling the Metal (function of the lungs), and this influence was reflected in the pulse readings. The Yin or deficient Earth pulse for the spleen was indication of the immune/lymphatic system problems. The first order of business was to teach Roger some self-help techniques so he could put moderate finger pressure on specific acupuncture points that would help his medication relax the contractions around his airway. This gave him an immediate sense of empowerment, enabling him to begin taking control of the problem. Secondly, we began treatments on the meridian systems to rebalance the Chi energy to a more normalized state.

This approach meant 1) Using the acupuncture points to open up the channel blockages in Fire (Heart and Small Intestine Meridians), tonifying (bringing energy into) the Earth (especially the Spleen); 2) Releasing the blocked energy of Metal (Lung and Large Intestine meridians) into the Water Element; and 3) Using some transfer-point energies in the Wood element into Fire to complete the circuit and balance the flow of Chi.

In essence, the goal was to release blockages in order to get the energy flowing again throughout the system by taking the Chi from excessive areas and moving it into the deficient meridians. Once the physical work had begun, we focused on aspects of the Five Element system. Over the ensuing weeks, I began to casually ask Roger about his life and lifestyle.

The first thing that became almost comical was that for every simple question asked, I would get at least a fifteen-minute answer. His excessive Fire element qualities sure were borne out by his loquaciousness. Roger was a burly man, about thirty pounds overweight. In addition to the asthma, he suffered from severe hemorrhoids (Metal-Lung and Large intestine are a Yin/Yang pair). He was a typical hardworking father whose wife stayed at home taking care of their three kids. Both of Roger's parents were dead, as was his younger brother, who had died in a kayaking accident. Roger had been married once before at an early age, but his wife had died quickly of an undiagnosed ovarian tumor. Roger was hugely afraid of flying. He hated the thought of dying in a plane crash. Of course, each time he mentioned death, my mind immediately registered that grief is the emotion associated with the Metal (Lung) element. When I asked the loaded question "How did you handle the grief of all those terrible losses in your life?" his answer was far too brief when he said that he didn't let death get to him "so much." Alarm bells began ringing in my head. Clearly, Roger was totally blocked in the Metal process of "Letting-go."

After the third week, Roger started to improve ever so slightly. At least the frequency and severity of his attacks began diminishing. About that time, I got a rather curious mental image while working on him. Since our energy systems were literally plugged into each other through the Chi energy work I was doing on him, this hit of mine was worth mentioning. I told him that I saw a brief glimpse of a little boy standing in the rain under an airplane wing. When I asked him if that image meant anything to him, he said, "Not that I know of." End of discussion!

Again, because Roger's normal pattern was to talk and talk and talk, I suspected there was more to the image than he was revealing. My suspicions grew even more when he cancelled his next appointment, offering a flimsy excuse about being too tired to drive the two miles to my office.

When Roger did finally come back in, he had a different look about him. He appeared tired and depleted, and he didn't know if our approach was really working because the asthma had come back in full force. For me the resurgence, though disappointing, seemed highly significant.

Roger continued to complain that he wasn't sleeping because he had many bad dreams. He believed the nightmares had something to do with that brief image I had shared the week before. Roger related that he felt the little boy was indeed himself, a long time ago. Something bad had happened in his childhood that he had tried to forget. When I asked if he thought it had something to do with the asthma returning, his eyes lit up. For him it was that "aha" moment when he made the connection of mind and body. He was intrigued and awestruck by the possibility that stirring images of that long-forgotten episode in his life might have triggered his terrible asthma episodes.

Asked if he would do some Voice Dialogue work, Roger agreed. Over the next several weeks, that child in his dreams emerged and slowly revealed a rather sad and profoundly significant story:

On a particularly blustery autumn day (Metal) in upper New York, eight-year-old Roger was suddenly pulled out of class and taken to the principal's office. A very sensitive lad, Roger wondered what was going on. However, past experience with his stoic mother, who was of Old World European stock, had conditioned him to mostly be seen and not heard. Roger knew something was wrong. The receptionist let it slip that something had happened to his father. Eventually, his uncle picked him up and told him they needed to fly to Cape Cod, where the relatives were gathering at the family compound. They drove to a small local airport (Metal). Little Roger's uncle was a pilot, and dropped the boy off at the plane while he went to file the flight plan for the short hop over to the cape.

Roger didn't know that his father had died from pneumonia earlier in the day, but he did know that something very bad had happened. As it began to rain, the boy, scared and alone, began to cry. The sobs were so strong and the weather so wet that cough-ing spasms overtook the hysterical child (Metal). When the uncle returned to the plane and saw the boy coughing, he administered "the cure": he slapped Roger hard on the back and told him that he had to "pull out of it!" The uncle ordered him to "stop crying," and said that he had to be a "brave little man." In a demanding tone the uncle instructed that the little boy had to be the "man of the family" because his father had died that morning. One can only imagine the emotional trauma when the uncle added, "Your daddy wouldn't want you to cry!" (Metal)

Of course, Roger was a very obedient young man and did *exactly* as he was told. He stopped crying then, and did not cry again for over thirty years. The asthma attacks began two weeks after his father's funeral, and got progressively worse when his mother died a few years later. Roger didn't cry at her funeral either, but took care of the details as the responsible person he'd grown to be. When his brother died, Roger did the same. When his wife died, Roger did the same. With every death and tear not shed, his asthma and hemorrhoids got worse.

When I showed Roger the Five Element chart, and he saw that the Metal-element emotion associated with the lungs was grief, he was silent for the longest time. He finally said, "It all makes sense, doesn't it?"

Then the work began in earnest. It took months to get Roger to the point where the grandparent controller system bound to the Fire element would allow those blocked grieving voices in the Metal element to speak at all. It took an extremely long time for the dutiful child to let go and shed that first tear, but once they started, they couldn't help but flow and flow and flow. When we revisited the long-ago funeral scene of his father, Roger finally released his pent-up grief in what was perhaps the most cathartic session I had ever witnessed. He used up a whole box of tissues.

After that long session I was quite concerned about any ill effects that such crying might have on Roger's overly sensitive respiratory system. To my great surprise and relief, his lung Chi pulses were the most normal I had ever felt in him.

Of course, more "elements" and "selves" required attention. We worked on the Earth-element nurturer part of him, which in a Yang way needed to take care of others. It gave rise in time to the Yin (disowned side) of that energetic, which longed to be nurtured by something other than spicy Mexican food (Metal element-Yang) Constipation from that diet was probably the source of the hemorrhoids. He changed his diet and solved that issue. The part of Roger that feared flying made great progress, and he finally went up in a small plane to "test" himself.

Over the course of one year, many voices got a chance to speak, and Roger's asthma slowly began to subside. After two years, his Western doctors discontinued Roger's asthma medications because this middle-aged man had mysteriously "outgrown" his disease. To this day, he still has occasional allergy attacks and his chest tightness in the springtime pollen bloom, but he copes with the symptoms and doesn't get excessively alarmed. The triggering mechanisms no longer cause the entire system to overreact.

Of course, much more went on with Roger than can be presented in a brief summary. Hopefully, the reader can get a glimpse of how, in Roger's case, the blending of ancient Asian Five Element observations, and the modern treatment tool of Voice Dialogue, aided Roger in "outgrowing" his previously severe and chronic medical problem.

Summary and Conclusion

In the two case studies above, the addition of Voice Dialogue to the therapeutic mix appeared to be extremely helpful. The conscious awareness created from having many inner voices speak about the real lifestyle choices and roadblocks, which had created such extreme health issues, made the transformation on a purely physical level much easier. Of course, not all patients have such dramatic results from the process of integrating Eastern and Western modalities; some have no good results at all. For me the value lies with the ones with whom it did work. If we can repeat and refine the elements involved in those processes, then we begin to understand how to effect cures.

It is said in Chinese medicine: "One needle cures all diseases." Though it seems rather idealistic, the notion is that if one can find and open the exact key point unbalancing the entire system, then everything else will fall into place. Of course, life is *never* that simple. We are far too complex creatures. Physical/mental/spiritual health is dependent on many factors ranging from genetics to lifestyles to emotions to traumas to the weather and pollution in our environment; the list goes on and on. Just like the doctors of old, modern healthcare professionals are beginning to understand the many-layered and interrelated causes of disease and the value of a multifaceted, multi-disciplined approach to cure. I predict that in the future, a more updated version of the Five Element chart will be integral in creating a tapestry that defines well-being.

References

Amber, R., and A. Babey-Brooke. *The Pulse: In Occident and Orient.* New York, NY: Santa Barbara Press, 1966.

Chang S. *The Complete Book of Acupuncture.* Milbrae, CA: Celestial Arts Press, 1976.

Connelly, D. *Traditional Acupuncture: The Law of the Five Elements,* Columbia, MD: Columbia Press, 1975.

Feng, G., and J. English. *Tao Te Ching, trans.* New York, NY: Knopf Press, 1972.

Hsu, P. *Introduction to Chinese Medicine.* Dallas, TX: McCartney Printing Press, 1976.

Kaptchuk, T. *The Web That Has No Weaver.* New York: Congdon & Weed Press, 1983.

Matsumoto, K. and S. Birch. *Five Elements and Ten Stems.* Brookline, MA: Paradigm Publications, 1983.

McGarey, W. *Acupuncture and Body Energetics.* Phoenix, AZ: Gabriel Press, 1974.

Porkert, M. *Theoretical Foundations of Chinese Medicine.* Cambridge, MA: The MIT Press, 1974.

Veith, I. *Nei Ching, The Yellow Emperor's Classsic of Internal Medicine.* Berkeley, CA: University of California Press, 1972.

Homeopathy and Voice Dialogue

Gabrielle Pinto, BSc, RS Hom

The dream of the pure scientist is to practice in a manner unsullied by temperament or contaminated by other disciplines — to find a healing discipline that is, of itself, both complete and efficacious.

Unfortunately for such dreamers, and, I believe, fortunately for patients, this is a utopian notion in which the dream serves only itself and the drug companies. For a discipline to be uncontaminated is of no importance whatsoever to the patient, who expects the physician to bring every ounce of knowledge that she can muster to the "cure." Patients care less about purity than they do about results. As Popeye says, "What woykes woykes."

I have practiced as a homeopath since 1984, and for over a quarter century I have amalgamated Voice Dialogue into my work. I discovered early in my practice that homeopathy could provide support for emotional problems, and later learnt that when homeopathy is combined with Voice Dialogue, patients experienced insightful, long-lasting changes in their lives. This interlacing of the two disciplines happened because I had a strong bias toward helping clients with depression and relationship difficulties. I also loved working with families, and sometimes wives have even brought their husbands.

What enabled me to help emotional problems using homeopathy was reading the psychologies of the remedies (medicines) in diverse materia medica. These are expert discourses on the nature of the homeopathic remedies. Samuel Hahnemann, the founder of homeopathy, noticed that each remedy had a temperament as well as corresponding physical problems. It was this idea that mental and emotional distress, as well as physical suffering, could be helped that drew me to become a homeopath.

Hahnemann was insistent that sickness in an individual relates to the whole person, not just to a part or an organ. He said that the homeopath must clearly perceive what is dis-eased in a client, and choose a remedy that will match all the symptoms and thus act curatively. I am a little wary of the word "cure" here because that would indicate an elimination of the problem (as if it had never happened). Of course the problem did happen, and it enabled change to take place. I would prefer to say that remedies facilitate transitions. One of our homeopathic principles is that "health is the ability to adapt to change."

Intrigued with the remedy pictures, I began an intensive study of their psychological aspects, and, as I will explain, I found that the descriptions correspond well with primary and vulnerable selves.

As an introduction to this arcane science, I will describe three common homeopathic remedies. Then I will show you two cases that illustrate my integrated approach. It may appear that the temperaments of these remedies are quite negative; however, homeopaths do not prescribe on the client's strengths, but on the problematical aspects of the defenses or primary selves and the vulnerabilities.

Nux Vomica

You could say that this remedy is one that belongs to our age. It fits workaholics, and I have often used it for men and women who over-work in business. They have primary selves or defenses that are hurried, competitive, and industrious. They are very impatient, irritable, and dictatorial. They admit that they can shout at their partner or their secretary, and they use alcohol or drugs to unwind, whereupon they become really abusive.

Their vulnerable side or self emerges in the night. They wake up at 3:00 a.m., highly anxious about business, and they often suffer gastric disorders.

Occasionally I have had the opportunity to dialogue with these business parts. What I have mostly observed is that after Nux Vomica treatment there is a great relaxation in the behavior of the primary selves, as if the density of the heavyweight primary selves diminishes. The sleep improves, and partners say how much nicer their mates have become. In such cases I am working with family dynamics and homeopathy, and I have no doubt that the remedy has acted by affecting the primary selves, but how it does so remains a mystery.

A general use for Nux Vomica (which many of you may already know) is simply for indigestion after a large meal, but it will not affect the primary selves if the mental-emotional disposition as described above is not there.

Arsenicum and Fear of Death

Arsenicum is made from arsenic, highly poisonous in a crude form, but wonderful in the tiny amounts used in homeopathy. The disposition in this remedy is for the highly anxious and insecure. The primary selves are apprehensive about health, and often become hypochondriacal. Like Nux Vomica types, they are competitive, arrogant, and compulsive. They have a fastidious part, which is an obsessive planner and needs to be in control of the environment.

Vulnerability emerges in the early hours of the night; they wake up between midnight and 2:00 a.m. in a panic attack, thinking that they will die. I treated a record producer who benefited from Arsenicum; he had terrible fear of death, and thought about lying in his grave at 2:00 a.m.. We had the opportunity to discuss this frightened part of him, and he was able to make links to his early childhood, when his father would come home drunk at night.

Silica and the Medium

In our materia medica, a silica patient is described as "lacking grit." This remedy is for delicate and highly refined, yielding primary selves. Patients worry about what others think of them, and are always trying to fulfill the image of what is wanted. There is another self that is highly perceptive, so much so that they can become easily become true mediums. This is because the lack of stamina or grit is also seen on a mental level, which is where they are very open to psychic impressions. Unfortunately, they are often quite ill on a physical level, with tiredness, weakness, and swollen glands. I find this remedy very helpful for these difficulties, but I do warn those who are psychic that as their health improves with the treatment, the psychic abilities may lessen, as it is not really a healthy state to be so open.

Let me cite a couple of case histories that can illustrate some of the most powerful transformations I have seen. These have been in the lives of clients whom I have had the opportunity to treat with both homeopathy and Voice Dialogue.

Calcarea Carbonica

Sarah and Her Dreams

On a sunny July day in 2009, Sarah, a thirty-five-year-old science teacher, came to my office for her first appointment. She said that she felt frightened, and that over the past year she had felt levels of anxiety that seemed out of proportion to the life she led. Sarah regarded herself as very sensitive because she avoided confrontations and rows.

As I listened, I warmed to Sarah. She was polite, generous, and eager to please, the sort of person who is always willing to help others. She said she had strong spiritual beliefs, and constantly wanted to send loving-kindness to others. She believed that if she was nice and hardworking, then life would work out for her, but things were not going her way.

Sarah's presenting physical complaint was sciatica and lower back pain. Although she was always responsible, and tried never to miss a day through illness, the pain had kept her from school. She had a demanding boss, and had recently had a distressing falling-out with an old friend. At the same time, a neighbor had bullied her into cutting some trees in her garden, even though she didn't want to.

When Sarah tried to return to teaching, her back became much worse. She was so overwhelmed with her work at the school that she had been trying to change jobs; however, the new job she was considering might require even more of her than her present job. She felt stuck and upset.

For quite some time, perhaps a year, Sarah had awakened in the night after recurrent nightmares. She found herself swimming in the sea in dark, dangerous waters that were full of sharks. Also, she had dreams of being chased by rough street people, and sometimes of driving in a car that was out of control.

I felt strongly that Sarah would benefit from homeopathy and Voice Dialogue. Her primary selves were the responsible, hardworking Mother, the Pleaser, and a Spiritual voice that believed in loving-kindness. These primary selves eventually became overwhelmed, which created anxiety in the vulnerable selves, who often develop a wide variety of fears as well as nightmares. Sarah had become exhausted and developed a bad back.

Calcarea Carbonica is a remedy made from oyster shell. Homeopaths have found that patients needing Calcarea often feel as if they have little or no protection from the demands people make on them, as if they have weak boundaries or "are missing the shell that protects them." They have primary selves that are highly responsible and dutiful. Everyone likes them, as they are such Pleasers. Unfortunately, they also have strong Pushers that keep them going, even when they are ill or in pain. It is common that patients who, like Sarah, overwork and then get bad backs are in need of Calcarea Carbonica. When it is truly indicated, the chance for resolution of the problem is favorable. Sarah was given this remedy.

We met two weeks later for a follow-up. Sarah was much better; she had started to take more time to rest, her pain was under control, but curiously, every time she wanted to go back to work, her back became bad again. She was confused and didn't know what to do.

After I have prescribed in cases like Sarah's, I ask if the patients would like the opportunity to look at what their dreams might mean. If they would, I give a small introductory talk on the Psychology of Selves. Then we discuss the dreams, and what they might represent, using Voice Dialogue as a model for understanding them. I explain how parts of our self that we do not honor in our waking life could manifest in our dreams.

I asked Sarah to tell me what she thought about her dreams and to discuss her fears. She felt that the sharks and the street people might be connected to the nastiness and bullying that she had felt around her these last few months. She found it really hard to say no when people made demands on her. I asked her if she thought the street people would be nice if asked to do things they did not want to do. She understood immediately.

She said she knew that she must "toughen up." Perhaps leaving her current job was not the issue, and that confronting her head teacher about being so demanding might be a better option.

Five weeks later, during her follow-up appointment, Sarah reported a beautiful dream: she was diving under the sea, and instead of being scared she found herself swimming with green turtles.

In her daily life, her pain was much better. She had confronted the head teacher about her workload, and the conversation had gone very well. Sarah had slowed down, the dreams of driving a car out of control were gone, and she no longer wanted to leave her job.

In Sarah's case, her dream narrative mirrored the emotional position of her waking life. She felt defenseless against her boss, the friend who had turned against her, and her bullying neighbor. Her "disowned parts" were symbolized in dreams by the energy of the sharks and streetwise boys. Sarah needed to integrate these energies.

What was curious to me, as a homeopath, is that she felt unprotected. Calcarea Carbonica activated some protective vitality, and, as her back got better, Sarah could begin to have the conversation with me about her dreams and what they represented.

By adopting or integrating some energy of the sharks or the streetwise boys, she could gain the protection (or the boundaries) she needed to deal effectively with what she perceived as attacks. Certainly I did not wish her to become like a shark when dealing with her boss, but rather to take on a tiny part of that shark energy — a homeopathic dose that would help her rectify the balance of the selves system.

I knew from the dream of the green turtles that Sarah was now in her process of change. She had begun the integration of the disowned voices. In this way, her back, which hurt and was her discharge from responsibility, could get better. The back pain and her dreams became Sarah's inner teacher.

Sepia

Emma's Tears

I have always admired Emma because she was a great mother to her four children. She relied on me like an old-fashioned family physician. I was always her first stop for help when the children were ill or life was difficult. In the Autumn of 2008 she came to see me, in tears. She reported:

> I'm so irritable, teary, and restless since the school holidays, I don't feel any love toward my children, they are all annoying me. I certainly don't want sex with my husband. I've lost interest in everything. I'm sure I'm depressed, as I want to run away.

Knowing Emma well, and being confident that homeopathy has some very good treatments for worn-out, overworked mothers, I gave her Sepia, which fitted her emotional state and her loss of interest in sex perfectly. In Sepia, the primary selves are the nurturing Mother and a very hardworking part: these join together to become Superwoman. Some women can sustain this combination for a while and seem to be truly remarkable, but sometimes the intense amount of mothering and the extreme busyness destabilize everything (including the hormonal system), which is also why women lose interest in sex. Sexual energy commonly drops in women when they become overtired; it's simply a way of the body conserving energy. I do expect it to return, however, after the correct homeopathic treatment, as the general energy and emotions improve.

(I am always available during treatment for extra telephone support, but rather than rely on phone conversations, I prefer to see what the remedy facilitates.)

One month after taking Sepia, Emma was already feeling better in herself, and her extreme irritability and tearfulness had subsided. She still had no sexual energy, but I explained that it might take a couple of menstrual cycles before it returned.

I find it easier to discuss Voice Dialogue theory after a client who needs Sepia starts to feel better, when her depression lifts. Sepia women can cut themselves off from communication with others, especially anyone who appears to offer consolation. It aggravates them. They can descend into an impersonal, numb part, and it's hard for them to hear what the therapist is saying.

During this second appointment, I did not facilitate the parts, but only discussed them. Emma quickly understood that she was primarily identified with Superwoman, who joined hands with the Critic and the Pusher. Together we listed all of her daily tasks, and then had a hilarious session as we actually found out exactly how long each job really took. Looking at the hours in the day required to do all the tasks, we found out it was impossible to achieve Superwoman's goals.

Emma said, from an aware perspective, " I really can't think how I could make those long lists and somehow believe that I could achieve it all. Now that we've looked at how impossible I had made my life, from this perspective it's funny. I still don't know how I'm going to change it all, but I know I must. I do feel so much better, but I am afraid that if I go back into the long lists I will lose the benefit of this change of vision."

I explained that we would need to do some Voice Dialogue sessions together to help her stabilize and allow her to separate from her busy, pushing side, which is such a strong primary self for her.

Once there had been a separation from Superwoman, the remedy and the work on the selves allowed Emma to feel more connected again to her husband and children.

She came back at the next session and spontaneously reported, "I really have felt so much calmer, and my husband has noticed. He suggested that we go out once a week for dinner, just for us, no chats about the business or the children, just time out for us. I don't always want to go, but when we do I feel so much happier. We are starting to reconnect again. I certainly don't feel like leaving them all as I did two months ago."

I see Emma twice a year for herself, and when her balance slips I repeat Sepia. If necessary we dialogue the primary selves that overwork, and then she feels in control again, with more awareness of what destabilizes her.

Integrating Voice Dialogue and homeopathy has created a new way of working for me. It began almost unnoticed at first, but over the last fifteen years it has profoundly changed my approach to illness, pain, and family dynamics. I hope, in writing this article, to give you an understanding of how well the two disciplines intertwine.

Healing is a mysterious process, and because no one yet knows how homeopathy works, adherents to scientism tend to ignore the good results and accuse homeopaths of relying on the placebo effect. This is rather like a French client who, puzzled by the almost instant disappearance of his long-standing malady, anxiously demanded: "Okay, now I know it works in practice, but does it work in theory?"

The answer to that is probably no. Just as a bumblebee flies despite being an aerodynamic disaster, homeopathy flies in the face of scientific dogma, yet when you get it right it works wonderfully, and when you put Voice Dialogue and homeopathy together, there are opportunities for powerful transformations.

References

Morrison, R. *Desktop Guides to Keynotes and Confirmatory Symptoms*. California: Hahnemann Clinic Publishing, 1993.

Pinto, G., and M. Feldman. *Homeopathy for Children*. Saffron Walden: C.F.W. Daniels. Random House, 2000.

Sankaran, R. *The Soul of Remedies*. Santa Cruz, CA: Bombay Homeopathic Medical Publishers, 1997.

Vithoulkas, G. *The Science of Homeopathy*. New York: Grove Press, Inc, 1980.

Vithoulkas, G. and E. V. Woensel. *Levels of Health*. Alonissos, Greece: International Academy of Classical Homeopathy, 2010.

INTELLIGENCE OF SELF:
VOICE DIALOGUE AND PERSONALITY TYPE

Geneviève Cailloux, IDF, and Pierre Cauvin, IDF

Introduction

In France during the 1980s, we introduced and developed the Jungian Type approach to our work of Organizational Development through combination with the Myers-Briggs Type Indicator. Though we were convinced of its usefulness, we were still unsatisfied because of the method of development beyond the mere knowledge of the type. When we encountered Voice Dialogue, we became aficionados. We studied in Europe, and then became regular visitors to Mendocino, California, working with Hal and Sidra Stone yearly.

At the beginning of the 3rd millennium, we gave a new orientation to our approach to Types and integrated it with Voice Dialogue. This led to what we now call "Intelligence of Self," based on our personal journey as individuals and as a couple, and our experiences with clients.

Since most if not all readers are knowledgeable about Voice Dialogue, we will not present its principles; however, it is necessary to explain our view about Types. We will then be able to see how they combine and what the benefits are.

Type Explained

A Bit of History

The fundamental idea of Jung's typology is that the functioning of the psyche is based on eight major processes or "functions." We are born with these, but they do not develop over time in the same way. Some, already present at the earliest age, are often called "preferred." Others are linked with our shadow, and it takes more time to integrate them, if we are ever able to do so.

The Jungian approach to Types developed very quickly in the 1980s, first in the US, and soon after in many other countries when it became of easily accessible through diverse sources. This had advantages and pitfalls.

The success allowed many people to benefit from this approach; it opened new fields of application, therapy, counseling, career orientation, and team building, to name a few. And it provided an enormous amount of data and research.

On the other hand, it simplified, and in many cases oversimplified, Jung's approach. The eight functions were translated into four dimensions, which were much more static than the interplay of the functions. The dynamics of the psyche (which is one of the main themes of Jung's thinking) was seldom used in practice, and almost never researched in theory.

At the end of the 1990s and beginning of the 2000s, a few practitioners, including us, started to give more emphasis to the functions and dynamics. We will present the eight functions and their interaction in this new way. Readers used to the "classical" approach to Types will find a table of conversion at the end of this paper (table 1).

The Eight Functions

The eight functions can be distributed in two groups:

1. The functions of perception, which deal with the way we collect information; and

2. The functions of judgment, which deal with the ways we make decisions.

In each group there are two pairs of opposites. Each function is designated by two initials, the first in uppercase letters, indicating the function itself, and the second in lowercase, referring to the orientation of the function, either toward the outside world (extraversion) or the inside world (introversion).

Functions of Perception

Extraverted Sensing (Se) vs. Introverted Intuition (Ni)

EXTRAVERTED SENSING
Ability to go with the flow, the here and now, and to experience the outside world with all the senses; learns by experimentation, finds practical solutions, leads by one's example.

INTROVERTED INTUITION
Ability to perceive the underlying relationships between the elements, and to synthesize them in a long-term vision; learns by readings, strategist, guided by one's vision.

Introverted Sensing (Si) vs. Extraverted Intuition (Ne)

INTROVERTED SENSING
Ability to catalog all relevant data and retrieve them easily; follows tested methods, starts from what already exists, leads hierarchically.

EXTRAVERTED INTUITION
Ability to let spring a flow of new ideas in any situation; learns by discussing, has the talent to adopt new viewpoint, leads by the strength of one's insights.

Functions of Decision

Extraverted Thinking (Te) vs. Introverted Feeling (Fi)

EXTRAVERTED THINKING
Ability to organize and structure the environment in a rational and orderly way; learns methodically, makes quick decisions, leads naturally.

INTROVERTED FEELING
Ability to create harmony around personal values deeply felt. Seeks meaning, makes decisions according to personal ethics, leads by influence.

Introverted Thinking (Ti) vs. Extraverted Feeling (Fe)

INTROVERTED THINKING
Ability to look for the rational explanation of everything through continuous questioning; learns by criticizing, makes decisions based on rational principles, leads by clarity of conception.

EXTRAVERTED FEELING
Ability to be in coherence with socially shared values; learns by interacting with others, makes decisions based on people's needs, leads by the strength of one's values.

The functions dynamics:

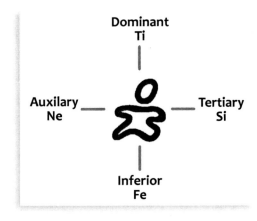

These eight functions are organized in the psyche according to a model that has been elaborated over time by practitioners and scientists following Jung's example of positioning the functions on a cross made up of two axes — the functions of judgment and the functions of perception.

To keep things simple we will limit the model to the first four functions. As an example, we will choose what is commonly supposed to be Jung's type.

The first function to develop is usually called the dominant. It gives the main orientation of the psyche, and is usually the one we use to tackle a problem. It manifests early, around the "age of reason." Jung's dominant function is most probably the Introverted Thinking, a characteristic of many scientists. Jung devoted his life to understanding the human psyche, and kept asking questions and deepening his theories all the time.

The second function, the auxiliary, strikes a balance with the dominant. It is introverted if the dominant is extraverted and vice versa. It is a perceiving function if the dominant is a judging one and vice versa. Usually, the auxiliary develops around adolescence. For Jung, it was probably the Extraverted Intuition: his scope of interests was extremely broad, his curiosity was boundless, and he was able to draw examples from many different cultures.

These two functions are the basis of the psyche, those we are familiar with and can serve to regulate. We can describe someone's psychological type with the initials of these two main functions. In Jung's case, it would be TiNe. But these two functions are just a part of the psyche: the aim of the development is to integrate their polar opposites, which make up the shadow side.

The tertiary function is more difficult to reach and use. It becomes somewhat reliable around adulthood. Then it may be a new source of energy and open a new domain of activity. Jung's Introverted Sensing manifested itself when he was building his tower in Bollingen or carving stones.

The inferior function is even more difficult to integrate. It is around the inferior function that we are overly sensitive, make repetitive errors, and feel threatened and vulnerable. Extraverted Feeling was probably

Jung's inferior function. His love life was a bit chaotic. The integration of the auxiliary with the tertiary opens the way to the integration of the inferior with the dominant, giving access to the Self through the transcendent function.

Obviously, this is just a broad sketch; interested readers are referred to the bibliography.

Links between Types and Voice Dialogue

Some links may have popped into the reader's mind. Let us delineate some from two viewpoints: 1) What Types and Voice Dialogue have in common; and 2) how they combine.

Features Common to Types and Voice Dialogue

Voice Dialogue and Types originating in Jung's vision of the psyche share necessarily some fundamental principles:

- ◆ Psychic energy is based on polar opposites. For each primary self there is a disowned self; for each preferred function there is a function in the shadow.

- ◆ Development does not consist of switching from one pole to the other but learning to integrate both polarities.

- ◆ There is nothing good or bad in a self or in a function; they all have their qualities and their limitations. Problems arise when a polarity makes a takeover on its opposite without an Aware Ego.

These common characteristics make Types and Voice Dialogue "compatible." The two approaches potentialize each other, as we will see in the next paragraphs.

Possible combinations of Types and Voice Dialogue

There are many different links between functions and selves. For instance:

♦ Primary selves and functions may be identical to the point of being archetypal. For instance, Extraverted Sensing is often the dominant function of the clever, resourceful "Jack of all trades."

♦ When describing this function to workshop participants, they frequently exclaim, "Oh, yes, MacGyver!"

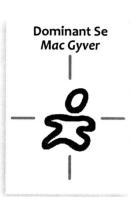

**Dominant Se
Mac Gyver**

The dominant and auxiliary functions are usually part of the Operating Ego. In Jung's example, it's easy to see how his combination of Introverted Thinking (looking for rational explanations) and Extraverted Intuition (constant curiosity) contributed to make him the fabulous explorer of the mind he was.

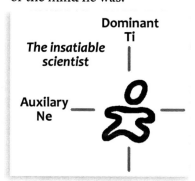

**Dominant
Ti**

*The insatiable
scientist*

**Auxilary
Ne**

An alliance between extraverted functions or, less frequently, introverted ones, may happen. In that case, the operating ego is closely associated to the extraverted side of the psyche, throwing the introverted side back into the shadow. This may appear in women of the Extraverted Intuition/Introverted Feeling type (NeFi), working in a male competitive business environment. They have to fight harder than the men, and therefore have to use their Extraverted Thinking more than their Introverted Feeling. This leads to great professional success before complete personal burnout.

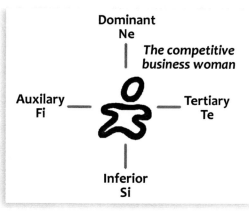

**Dominant
Ne**

*The competitive
business woman*

**Auxilary
Fi**

**Tertiary
Te**

**Inferior
Si**

The function dynamics are also helpful in looking at the disowned selves. Jacques is a NiTe. As such, his talent is to implement creative, long-term ideas. Reinforced by education, this talent becomes over the years a very strong operating ego who cannot stop implementing ideas as soon as they are expressed. He calls it the "Noria of ideas," referring to the donkey that cannot stop moving in the same circle to draw water. Opposite to NiTe are the tertiary and inferior functions SeFi. This type is the life and soul of a party, the good friend who brings people together to play and have fun. Jacques cannot help seeing him as the "lazy beach boy." Nonetheless, it is the side he has to integrate in order to have better relationships with his friends, his family, and even his clients.

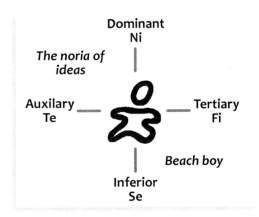

There are many possibilities. This function-dynamics cross can be used as a way of mapping the selves, of better understanding their functioning, and of clarifying the relationships between them. It also helps to get the "flavor" of each self. The Professional is always different, whether it is linked to the Introverted Sensing or the Extraverted Intuition.

As an example, below is Liz's map of the selves. Liz is a NeTi, who had led a very independent life. Artemis and the Professional are the selves who have conducted her successful professional life, her preferred functions that give her both creativity and logic. Liz was attracted to power, and easily climbed the hierarchical ladder to a high position in the Human Resources department at the headquarters of a large multinational company. In order not to be swallowed by the structure, she developed a counterdependent Little Savage, which her Extraverted Intuition was too happy to help. On the other side, with her friends, this function transformed itself in a Clown. In her late thirties, Liz married and had a child. It was clearly the time of the tertiary function, the Extraverted Feeling, which led to the Loving Mother.

Not by coincidence, the Inner Patriarch, who had been very silent (he was an Introvert), made his entry, to her great surprise. Then, Liz started a professional training in Voice Dialogue, and discovered three selves linked to her inferior function, the Introverted Sensing (the ability to be precise, organized, structured). This function had been quite absent in Liz's life. When she got in touch with it, she discovered neglected disowned selves — the Poor Me and the Shapeless Effete. In recognizing the existence of this part of her, she gave birth to a new energy, the mix of Senses and Feelings, Aphrodite.

The Benefits of Combining Types and Voice Dialogue

Some Benefits

Based on twenty years of the combined use of Types and Voice Dialogue, we not only believe but also know through experience that this combination has enormous benefits:

◆ It provides a global view of the psyche, which is made of both inborn processes and acquired strategies. Voice Dialogue emphasizes the latter; Types deal with the former. The combination allows us to see all sides and to analyze their interplay.

◆ Types give a frame to the variability of the selves. Types are structured: there are eight functions, paired as opposites. Selves are many and vary. Combining them is like finding an Aware Ego between structure and no structure.

◆ In a business environment, Types are easier to present. Going step by step deeper into the use of Types paves the way to Voice Dialogue.

◆ Types are a compass that gives us an idea of where to go, and Voice Dialogue allows us to go there. For the facilitator, Types give an indication of the area where the disowned selves probably are.

An Example: the Projections

Projection, or the fact of attributing to someone a characteristic, positive or negative, that is actually in us, is a very important phenomenon of the psyche:

◆ Projections happen all the time and lead to many misunderstandings, personal or social clashes and fights.

◆ Projections are what primary selves do in order to avoid being challenged.

- Primary selves project onto other people or onto own disowned selves.

- Projections are many — it would be impossible to list all of them. Here also, Types provide a framework to get a feeling of what the projections can look like. Hence the following two tables.

Conclusion

Intelligence is the ability to adapt to new situations and find solutions to the problems encountered. In that sense, we think that the combination of Voice Dialogue and Types makes us more intelligent. This is why we have called it Intelligence of Self... and others.

Table 1: Conversion of Four-letter Code and Type Dynamics Code

Four-letter code	Type Dynamics	Four-letter code	Type Dynamics
ISTJ	SiTe	ESTP	SeTi
ISFJ	SiFe	ESFP	SeFi
INFJ	NiFe	ENFP	NeFi
INTJ	NiTe	ENTP	NeTi
ISTP	TiSe	ESTJ	TeSi
ISFP	FiSe	ESFJ	FeSi
INFP	FiNe	ENFJ	FeNi
INTP	TiNe	ENTJ	TeNi

Table 2. Projections from One Function Toward Its Opposite

Function	Positive Projection	Negative Projection
From extraverted Sensation toward introverted Intuition	I wish I had this wonderful ability to reach so far; I'm ready to follow someone who has such a long-term vision.	These abstract thinkers get on my nerves. They have their heads in the clouds, but their feet don't touch the ground.
From introverted Sensation toward extraverted Intuition	I am in awe of this creativity; I feel like a worthless drudge.	It's easy to say whatever pops into your mind when someone else does the hard work.
From extraverted Intuition to introverted Sensation	How lucky they are to be down-to-earth and find at once what they need.	I hate these fussy, stubborn bureaucrats. They spoil my life.
From introverted Intuition toward extraverted Sensation	I admire their savoir-faire; everything seems easy to them.	Life is easy when you spend it sunbathing. What a lack of responsibility!
From extraverted Thinking toward introverted Feeling	When I see him/her, I feel out of place. If only I had such finesse.	One must live in a different world if one has time to discuss forever every nuance.
From introverted Thinking toward extraverted Feeling	What a social facility for bringing people together. I feel like a mouse in its corner.	Help! Missionaries are coming to convert us.
From extraverted Feeling toward introverted Thinking	I admire these people who have enough distance not to be swallowed by others. I would not be the all-loving mother.	One must have a stone instead of a heart to split hairs when there's so much suffering around.
From introverted Feeling to extraverted Thinking	I wish I had this wonderful ability to take a stand instead of letting people step on my toes.	It's easy to take drastic action when you don't care about people.

Projection to One Function Toward the Same One in the Opposite Orientation		
Function	*Positive projection*	*Negative projection*
From extraverted Sensation toward intro-verted Sensation	I wish I were so well organized; I would have more time to enjoy life.	These know-it-all people are just able to throw a monkey wrench into our plans.
From introverted Sensation toward extra-verted Sensation	If only I weren't so fussy about everything and able to enjoy life as they do.	It's totally stupid to reinvent the wheel instead of asking for information.
From extraverted Intuition toward intro-verted Intuition	If only I could take the time as they do to think things through before opening my big mouth.	It's easy to look intel-ligent afterward when others have taken the initiative to propose the ideas.
From introverted Intuition toward extra-verted Intuition	How lucky they are to be so spontaneous; I feel blocked.	How upsetting to pro-pose any idea that pops up without previous thinking! Any idiot can do that.
From extraverted Thinking toward intro-verted Thinking	I wish I were able to make a decision when the time was ripe, in-stead of just making it as soon as possible.	Ratiocination and pro-crastination are the privilege of people who don't have any responsibility.
From introverted Thinking toward extra-verted Thinking	My dream: to be as able as they are to make a decision without end-less pondering.	I can't stand people who confuse thinking and bring things to an abrupt conclusion.
From extraverted Feeling toward intro-verted Feeling	How do they find the core value right away when I have to discuss it with a lot of people?	How can one spend so much time taking care of one's soul when peo-ple are dying out there?
From introverted Feeling to extraverted Feeling	I admire his/her enthu-siasm and generos-ity. I feel selfish and worthless.	Could he/she stop preaching all the time? What a lack of modesty!

References

Hundreds of books could be listed regarding Voice Dialogue or Jung's typology. We cite here only those that have a link with our topic.

Beebe, John. *Evolving the 8-function model.* www.typeinsights.com/eightfunctionmodel.html

Cauvin, Pierre, et Geneviève Cailloux. *L'intelligence de Soi… et de l'autre.* Paris: Dunod, 2009.

Cauvin, Pierre, et Geneviève Cailloux. *Tipos de Personalidad.* Bilbao: Mensajero, 2001.

Cauvin, Pierre, et Geneviève Cailloux. *Les types de personnalité.* 8th edition. Paris: ESF, 2009.

Cauvin, Pierre, et Geneviève Cailloux. *Deviens qui tu es.* 4th edition. Barret: Le Souffle d'Or, 2007.

Cauvin, Pierre, et Geneviève Cailloux. *Embrassez vos opposes.* Le Souffle d'Or, 2001, 2007.

Cauvin, Pierre, et Geneviève Cailloux. *La dynamique du Moi Conscient,* Osiris Éditions, Vernou, 2006.

Cauvin, Pierre, et Geneviève Cailloux. *La dynamique des fonctions,* Osiris Éditions, Vernou, 2005.

Cauvin, Pierre, and Geneviève Cailloux. "The Aware Ego and the Laws of the Psyche." *Bulletin of Psychological Type,* Vol. 29, No 1, 2006.

Cauvin, Pierre, and Geneviève Cailloux. "Three Levels of Typology and Five Ways of Using Function Dynamics." *Bulletin of Psychological Type,* Vol. 28, No 2, 2005.

Corlett, Eleanor and Nancy Millner. *Navigating Midlife, using typology as a guide,* Palo Alto, CA: CPP, 1993.

Franz (von) Marie-Louise. *The inferior function in "Jung's Typology."* Dallas, TX: Spring Publications, 1986.

Jung, Carl Gustav. *Psychological Types*, Bollingen – A revision, 1992.

Jung, Carl Gustav. *Modern Man in Search of a Soul*, Mariner Books, 1955.

Spotto, Angelo. *Jung's Typology in Perspective*. Willmette, IL: Chiron Publications, 1995.

Thompson, Henry. *Jung's Function-Attitudes Explained*. Watkinsville, GA: Wormhole Publishing, 1997.

The Psychic Fingerprint:
Voice Dialogue Seen from a James Hillman and Depth Psychology Perspective

J'aime ona Pangaia, RN

Once upon a time, a tigress was about to give birth. One day when she was out hunting she came upon a herd of goats. She gave chase and, even in her condition, managed to kill one, but the stress of the chase forced her into labor, and she died as she gave birth to a male cub. The goats, which had run away, returned when they sensed that the danger was over. Approaching the dead tigress, they discovered her newborn cub and adopted him into their herd.

The tiger cub grew up among the goats believing that he too was a goat. He bleated as well as he could, he smelled like a goat, and ate only vegetation; in every respect he behaved like a goat, yet within him, as we are well aware, beat the heart of a tiger.

All went well until the day that an older tiger approached the herd and attacked and killed one of the goats. The rest of the goats ran away as soon as they saw the old tiger, but our tiger/goat saw no reason to run, for he sensed no danger.

Although the old tiger was a veteran of many hunts, he had never in his life been as shocked as he was when he confronted this full-grown tiger that smelled like a goat, bleated like a goat, and in every other way acted like a goat. Being a rather gruff old duffer, and not particularly sympathetic, the old tiger grabbed the young one by the scruff of the neck, dragged him to a nearby creek, and showed him his reflection in the water. But the young tiger was unimpressed with his own reflection; it meant nothing to him, and he failed to see his similarity to the old tiger.

Frustrated by this lack of comprehension, the old cat dragged the young one back to the place where he had made his kill. There he ripped a piece of meat from the dead goat and shoved it into the mouth of our young friend.

We can well imagine the young tiger's shock and consternation. At first he gagged and tried spitting out the raw flesh, but the old tiger was determined to show the young one who he really was, and made sure the cub swallowed this new food. When he was sure the cub had swallowed it all, the old tiger shoved another piece of meat into him, and this time there was a change.

Our young tiger now allowed himself to taste the raw flesh and the warm blood, and he ate this piece with gusto. When he finished, the young tiger stretched, and then, for the first time in his young life, he let out a powerful roar — the roar of a jungle cat. Then the two tigers disappeared together into the forest.

— Stone and Stone, 1989

◆

"The Roar of Awakening," the African folktale that begins *Embracing Our Selves*, speaks both to the sense of early conditions being the source of primary and disowned selves and to the inherent soul qualities of the individual that are waiting to be uncovered and reclaimed.

When we consider the reality of sub-personalities, or inner selves, in Voice Dialogue, one important aspect is their origins — how they came to exist in a person. As we listen to their subjective stories about their past, we usually focus on what are considered to be their formative experiences with an eye to how it is that they came to be so primary or disowned in that person's life. Although the Stones speak of other factors (the unique qualities or "nature" of the individual) that determine the dominance of certain selves, such as genetic predispositions, the existence of archetypes, the psychic fingerprint, and other, more soul-related, determining factors, they do not elaborate on these. And, in the general practice of Voice Dialogue, more attention is given to "nurture," or the more apparent formative factors, than to "nature," or the incoming soul reality of the individual.

If, however, we interact *solely* from this viewpoint, the emphasis upon nurture as opposed to nature, we risk falling into a dualistic "self system" that sees the world primarily in terms of traumas, mishaps, and riveting experiences that happened *to us* (victim/ subject), and our reactive psychological efforts at managing pain and fear by learning and adopting (both consciously and subconsciously) beliefs and behaviors, i.e. selves, that save us (hero) from a threatening, harsh world (other). Unless we're vigilant, we can even mistake the Aware Ego Process as some kind of consciously aware hero who exists to manage life by managing selves" "If I have an Aware Ego Process, I'll be balanced and won't suffer or fear anymore."

This article takes an alternative and archetypal look at the selves and their relationship to what we refer to in Voice Dialogue as *the psychic fingerprint*. In the *practice* of Voice Dialogue, more attention could be given to the acknowledgment of our incoming nature, which the Stones named the psychic fingerprint, a term coined to refer to something that has long been recognized by many cultures and philosophers (since the days of Socrates, Plato, and Aristotle). It refers to that unique essence that each of us is born with.

In other times and cultures, this essence has been considered to have been brought forward and fostered in life by something that has variously been called our inner daimon, our spirit, our guiding angel, our genius, our soul's image, and the seed of the soul. (I'll use these names interchangeably in this article). It has been seen as the carrier of our fate and destiny, and is that which knows our path. As a carrier of our destiny, it is with us not only at birth but it also shines forth at every turn of events. As daimon, as soul image, it is timeless, so it always exists at all points in our lives. We are recognizably born with it as an infant, but *it* is already timeless, ageless, eternal — *not* infantile, not belonging exclusively to the child archetype.

We can look back over our lives and see that our essential soul print is always there. Also, we can look forward and feel its call to us to become our genius more fully in time and substance. As we interact with the world, its peoples, and life's constraints and opportunities, this psychic fingerprint is what guides us in the guise of spontaneous urges, thrills, forebodings, stylistic inclinations, etc., that not only direct our fate but also reveal something about our Psyche. It is most likely, given the pressing weight of evidence, that the aspirations of our soul (unlike that of our ego states) isn't to live a happy or contented or peaceful or even necessarily an egotistically self-aware life. It is, rather, to experience *yet another* expression of its creative potential here, in this life. Quite often this happens in ways that cause our conscious ego, living in a realm of dualities, to suffer, and as a result the ego can judge its fate harshly.

While the Voice Dialogue story of our becoming a personality has at its very beginning the recognition of this psychic fingerprint, we can also pay attention to how we hold the conceptual framework of our practice. An essential quality in the journey to being able to experience the Aware Ego Process is the development of our ability to directly, consciously experience and relate to our (and others') vulnerability with dispassionate/compassionate acceptance. It is commonly recognized that it is in this encounter with vulnerability that we most encounter our psychic fingerprint. Let me suggest that we also experience this soul essence in those parts of us we call the power selves, the primary self system.

If we were to absorb the perspectives of our philosophical ancestors, we would imagine that as the carrier of our unique Soul destiny, our psychic fingerprint is also a magnet of sorts for not only the singular events of a life but also for the powers of character that will best unfold them. In this case, those power selves, being archetypally derived, would have risen to the fore (primacy) as much through our ideas about early childhood conditioning as by the inner daimon that requires these very conditions — and inner selves — to fulfill its destiny for *this* life.

Here's what James Hillman has to say about archetypes:

> Let us imagine archetypes as the deepest patterns of psychic function-ing, the roots of the soul governing perspectives we have of ourselves and the world.
>
> All ways of speaking of archetypes are translations from one metaphor to another. Even sober operational definitions in the language of science or logic are no less metaphorical than an image which presents the archetypes as root ideas, psychic organs, figures of myth, typical styles of existence, or dominant fantasies that govern consciousness. There are many other metaphors for describing them: immaterial potentials of structure, like invisible crystals in solution or form in plants that suddenly show forth under certain conditions; patterns of instinctual behavior like those in animals that direct actions along unswerving paths; the genres and topoi in literature; the recurring typicalities in history; the basic syndromes in psychiatry; the paradigmatic thought models in science; the world-wide figures, rituals and relationships in anthropology. But one thing is absolutely essential to the notion of archetypes: their emotional possessive effect, their bedazzlement of consciousness so that it becomes blind to its own stance.
>
> — Hillman, 1996

This is another raison d'être for the Aware Ego Process, not only to consciously manage energetic forces but also to simply open more fully to the energetic nature of life and our soul presence within it. There is an experience that accompanies the Aware Ego Process, the awareness that "I am not that/I experience that." There's a feeling of both empti-ness and fullness of presence. It's here too, I sense, that we feel into an awareness of the tones of soul presence, a soul who has experiences of life *through* these psychic energies (selves) and mutable physical body experiences. In dreams too, when we feel the current that carries the images and sense the overarching themes that are revealed in countless dream stories, we in our Aware Ego Process — that separation from and holding of all those story images — are apprehending our source waters.

Another relevant ancient tradition that practices from this awareness and integration of soul destiny (the soul's course) is astrology. In *Cosmos and Psyche*, Richard Tarnas (Depth Psychologist and archetypal astrologer) goes a long way toward redeeming the archetypal roots of astrology. In the book, he presents an exhaustive research on the horoscopes of historical personages. Horoscopes have historically been used to ascertain the archetypal energies that influence persons, places, or events. The planets and constellations and their relationships are seen literally as cosmic reflections of archetypal energies. Through his research on historical figures, Tarnas clearly demonstrates how they were born for their times, as indicated by the planetary influences (archetypes) that predominated in their birth horoscope charts. They *became* important movers and shakers, he argues persuasively, *because* it was their soul destiny, as pictured in their charts. We could say that their psychic fingerprint is pictured archetypally in their charts. Their personalities (primary and disowned selves) uniquely coincided with the planetary influences of the time and of the planet as a whole. He might argue that "the times" brought forth these personalities, with their unique potentials; those people who were the ones most *coherently* in harmony with the archetypal energies of the day. In other words, the psychic fingerprint arrives in an archetypally harmonic way within the cosmic and physical universe.

How might all this influence the way we hold the philosophy and practice of Voice Dialogue? I'm not suggesting that we dismiss the ways that primary and disowned selves experience their histories, pains, and triumphs; these stories that selves tell are living dreams, myths, and personal realities that make up part of their nature as much as how they inhabit the body or interrelate with the environment or with others. At the same time, we would do well to listen to these stories with a mythically minded ear, as we do other dreams. We can pay attention to the possibility that a person's primary selves are as much a reflection of early life experience as they are of a soul who needed those particular early experiences so that those very power selves (and their abilities) would rise to the foreground.

In the fairytale told at the opening of this article, the Stones tell a story about losing touch with one's true nature, one's destiny (in this case, to be a tiger), one's psychic fingerprint, and the roar of awakening back to that essence. Being a tale ("Once upon a time"), it is, like all dreams and myths, richly layered. Its different layers offer up unique dimensions of meaning. This reading of the tale alerts us to an archetypal drama of being confused and then clear, of being false and then true, of being ignorant/innocent and then informed/initiated.

Engaging this story from yet another layer, we might also consider it actually to be part of this young tiger's psychic fingerprint, his soul's nature, to actualize a destiny that includes being orphaned, lost to himself, being found by an elder, initiated, and becoming a being who can know and hold two paradoxical true energies, those of tiger *and* goat.

His was a different fate from that of the old tiger who finds him. This orphaning and adoption and conditioning by "an other" is not merely a loss, a trauma to overcome; it is an essential condition, a gift even, and necessary for his larger soul potential to exist. The whorls of his psychic fingerprint had the map written through it of his potentials for both a tiger and a goat life. There was something in those whorls that required orphaning and adoption outside the tribe of tigers, and mentoring in the ways of the goat so that those qualities of the psychic fingerprint, the soul's image, could more fully be lived. It was equally part of his destiny to be found and reclaimed and awakened to his tiger potential as well. We could say that his psychic fingerprint was destined to eventually express both tiger and goat power energies. His primary goat self is part of his soul's true nature, not merely a result of social conditioning by the herd.

The same holds true for us as we relate to the stories of our life. I encourage us to expand beyond a trauma focus as the only model for how we came to be who we think we are, to include a more nuanced memory of and feeling for our soulful histories and pathways and its revelations. This means that we begin to more fully appreciate primary selves as also being expressions of our psychic fingerprint. This means that as we develop a capacity for an Aware Ego Process, there's as much a possible quality of consciously *surrendering to* and *being with* as there is *controlling/managing of* energies with awareness.

The old man tiger acts from a different destiny, a different archetype. Being a fairytale old tiger, he has always been old. His purpose in the story is to maintain the natural order, the rules of engagement: tigers should be tigers, and goats, goats. He initiates the young tiger into this proper order and back into tiger-hood. The old tiger is the Senex, the old man who maintains traditions. His is Saturn energy. He is vulnerable about loss of order in the kingdom, although he doesn't reveal his vulnerability. His path, his soul's work, is also to find someone who is lost, errant, and teach him, even impose upon him, the rules and traditions. This is one of his primary selves. Would this old tiger act differently, with an Aware Ego Process, if he knew of his underlying vulnerability? Perhaps not: perhaps his Aware Ego Process would allow him to surrender to a psychic fingerprinting that comes to be a Senex, an initiator for that goat-tiger.

Using this story of the goat-tiger, our own Aware Ego Process would have us discover both our old and young tigers, and our goat. The story exists the way myths do — they happened. We too live out myths, myths that are not to be and cannot be controlled; we "happen." The Aware Ego Process helps us to better appreciate, enjoy, suffer, and live for and through our psychic fingerprint, our soul's image, with all its incarnated character cast of selves and senses. Taking more account of our psychic fingerprint as a force of soul causes us to consider the relationship of ego, even in an Aware Ego Process, with our soul nature.

As teachers and facilitators of Voice Dialogue, we might orient our subjects (students/clients) to notice how our power selves exist not only as protectors from loss and suffering but also how they fulfill certain kinds of experience. A primary goat self may tell a story about needing to be goat-like to compensate for a loss or to assure its belonging with the herd. As we continue to look, however, it may also tell of simply enjoying the fine love of being an ordinary herd being, and of being sure, unmovable, even stubborn And the primary old tiger self may tell a story about how the world goes to hell in a hand basket when order isn't maintained, and, from the point of view of the soul, it speaks of the beauty of things lining up in a predictable, stable, orderly manner.

Then, *ahhh*, so it is. An aspect of soul has been painted, rendered, and become itself in space, as the quality of goat-like fixedness, or of Order itself, not simply confined to the borders of skin and ego self but as soul becoming an event in time and space.

References

Hillman, J. *The Soul's Code.* New York: Random House, 1996.

Hillman, J. *Revisioning Psychology.* New York: Harper Perennial, 1976.

Norton, M. *The Kitten who thought it was a MOUSE.* New York: Simon & Schuster, 1954.

Plato. *Republic.* (Waterfield, R., Trans.) New York: Oxford University Press, 1993.

Sheldrake, R. *A New Science of Life.* California: J. P. Tarcher, 1981.

Stone, H., and S. Stone. *Embracing Our Selves,* California: New World Library, 1989.

Stone, H., and S. Stone. *Meeting the Selves,* (cd) Mendocino, CA: Delos, Inc., 1990–2004.

Tarnas, R. *Cosmos and Psyche,* New York: Viking, 2006.

The Brain and the Aware Ego Process

LeAnne Dougherty, DSW, LCSW

I love all men who dive. Any fish can swim near the surface,
But it takes a great whale to go down stairs five miles or more:
& if he don't attain the bottom why, all the lead in Galena
Can't fashion the plummet that will. I'm not talking of Mr.
Emerson now – but of the whole corps of thought-divers, that
Have been diving & coming up again with bloodshot eyes since
The world began.

— Herman Melville, 1849

Introduction

Welcome to my personal and professional musings from thirty-five years
of marriage and the coming together of neuroscience and psychotherapy.
The early years include my husband, John's, training as a neurologist at
New York Hospital, Cornell, and my work at New York Hospital, West-
chester Division, personal analysis, and completing a doctorate in social
work at Columbia University. We had many lively debates and bonding
patterns with the rational mind and psychological knower. We were
lucky enough to be on the cutting edge of both neuroscience and social
work. Mike Gazzaniga was then at Cornell, and we were privileged to

experience firsthand the original split-brain studies. These would reveal that the brain would process only what the neurological circuits had access to. Social work has always been about the "fit between person and environment," and rich with research about their effects on each other.

While John and I had enough common sense to know it couldn't be all nature or nurture, we would value different sides in our quest to help others. My skills were on the nurture side, and John's training focused on the mechanisms of the brain. Having two children with very different temperaments and needs forced us to go beyond nature and nurture. Becoming parents stressed our systems because we had to deal with selves beyond the mind and psychological knower. Both in psychotherapy (crisis theory) and neuroscience (neuroplasticity), the power of stress to trigger new learning is a key element of success in human growth. We were both challenged.

To bond, to accept children, to balance a whole new set of physiological firings of motherhood along with the voices of individual, professional, wife, friend, etc., meant a reorganization of body, mind, and spirit. The necessity for inclusiveness of the whole rather than single-pointed perfection was a daily requirement. We were faced with the terrible and beautiful task of growth, which resulted in accepting the diversity of what felt like ten thousand new things. Our motto came from Faulkner's *The Sound and The Fury:* "we will not only endure but prevail."

Holding the opposites of enduring and moving forward left us open to live and learn. When the Psychology of Selves entered our lives twenty years ago, we had the theory and people to provide the method and support we needed for continued growth. I felt like I was coming home when I listened to Sidra say that the hardest part of evolving, was "giving up the juiciness of righteous indignation." This was permission not to have to find the right way and to be happy.

The teachings from neuroscience assume an "average expectable brain" similar to the "average expectable environment" of Object Relation theory. This sharing is not comprehensive and will not provide information about brain damage or specific brain diseases. The intention is a personal sharing of the knowledge that has enriched my clients and me. It has given us an understanding and awareness of the processes of the brain and brain development rather than a focus on pathology or judgments.

Neuroscience and Voice Dialogue

Start with appreciating that adults have about 100 billion neurons that, on average, have 7,000 to 10,000 synaptic connections to other neurons, creating 2 million miles of neural highways in our brains (Siegel, 1999). Human growth across the lifespan involves changes in the structure and function of these neural pathways in the brain, which give rise to the emergent mind. As Voice Dialogue facilitators, we appreciate that a simple "single-skull" view of the neural activity is inadequate. We must also be aware of how these fundamental aspects of memory, emotion, and thought are influenced by interpersonal relationships and the patterns of connection with each other.

As Hal and Sidra's experience has moved psychotherapy beyond analysis of one mind to the "juice" of knowing ourselves through our bonding patterns and judgments, understanding of the brain will come from the relationship between the structure and function of the parts.

Neuroscience initially focused on objective data to create a model of the brain and mind. Science has mapped how the brain and nervous system are built, neuron by neuron, through the interaction of genetic programming and environmental influences. Cozolino defines the brain as neither predetermined nor unchanging, calling it an organ of adaptation. The development of the brain is use-dependent.

Models of the brain do not give the precise mechanisms of the synaptic chemistry or outline the complexity at work in a single moment. However, Paul MacLean's model of the evolutionary brain is a useful starting point.

MacLean described the human brain as a three-part phylogenetic system reflecting our evolutionary connection to both reptiles and lower animals. Think of it as a brain within a brain within a brain. Each successive layer is devoted to increasingly complex functions and abilities. At the core is the reptilian brain, little changed through evolutionary history and responsible for activation, arousal, homeostasis of the organism, and reproductive drives. The paleomammalian brain (or limbic system) is involved with learning, memory, and emotion and wraps around the reptilian brain. The highest layer, the neomammalian brain, is primarily the cerebral cortex and a large portion of the corpus callosum, and is required for conscious thought and self-awareness (Cozolino, 2002, p.8).

Because of their different functions, these three brains do not necessarily work well together. Hampden-Turner (1981) has referred to this as the therapist challenge of simultaneously treating a human, a horse, and a crocodile. Stress would bring the energies of the crocodile, and from that place, choices are very limited — thus the saying "stress makes us stupid." This model of the brain (as with the method of Voice Dialogue) carries no shame or blame, and becoming conscious of that "is-ness" provides a nonjudgmental way to move out of the crocodile and into human consciousness.

In his book *From Axons to Identity* (2009), Todd Feinberg organized knowledge from neurology focusing on how the complex system of the brain creates a self. His model adds depth to MacLean, and provides scientific information that supports our work with the Aware Ego Process. Feinberg's model views the self as related to three hierarchically arranged and interrelated systems: the Interoself, the Exterosensorimotor system, and the integrative self system.

The Interoself System is located within either the brainstem or forebrain, and contributes to the organism's relationship to the internal milieu. It serves homeostatic and self-preservative functions.

The Exterosensorimotor System corresponds to the lateral brainstem and cortical regions in closest communication with and having the greatest responsiveness to the external environment. This system does contain an implicit sense of self. For example, an animal with an implicit self can also distinguish itself from the environment and other animals.

The Integrative Self System serves to assimilate the interoself systems with the extero systems, and to mediate the organism's internal needs with the external environment. This system includes the development of the "episodic memory system," which is unique to the human species.

It holds the capacity for mental time travel, for envisioning one's past, and for re-experiencing specific events. It also allows the emergence of self, self-awareness, identity, autobiographical identity, and a sense of subjective time. It is dependent on frontal lobe structures. It is clear that the activation and health of this system is mandatory for the Aware Ego Process.

This dependency on frontal lobe structures underlines the centrality of relational experiences and validates the importance of attachment theories. The Attachment Theory hypothesis is that it is in relationship that these areas grow. It is now believed that even in utero there are powerful interactions with the mother's innate neural firings that encode and strengthen certain states of mind both in mother and infant. Neuroscience sheds light on how this internalization process might work. We are relational beings as soon as there is neural equipment available, and states of mind effect this development

We are most in need of contact in infancy because of our physical and emotional dependency and because of the way parenting relationships help form a view of self. How the three systems of our brains are working together will determine how we bond with a child, and thus determine the cast of characters that will become primary and disowned selves.

This paper emphasizes the important scientific view that the brain will not develop without relationships, and that at no time in life do interpersonal processes stop shaping our lives.

Evolutional Hierarchy and Organizing Principle

We honor the organizing principle of the primary self by asking its permission to speak to the other side. The evolutionary process of the brain progresses in a hierarchical fashion in order for biological advances to be preserved. Previous levels of organization must be reorganized into new stable subassemblies (selves), or else every time there is a major biological change (or separation form the primary self), the entire previously organized system would fragment. The following parable illustrates this point:

Two watchmakers assemble fine watches, each watch containing 10,000 parts. Each watchmaker is interrupted frequently to answer the phone. The first has organized his total assembly operation into a sequence of subassemblies; each subassembly is a stable arrangement of one hundred subassemblies. The second watchmaker has developed no such organization. The average interval between phone interruptions is long enough to assemble about 150 elements. An interruption causes any set of elements that does not yet form a stable system to fall apart completely. By the time he has answered about eleven phone calls, the first watchmaker will usually have finished assembling a watch. The second watchmaker will almost never succeed in assembling one.

— Nieuwenhuys, et al, 2008

The external environment acts on the higher biological units. The traits of the higher units will act on variations arising in lower units. For example, the Interself System sends a signal of hunger, which cannot be fulfilled without higher functions and contact with the external world. Our choice of how to fulfill that hunger is therefore dependent on traits expressed in the higher units. The lower more primitive traits are located in the brain the more difficult it is to promote evolutionary change. Our attention must therefore be concentrated on the higher units of brain function.

As we understand from Voice Dialogue, a Pleaser may be born to meet the needs of the system. It will also form a conservative belief "If I am not nice then I am not safe." Thus anytime there is a need from the lower brain, the first message will be to be nice. If the higher forms do not evolve to hold the opposites of pleasing others, and being in touch with one's own needs and emotions, the person will eventually receive a "slap," experience a symptom, or stay in the victim position. By experiencing the separation from the Pleaser, and thus having access to a realization of the complexity of the brain, mind, and consciousness, the neural firings in the higher system have increased energy. The process of Voice Dialogue allows emergent selves that we may not have been aware of before to have a voice. Neuroscience also gives much discussion to the "emergent" aspects and possibilities of the brain. Roger Sperry, who won a Nobel Prize for split-brain research, proposes that the self and mind emerge in a unified fashion from the diverse parts of the brain. He defines the self as more than the sum of the parts of the brain that create it. He believes that a unified self and consciousness emerge at the topmost part of the nervous system. This theory supports the concept of the emerging Aware Ego Process.

Sperry defines two different kinds of emergence, which resonates with my understanding of first- and second-order change in psychotherapy. Weak emergence simply states that there are higher-order properties of a system, which are novel relative to a specific part.

Radical emergence claims that there are emergent properties that cannot, in principle, ever be reduced to the component parts of the system. In other words, consciousness and the Aware Ego Process can never be reduced to the "simple" brain, by virtue of it being a radically emergent feature. After being facilitated for many years, my experience of coming to the Aware Ego has a different feel each time. My subjective experience is not that it's just my higher functioning that is different, but that all the selves, brain structures, and body chemistry are different. The information in my lower brain from earlier experience and wiring from the archetypes from the past are also affected by my higher-levels increase in awareness. Without this input to the higher system, we would be left to live out the archetypes and myths of our evolution without choice.

In her very readable book *An Alchemy of Mind* (2004), Diane Ackerman describes this process by quoting Francois Villon's poem "Winter": "Winter makes the wolf of the woods go pale."

> Imperceptibly influenced by breezes arriving from the round corners of one's life, one meets equally breeze-swayed others, all moving in a dynamic dance of infinite realignments. Even a minutely different environment is enough to sculpt noticeably different personalities and behaviors, just as it's enough to reform the geometry of snow on a tree limb.
>
> — Ackerman, p.150

Parenting two young children would often make me exclaim that it's not the connecting with each child that's hard, but the combustion between them. Thus the family environment was always shifting from the ricochets from our relationships with each other. I don't have a good metaphor for how in the brain everything affects everything else all at once, and how that meets the everything-ness of everyone else. Bonding patterns are a beginning, but they are in a specific moment and may be different with a change in the wind of one mind or another.

Nested and Control Hierarchies

It is helpful to appreciate how these biological hierarchies operate the concepts of non-nested control hierarchies and nested, or compositional, hierarchies. In a non-nested hierarchy, the higher levels are physically independent from the lower levels. Feinberg uses the metaphor of a general using a command such as "Take that hill," and notes that the general does not know how, when, or where the mission will be accomplished. He/she has only the big picture while the troops do the specifics. The non-nested hierarchy focuses on action, structure, and logic, and goes from the top down.

The nested hierarchy at any level of organization is entirely composed of its constituent parts. One of the defining features is that it is a process and system of communication. The lower levels are faster, as we see in the brain's stress response. As danger is communicated to higher levels, the process of determining the reality of the danger is set in motion for all the systems of the brain. For example, when I'm riding a bicycle and I hear a dog bark, I immediately pedal faster, then check to see if the dog is contained. As this has happened many times, the process of checking reality comes faster. Just as my lower brain can respond instantly to being told what to do with a rebel response (thanks to the Voice Dialogue process), I can now access the reality that I am not a child and I have a choice before the bonding pattern is full-blown. This nested hierarchy of the brain allows for increased complexity of the emergent qualities of awareness, choice, and the organizing principle illustrated in the watchmaker parable.

The Brain and "Aha" Moments

As referred to earlier, the minute we have neurons, our brains are doing something, and processing innate and environmental stimuli. It's impossible, however, to be aware of all these processes, as evidenced by the work the brain does in dreaming during sleep or daydreaming. I recently bought John a picture of a bicycle with the quote from Albert Einstein: "I thought of it on my bike." Researchers have been studying these "aha" moments by recording brainwave patterns and imaging the neural circuits that become active as volunteers struggle to solve anagrams, riddles, and other brainteasers.

We have all had the "aha" moments that allow us to see something from a different view. As a therapist, it's music to my ears when a client stops and says, " I hadn't thought about it in that way before." It is the beginning of a new neural pathway with insight.

Researchers have found that these sudden insights are the culmination of an intense and complex series of brain states that require more neural resources than methodological reasoning. "Solving a problem with insight is fundamentally different from solving a problem analytically. There really are different brain mechanisms involved" (Kounios, 2009).

Just as we now know that we are not tabulae rasae at birth, the technology of PET scans and fMRIs confirms that the brain may be most actively engaged when the mind is wandering. As measured by brain activity, a mind wandering is much more active than during reasoning with a complex problem. An unfocused mind may trap new ideas and unexpected associations more effectively than by methodical reasoning. While no one knows now why problems sometimes trigger insights, research does indicate that a positive mood makes insight more likely. Our state of mind can affect whether or not we will resort to insightful thinking.

I have struggled to make sense of what Hal meant when he suggested that the Aware Ego Process is supported with time out of ordinary reality. The above research would support that it's when we don't notice our thoughts that we may be thinking most creatively. These studies also suggest that all systems of the brain work in unison during dreaming.

As a Voice Dialogue facilitator, I've learned that when I have preconceived notions (what Bateson refers to as the "dangers of conscious purpose"), I often over-interpret. We can be responsible for our ability to energetically connect with awareness of the moment-to-moment interactions. Energetic connection, keeping the mystery, faith in the process, and holding the sacred space of therapy would facilitate a state of mind receptive to insightful thinking.

Allen Combs (2009) terms the emerging direction as a transcendental evolutionary model in which consciousness unfolds in stages. A major point for him is that no step can be omitted or passed over. There is no magic bullet for consciousness, as the brain is governed by emergent and organizing principles. Our challenge is the integration and movement to a non-dualistic way of understanding.

Conclusion

We now come back to Hal and Sidra's original definition of consciousness in 1985, and I feel like it is T. S. Eliot's experience of coming to the beginning and knowing it for the first time.

> What we will be defining is not consciousness but the consciousness process. We will be calling it consciousness but we are not talking about a condition of being. As far as we are concerned, one does not become simply conscious: consciousness is not simply something that we strive to achieve. Consciousness is a process that we must live out — an evolutionary process continually changing, fluctuating, from one moment to the next.
>
> — Stone and Stone, 1985

The Stones were appreciating all the energies of the brain, and the wirings that become traits and states of being, because our nature and nurture allow us to arrive at a non-pathological "is-ness." Nature has created a hierarchical organizing principle that Voice Dialogue can nurture. There is a scientific leg to stand on, which supports that we are of two minds and many selves, and there is the capacity for the Aware

Ego Process to embrace all the qualities of the brain.

This article has been a quest to put theory and research into the Aware Ego Process. It was not my conscious intention, though the process was working within me, to incorporate Hal's idea of horizontal and vertical energies and the recruitment of the Aware Ego Process into my life experience.

From the theories of the self and consciousness cited here, the horizontal and vertical are like the warp and woof of a weaving. The self, or the fabric, would not hold together without a union of both the knowledge from the limbic system and the cerebral cortex, and the connections to the left and right brain.

When Hal talked about activating the Aware Ego Process he listed three tasks:

1. Surrender to the energies (which referred to the work of the primary selves).

2. Surrender to the universe (the intelligence of the dream process).

3. Experiencing these processes will develop the ability to experience the organizational elements and energies of the self.

My research would support that we are wired for that organizational energy. Our brain holds how we think and feel all the time. Having the skills to hold the vulnerability and experience the opposites will give the power to the Aware Ego Process as a method of psychological and spiritual growth.

It is now time to go beyond the "hard problem" of questioning how subjective experience emerges from the objective workings of the physical brain. The objective knowledge leads us to the mystery and complexity of the developmental process, and the state of mind of the brain to the tasks at hand. To achieve non-duality, we must hold both the objective and the mystery, and move toward integration. The "sweat" for increased knowledge of consciousness, as with success in the Voice Dialogue process, comes with valuing both and surrendering to the fact that our brain and selves are working without our conscious awareness. Keeping our evolutionary process going with curiosity will leave space for the brain to do what it was created to do and emerge with increased insight and integration.

As with Melville's words, we have to keep diving deep and surfacing. As I conclude my musings on the brain and mind, it would seem that the way to consciousness is through the awareness of our conflicts. By welcoming the bonding patterns, internally and externally, we open to the process that makes aware integration possible. The most human quality of mind may not be consciousness but conflict.

References

Ackerman, Diane. *An Alchemy of Mind.* Scribner, 2004.

Badenoch, Bonnie. *Being A Brain-Wise Therapist: A practical guide to interpersonal neurobiology.* W. W. Norton & Co., 2008.

Combs, Allen. *Consciousness Better Explained: Toward an Integral Understanding of the Multifaced Nature of Consciousness.* Paragon House, 2009.

Cozolino, Louis, "It's a Jungle in There." *Psychotherapy Networker,* Sept./Oct. 2008, pp.20–27.

Cozolino, Louis. *The Neuroscience of Psychotherapy.* W. W. Norton & Co. 2002.

Epstein, Mark. Thoughts without a thinker. Basic Book, 1995.

Feinberg, Todd, M.D. *Altered Egos: How the Brain Creates the Self.* Oxford University Press, 2001.

Feinberg, Todd, M.D. *From Axons to Identity: Neurological Explorations of the Nature of the Self.* W. W. Norton & Co., 2009.

Gazzaniga, Michael. *Mind Matters: How the Mind & Brain Interact to Create our Conscious Lives.* Houghton Mifflin Co., 1988.

Flotz, Robert Lee. "A Wandering Mind Heads Straight toward Insight," *Wall Street Journal,* June 19, 2009, Section A, p.11.

Nieuwenhuys, R., J. Voogd, and C. v. Huijzen. *The Human Central Nervous System: A Synopsis And Atlas*. Springer-Verlag, 2008.

Siegel, Daniel. "Foreword" in *The Neuroscience of Psychotherapy*. Cozolino, 2002.

Stone, Hal, PhD, and Sidra Stone, PhD. *Embracing Our Selves*. New World Library, 1985.

Wilson, Stephen (ed). *The Book of Mind*. Bloomsbury, 2003.

Transpersonal Dialogue: Voice Dialogue as a Transformative Practice

Ana Barner

This article is about the potential of Voice Dialogue to provide not only an excellent map and method for developing our personality but also a skillful tool for including our spiritual essence in this exploration. I have been involved with Voice Dialogue since the mid-1980s, and it has been an incredibly rewarding journey, not only professionally but also personally. In order to be an effective Voice Dialogue facilitator, I need to keep doing my own personal inquiry, discovering new primary and disowned selves, learning other ways of taking care of my vulnerability, and developing an ever-increasing Aware Ego Process. In particular, working with the Transpersonal challenges me to keep my connection with Essence alive in myself, integrating it into my work and daily life. In this way Voice Dialogue has become a transformative practice for me.

When I talk about Transpersonal, I mean beyond personality; the energy in us that is without boundaries, deeply connected to everything and everyone. Most of us have had glimpses of this reality through meditation, peak experiences, making love, being creative, being in nature, etc. Once we connect with this expansive energy it feels like coming home. We often do not know how to stay immersed in Being while being active in the world. I have found that Voice Dialogue is one of the most effective tools to give us direct access to this space, and support us in integrating it into our day-to-day life.

I will describe the process of intentionally approaching and including the Transcendent within Voice Dialogue processes. I have called this work Transpersonal Dialogue, and started to integrate it into my Voice Dialogue practice over the last twelve years. Most of my individual sessions and trainings focus on traditional Voice Dialogue work (developing an Aware Ego Process), but I feel passionate about expanding Voice Dialogue in a number of ways. I hope this article will trigger discussion within our community; I am especially interested in how others work with this material and in developing advanced training programs.

My Personal Journey

When I started to write this article, I recognized that the development of Transpersonal Dialogue within my Voice Dialogue practice is connected to my own psycho-spiritual process. I therefore include some of my personal history, and introduce the development of Transpersonal Dialogue as it follows my own journey.

I have been interested in the human psyche since my mid-teens, and have always been a practical and experiential explorer. Apart from studying psychology and social work within a framework of socialism and feminism, I experimented with a range of alternative therapies in my early twenties, such as co-counseling and radical therapy. Looking for a more transpersonal dimension, I joined a spiritual movement that combined intense emotional release work with active and passive meditation practices. I participated in groups and trainings exploring rebirthing, primal, encounter groups, bioenergetics, and hypnotherapy.

Working as a rebirther in the mid-'80s, I discovered Voice Dialogue, and, together with a group of friends, organised Hal and Sidra Stone's first tour to Australia. I have been passionately involved with Voice Dialogue ever since.

Psychological Versus Spiritual

Because of my background and training, there was never a division for me between the exploration of the psyche and the search for what is beyond my personality. It was clear to me that in order to fully understand myself as a human being, I needed to explore my personality with all its primary and disowned aspects through a variety of psychological approaches. It was also important to go beyond the personal, to find my transcendent essence through meditation and other spiritual practices.

It seemed though that there was a gap between the approaches toward personality and soul. The psychological movement focused mainly on changing and fixing the personality, and the spiritual tradition endeavored to overcome and transcend the Ego. In my work with Voice Dialogue, I worked primarily with the integration of various parts of the personality through the Aware Ego Process. The spiritual dimension only showed up in sessions by talking to spiritual selves such as the Higher Self, a Wisdom Voice, or a sense of Being. I always approached them as parts of the personality, who were often disowned. Occasionally they were primary selves in clients identified with spirituality, protecting them from the experience of their vulnerability.

In the mid-'90s, I went through another spiritual deepening. This expanding three-month process catapulted me into an intense questioning of my life and work. I now experienced my personality as a vessel, something I inhabit just like my body. And like my body, it needs understanding, care, and focus. To me it feels like a house that I live in; if the roof leaks and the doors don't close, it's an uncomfortable place. If I live my life from an automatic Primary Self System, keep repeating unconscious patterns in relationships, and am not connected to my vulnerability, I will not enjoy being on earth. At the same time, it's important for me to stay connected to the knowledge that my personality is only a transient place, and that I am also a Transcendent Being. These insights became so important that I wanted to include the work with the Transpersonal within my Voice Dialogue practice in a more deliberate and focused way.

The Transpersonal

Even though the experience of essence is a very specific energetic space for me, it is difficult to talk about. I see it as a natural and accessible part of our being, but there are so many stories, myths, and misconceptions associated with it that I've been reluctant to talk about my experiences and work. In the spiritual texts and traditions it is described as emptiness, enlightenment, oneness, god, essence, etc. It is widely believed that we can attain oneness only through intense effort and discipline, and years of meditation and seclusion, and that we must overcome and transcend the ego in order to attain emptiness. There is also the idea that this space is separate from our daily lives and cannot be integrated into an active, involved human existence. Recently there has been a shift in these concepts. The Integral movement around Ken Wilber has been developing a much more modern, holistic model. I believe that Voice Dialogue is part of this development, and provides an incredibly skillful and elegant process linking personality and essence. This makes it possible to navigate our world with our personality being deeply connected to our internal spiritual reality.

Voice Dialogue as a Spiritual Enquiry

Once I started to focus on the exploration of the Transcendent within Voice Dialogue, I came to realize that Voice Dialogue in itself is a spiritual enquiry. It is a process of "emptying out." I acknowledge that all my thoughts, feelings and experiences are just parts of me that I can externalize and disidentify from. By physically placing them outside of my system and then questioning what remains, I become aware that I don't know who I am, and in the absence of my personality, I feel empty and filled with a luminous energy at the same time. The process of this "emptying out" includes all the traditional elements used in spiritual inquiry: mindfulness, awareness, non-judgment, compassion, disidentification, and choicelessness. If I keep following the thread and stay with the process, I start to realize that I am all of these different energies, but they are also all just parts of my personality. I can watch them and experience them outside of myself, so who is this "I" that is doing the watching?

This resembles some of the oldest spiritual techniques of self-inquiry to reach enlightenment. It is exciting to recognize that Voice Dialogue can help people integrate their transpersonal nature, not by trying to transcend their personality but by deeply exploring and accepting it.

Disowned Selves as Gateways

Apart from accessing our Essence through selves that are aligned with the energy, such as the Meditator, Seeker, or Higher Self, I also started to notice that Essence could show up in unexpected places. Often when I was supporting people to work deeply with parts of themselves that had been very disowned, they would experience a profound shift. It seems that if we intentionally and patiently stay within the discomfort of intimately experiencing a disowned self (e.g., fear, not knowing, grief, aloneness, depression, strong vulnerability, etc.), a space can open up that is so luminous and expansive that it is unmistakably a spiritual experience. The selves that we are most afraid of can be gateways to our transcendent nature if we allow ourselves to stay with the energy and not move into our usual primary selves.

There seem to be similarities in the way we experience the Transcendent. First there is usually a deepening and refining of the senses: sounds may be heard that we usually are too busy to notice, such as the wind, birds, our breathing. Everything may look luminous and three-dimensional, and the colors are intensified. We might smell things we were not aware of before and feel the breeze touch our skin. Energetically, we often feel expansive and without limits, there is no concept of time, the past and the future recede, and we are deeply present in the now.

The mind slows down, there are very few thoughts, and we tend to not give them much attention. Thoughts come and go but there is no attachment to or rejection of them. We may realize there are no problems right now, even though nothing has changed and nothing needs to. Everything is perfect as it is, including the personality. This is often very profound and surprising within a Voice Dialogue session, especially if we have just talked to the team (Rulemaker, Pusher, Critic) who are spending so much time and effort on improving the personality. The experience often leads to a strong feeling of compassion for the world and especially for the self. It can be accessed by anyone, even people who have had no prior spiritual background and training. We may recognize that this reality is always available; we just need to relax our intense identification with our personality and re-remember emptiness.

Transpersonal Dialogue

Once I had established that it was possible to include work with the Transcendent within traditional Voice Dialogue, I experimented with a variety of processes to make this more deliberate. Because the energy is contagious, it is possible to induce the experience in the client by connecting with it within myself. I started to extend and ground the energy by asking people to open their eyes, look around the room, connect with me, and even walk around and talk. My role as a facilitator is to keep being connected to the spaciousness, and to notice when they lose that experience. A whole range of parts will try to interrupt, for example the Pleaser who is aware of being watched and wants to do it right, the Critic who comments on this, the Rational Mind trying to understand what is going on, or some kind of Pusher wanting to make sure that the client remembers how to do this again next time. I support the client in being able to stay centered in Presence and let the parts of the personality come and go. This process can be compared to the technique of some traditional spiritual approaches, where we talk about being the sky and letting the thoughts that are like clouds drift through without attachment or rejection. Even if the client has experienced the Transpersonal before, this has usually happened when they were alone and inactive. It can be profoundly moving to experience being connected to another person and involved in a conversation while grounded in spaciousness.

Before going back to the Aware Ego I usually spend some time brainstorming with the client about ways to remember and access the

Transpersonal, such as meditation, being in nature, gardening, listening to certain kinds of music, etc. Sometimes it feels awkward and restricting to move back into the Aware Ego, but it's important to take some time at the end of a session to sit between the personality on one side and the Transcendent on the other. Then we can practice bringing both energies in and out, starting to have some choice about the intensity. This gives clients a real sense of being able to introduce the Transpersonal into their daily lives and ground this often very spacious energy.

Big Mind, Big Heart

The first time I made my work with the Transpersonal more public was during the 2002 Melbourne gathering with Hal and Sidra Stone. I facilitated a group inquiry around the exploration of the Transpersonal. We shared our experiences facilitating this energy within Voice Dialogue sessions, and during the discussion most of us dropped into the energy and experienced a profound connection to Being, stillness, and each other. This showed me again how powerfully energetic and contagious the energy is, and how it gets amplified within a group.

I then became interested in Genpo Roshi's Big Mind process. Genpo Roshi is an American Zen master who, after doing some work with Hal and Sidra Stone, started mixing traditional Zen with elements of Voice Dialogue. After some training with Genpo Roshi, I started to use elements of this process in my work.

Even though Big Mind is based on Voice Dialogue, there are a number of significant differences between the two modalities. Unlike Voice Dialogue, Big Mind has a clear agenda and goal: to introduce people to the Transpersonal. The process is usually done in a group, even though it can be used in individual sessions. The selves that are being explored are chosen and elicited by the facilitator, and instead of moving to different spaces in the room, the participants only move slightly in their chairs. Most important, Big Mind does not include an Aware Ego Process as its main focus, even though, a few years ago, Genpo Roshi introduced The Apex, which can be compared to the Aware Ego.

Integrating some Big Mind techniques into my Voice Dialogue practice allows me to introduce people very quickly and effectively to the Transpersonal. It enables me to work experientially with groups, not only with the Transcendent but also with general Voice Dialogue material. Because Genpo Roshi comes from a spiritual background, a whole network of people who are usually more interested in transcending the Ego than exploring their personality are introduced to the Psychology of Selves. The Integral movement has started to incorporate this work into their curriculum, and it's my hope that this will accelerate the development of Voice Dialogue on a much wider scale.

Training Other Facilitators

Once Transpersonal Dialogue became integrated into my work, I wanted to include it in my trainings. Even though I realize that not everyone is interested in the Transpersonal, I feel that it's important for facilitators to at least have some knowledge of and experience and skill with this energy. It is such an amazing resource in reducing some of the trauma and suffering people experience in their intense identification with personality.

We know that it's important as a facilitator to have access to a part in order to be able to facilitate it in any depth. This is especially the case with the transcendent energies, as they are so subtle and refined that their presence can easily be missed. On the other hand, people who are interested in working with the Transcendent are often unconsciously identified with it. Beingness has become a Primary Self protecting them from the experience of their vulnerability and other parts of their personality. In my trainings, I try to take students through some of the work necessary to develop an Aware Ego Process in regard to the Transpersonal.

Because the transcendent energy often comes through a deep experience of a disowned self, trainees have to become comfortable with and confident about working with disowned energies. They have to be able to walk into the jungle while holding the Aware Ego Process for the client and themselves.

It also takes some skill to notice the presence of a gateway, being able to intentionally access Beingness, and then help the client to keep out interrupting voices and expand the transcendent energy. If inducing and holding the space presents challenges, being able to connect with the client from emptiness and assist her/him in grounding the energy is often very confronting. A strong sense of intimacy opens up when we connect with someone in this way, and it can be difficult for the facilitator to allow this to happen and still be able to hold the impersonality of an Aware Ego at the same time.

The work with the Aware Ego Process at the end of the session is important as well. Trainees need to know how to help people bring in both energies (Personality and Transpersonal) and then consciously release the intense connection that often occurs between facilitator and client in this work.

As with all aspects of facilitating, the personal gains for the trainees are immense. I often teach facilitating to participants even though they will never become facilitators. Learning how to be with another person from an Aware Ego space with mindfulness, non-judgment, and total focus is an incredibly empowering and satisfying skill. And, if we can turn this compassionate attention and acceptance toward ourselves, so much of the suffering that is being caused, especially by the Critic, gets released. Facilitating the Transcendent teaches the trainees to deliberately tune into Beingness within themselves and function in connection with others without losing this link. Imagine being able to increasingly do this not just in sessions but also in your daily life!

Examples of Sessions

Flipping the Coin

My first memory of a session that changed from a typical Voice Dialogue encounter into a more Transpersonal one is from one of the last Summer Kamps with Hal and Sidra Stone in the States. I was on staff, working with one of the participants. We were exploring an energy that was very dark; he was feeling depressed, disconnected, alone, and at odds with

330 The Voice Dialogue Anthology

himself, the world, and god. This was a self he usually did not allow himself to enter into fully; his Primary Self System was more aligned with being positive, light, and empowered. We deliberately stayed with this Disowned Self for quite some time, until we experienced the fullness of the energy. I then asked him to imagine that this part was just one side of a coin and to allow himself to imagine what would happen if we flipped the coin. He immediately experienced a profound spiritual expansion. He felt deeply connected to everything, himself, other human beings, and the universe. It was a strong experience of essence and oneness.

The Critic and the Black Hole

Here is a more recent example of an individual session. The client was struggling with the voice of the Critic harassing him and creating a sense of depression, which he was trying to avoid and overcome. After working with the Critic in depth, the client moved back into the Aware Ego and explored the physical and energetic effect of the constant analysis and criticism. He became aware of a heaviness and depression, which he called the black hole.

We then moved into this disowned self, and the client became aware of a strong longing to just stop and give up. Surrendering to this feeling, the energy began to change, and he felt like he was sinking down into a different space. It was obvious that this disowned self was a gateway to the Transpersonal. Experiencing a total disidentification from his personality, the client began to feel still, present, and awake. We proceeded to deepen the experience of emptiness and depth by using metaphors that he expressed: the feeling that he was underwater and could breathe and relax, the image of the choppy water on the surface, and how much time he spent there. He likened that to the identification with the personality, the waves being the thoughts, feelings and body symptoms.

We used a range of other techniques to ground him in this energy. The client had his eyes closed during most of this process. I then invited him to stay connected to the depth of being still and present while communicating with the outside world by opening his eyes, making contact with me, and moving around the room.

At the end of the session, we came back to the Aware Ego and spent some time moving the two energies in and out, the identification with personality and the energy of presence. We talked about his ability to stay connected to this sense of essence while functioning in the world, and how he could integrate this into his daily life.

Intimacy

This group exploration happened in one of my regular advanced training meetings. We were exploring different primary selves around the issue of intimacy in relationships. Some people were more consumed with the fear of intimacy, wanting to keep themselves safe by creating a distance from other people. Their Primary Self System protected them by putting up walls, staying impersonal and distant and generally avoiding intimacy. Other participants were more interested in creating intimacy, and were desperately looking for closeness. They were trying to protect themselves from aloneness and abandonment by pushing for connection, often in a very demanding and intrusive way.

We explored the different primary selves, their fears, and some of the vulnerability underneath. I then asked the group as a whole to move into the voice of intimacy. They shared, one by one, how they perceived this energy, deepening and expanding the experience for everyone. We all felt intimately connected to ourselves, each other, and the world; the fears of the Primary Self System receded. Intimacy explored in this form revealed itself as an archetypal energy of the Transcendent.

The "Gang"

I work with the Transcendent in Voice Dialogue sessions in a number of ways. Below is one of my favorite techniques:

When we work with the Primary Self System, especially what I call the gang (Rulemaker, Perfectionist, Pusher, and Critic), the client often gets a sense of the overwhelming pressure and tightness of this group of selves once they move back to the Aware Ego position. It seems there is no way out. I then ask the client to find an energy that is not affected by this system and move there. This often connects them to the Transpersonal in a very easy and profound way. As we generally think that it's difficult to intentionally access Essence, experiencing this space just by moving to another physical place can be incredibly empowering.

Once we have shifted into this space, whenever a thought or feeling comes up, I ask the client to check if this belongs to the expanded space of Being or to the personality we just worked with. Usually, if it has any firm content, it belongs to the personality, and I ask the client to let it flow back to the space in the room that is taken up by the group of selves. This allows the experience of the Transcendent to deepen, and gives the client another way to learn how to disengage from the Primary Self System. Coming back to the Aware Ego position and learning to be centered between Personality and Essence grounds this experience.

The Transcendent in Voice Dialogue

I have been passionate about the potential of Voice Dialogue to bridge the work with personality and the transpersonal for a long time. I hope this article has shown how much the inclusion of Transpersonal Dialogue alongside more traditional Voice Dialogue can benefit facilitators and clients. We can finally make the transcendent aspects of ourselves more accessible in our day-to-day lives, not by trying to overcome our ego but by deeply engaging with parts of our personality and accepting all we find.

Learning how to have direct access to the transpersonal reality provides another clear resource for being able to separate from the often-painful restrictions of our personality and find more peace and joy. It can create deep compassion for others and for ourselves, and makes it possible to be fully in the world but not of it.

Transpersonal Dialogue can also shine a light on one basic aspect that we all share as human beings: our deeply painful sense of separation. Too much of our sense of self has been developed trying to avoid and overcome this experience of separateness. The stories of our wounds and vulnerabilities might be different, and the ways we try to hide and overcome them vary, but ultimately, when we drop down into our deepest fear and pain, the words we use to describe this reality are very similar.

We feel abandoned, alone and separate, and don't think we belong. No matter how hard we try to overcome this feeling and fill the hole, it runs like a deep current underneath our lives, and it resurfaces again and again. Some of these feelings are linked to traumatic experiences in our childhood and adulthood, and can be integrated and held by the Aware Ego Process, but even if we do this work, the sense of separation remains, and we feel alone. For me, this reality of separateness is inherent in being in a body and personality; it is our human condition. From my perspective, only a vivid experience of the Transpersonal, and the resulting realization of our connectedness, allows us to see that, from the soul's perspective, separateness is an illusion. Once we have this insight as a true experience and understanding, the identification with our personality and story softens. The Primary Self System so consumed with trying to overcome or distract us from the perceived sense of separateness can relax, and we are able to accept and be ourselves and feel compassion and understanding for others. I feel that Voice Dialogue used in this way can become a profoundly transformative practice personally and spiritually.

The Convergence of Voice Dialogue and Imago Relationship Therapy

Dorsey Cartwright, LMFT

The goal of this article is to convey some of the ways that I have used Voice Dialogue to enhance my work as an Imago Relationship therapist, and to show the personal as well as the professional value of combing the two.

Background

My journey of integrating Voice Dialogue and Imago Relationship Therapy occurred over a number of years. The following background highlights some of the events along the way.

My Discovery of Voice Dialogue

It was not the promotional flyer's description of our containing many selves that drew me to sign up for my first Voice Dialogue group in 1986. After ten years of clinical practice, I knew about selves or sub-personalities from my training in Gestalt, Psychosynthesis, Jung's Active Imagination, and NLP. What grabbed my attention was the second paragraph explaining that when two people fall in love, their inner selves start triggering each other, which can make relationships feel so crazy to the people in them. Three days earlier, after just four months, my current boyfriend (who'd moved from Boston to Houston to be with me) and I had mutually decided he had to move out. I was highly motivated to learn more about this triggering so that I'd never have to experience such pain again. I registered for the Voice Dialogue group.

My Discovery of Imago Relationship Therapy

I accepted an invitation in the spring of 1990 to speak to a large singles group on the "Psychological Approach to Finding a Mate." I planned to introduce them to the concept of selves and bonding patterns. However, my Inner Critic was anxiously reminding me that I had been divorced and single for fifteen years, and had no business telling others how to find a mate. My Rational Mind came to the rescue, suggesting I find additional books to read on the subject. A colleague who gave relationship workshops recommended Dr. Harville Hendrix's *Getting The Love You Want, A Guide for Couples.* He explained that while it was written for couples, it included excellent information and exercises for singles who want to have a good relationship.

I dashed to the bookstore, purchased a copy, and eagerly began to read. I was quickly rewarded when I read in the preface:

> Marriage is a psychological and spiritual journey that begins in the ecstasy of attraction, meanders through a rocky stretch of self-discovery, and culminates in the creation of an intimate lifelong union. Whether you realize the full potential of this vision depends not on your ability to attract the perfect mate, but on your willingness to acquire knowledge about hidden parts of yourself.
>
> — Hendrix, 1988

That last sentence delighted me personally as well as professionally. I had lost confidence in my ability to attract the perfect mate. Now, however, I had an excellent tool, Voice Dialogue, for acquiring knowledge about my hidden parts (as well as guiding my clients in exploring theirs).

As I read the book, I saw an overlap in the discoveries of Drs. Hal and Sidra Stone and those of Dr. Hendrix. With each chapter, I had a deepening intuitive sense that there was an important interfacing between these two models. I was being guided along a path that would enable me to finally be in a fulfilling committed relationship, and I would be able to help my clients achieve the same.

Being a Bridge

A year later, in 1991, I was certified as an Imago Relationship Therapist; three years later I became a workshop presenter for the *Getting the Love You Want* workshop for couples. The next year I was certified to present the *Keeping the Love You Find* workshop for singles. Out of this came a wide range of opportunities to act as a bridge between these two models and communities. Those opportunities included:

- I became a staff member at Voice Dialogue Summer Kamp, introducing Imago Relationship Therapy to campers, and teaching them how to use it with Voice Dialogue.

- I was invited by the Australian Voice Dialogue community to present Imago Relationship workshops to Australians, and to introduce Voice Dialogue and Imago to Australian therapists.

- As a member of the Association of Imago Relationship Therapists and Imago Relationships International, I was invited to present workshops on Voice Dialogue and Imago at a number of annual conferences.

- I became one of four coauthors of a resource manual for Imago therapists titled Deepening the Conscious Self: An Advanced Toolbox for Working with Individuals, Couples and Groups (in future referred to as the Toolbox). We contributed a number of exercises to help readers recognize their defenses and resistances as parts with important concerns to be understood and wisdom to draw on (Fein Baker, Cartwright, Kramer Slepian, & Slade, 2002).

◆ I was invited to be a member of the task force for updating the Keeping the Love You Find workshop and manual, in which we introduced the value of honoring and working with earlier primary selves as an integral step in embracing new behaviors and ways of being in relationships (Hendrix, 2007).

At the end of 1999, Voice Dialogue and Imago also dramatically impacted my personal life when they played a part in drawing to me my life partner Neil. Shortly after we met, Neil was introduced to Voice Dialogue at a workshop given by Shakti Gawain. He loved it immediately. Since that time, we have traveled throughout the United States, and to Greece and Israel, training Imago therapists and others in Voice Dialogue.

Imago Relationship Therapy in a Nutshell

Dr. Harville Hendrix and his wife, Dr. Helen LaKelly Hunt, are the originators of Imago Relationship Therapy. They used their own relationship as a laboratory, as Hal and Sidra Stone have done. Imago Relationship Therapy teaches that nature (or our unconscious) has led couples in a committed love relationships to just the right partner in order to help them heal their childhood wounds and grow into wholeness. In Imago, "healing" means getting the needs met that were not met in childhood, this time by an intimate partner. "Growth" means reclaiming the aspects of oneself that had to be disowned in the process of growing up. It seems that we are given a second chance through our relationship with a partner to become who we were born to be, by reclaiming what was lost or distorted in childhood.

How does this happen? It seems that while nature or the unconscious desires us to be healed by the one who wounded us, it will accept a reasonable facsimile. We are attracted to people who are similar to those who wounded us in childhood (this similarity is often enhanced by projection and provoking) The mechanism for this attraction is an image, imprinted from both our positive and negative experiences, of our primary caretakers and significant others in childhood. This image is called the Imago, and partners are seen as Imago Matches.

In the beginning of a love relationship (what Imago calls the romantic stage), we are only aware of the positive aspects of our imago in our partner. We have the subconscious fantasy: "I've finally met someone who will love me and be there for me in the way I wanted my parents to be." In the next stage (the power struggle), we've begun to experience the negative aspects of our imago. Usually one or both partners' vulnerabilities have been triggered, and the defenses from childhood have been activated. Rather than meeting our needs, our partner has now become a source of further wounding. These two stages are similar to the positive and negative bonding patterns in Voice Dialogue. Also like Voice Dialogue, Imago sees the power struggle as providing the opportunity for growth, healing, and greater consciousness. Imago therapists strive to educate partners to welcome the power struggle as "growth trying to happen." This means that frustrations left over from childhood are being repeated in order to be repaired, and each partner must grow for that to happen. There are a number of tools that Imago therapists use to enable couples to move through their power struggles with conscious intentionality rather than unconscious reactivity, and to grow into a mature love. This is an enduring love relationship, having both the safety of best friends and the passion of romantic love.

To me the process of becoming aware of one's reactivity (think of selves) and gaining the ability to intentionally act in ways that best serve the relationship is similar to Voice Dialogue's Aware Ego Process. It may well be that both are sourced by the same part of the brain. Neurologist and Voice Dialogue student John Dougherty, MD, hypothesizes that the Aware Ego Process resides in the anterior cingulate cortex (Dougherty, Dougherty, de Leonni Stanonik, and Licata, 2004). Daniel Siegel, MD, in *The Mindful Brain*, describes the anterior cingulate cortex as the "operating officer of the brain because it allocates attentional resources… also involved in the regulation of emotional arousal, esp. where there is conflict in attentional responses" (Siegel, p. 114).

Combining Imago Processes with Voice Dialogue Method

The Imago Dialogue

The major therapeutic tool Imago therapists use to enable partners to shift from an unconscious to a conscious relationship is the Imago Dialogue. This is a structured dialogue in which partners mirror, validate, and empathize with each other when addressing conflictual issues. At first these steps can seem rather stilted and mechanical; however, with practice, this process becomes a very rich and nuanced experience that restores and deepens the partners' connection.

In my practice as an Imago therapist, I begin with the Imago Dialogue, and when I hear or see a self coming in (perhaps a blaming, critical parent self) I gently guide the person to move into the Critical Parent, whose anger is now expressed to me rather than at the partner. I dialogue with that self, first hearing its frustration and then discovering what vulnerable self it is trying to protect. I may or may not move the person into the vulnerable self, but I certainly help them experience and connect with it. From a more Aware Ego position, I have the person use the Imago Dialogue with her partner to share insights from her Voice Dialogue experience. If time allows, the couple then resumes their original discussion with increased intentionality.

The Stretching Principle

A basic Imago premise is that what both partners most need for healing their childhood experiences is that which each one's partner is most defended against. Out of this comes the "stretching principle." If the defending partner can *stretch* toward giving what her partner needs in order to heal, the stretching partner will also reconnect with a part of him- or herself that was buried in the process of growing up. In other words, the stretching partner is reclaiming his or her wholeness. In Imago, the early defensive adaptations are labeled "character structure," and while respected as behaviors that enabled the person to survive childhood, the goal is to let go of these adaptations by growing out of them through the stretching principle.

The Behavior Change Request Dialogue

The Behavior Change Request Dialogue, one of the most important and powerful processes in Imago couples work, is based upon and activates this stretching principle. Couples learn that embedded in a recurring frustration is a childhood need, a desire. If they can learn to speak from that desire rather than from criticism, their partner can experience being a positive resource, instead of the "problem," and is therefore more likely to be motivated to change. They also learn that a recurring frustration usually indicates underlying childhood wounding in both partners, so if one partner stretches to meet the needs of the other, they risk re-wounding themselves. To address these dynamics, the Behavior Change Request Dialogue creates a structure for partners to voice not only their frustration but also their need and desire and, possibly, the childhood pain beneath it. With this tool, couples learn how to restructure their frustrations with one another into positive behavioral requests.

The partner asking for change makes small (baby-step), concrete behavior requests, stated positively, and relevant to the frustration or need. Imago stresses that these are requests, not demands, and that agreeing to any of them is a gift, not an obligation. It is important that the gifting partner agree only to what is doable for her/him, with some stretching.

The beauty of this exercise is that while partners are not responsible for what the parents of their partners did that their own behavior is now triggering, they do have a unique opportunity to play a healing role in each other's lives. There is growth for the partner stretching to meet the request, and healing for the partner whose request is met.

A challenge is that this process is often very moving, as the gifting partner experiences the wounded child beneath her/his partner's critical or demanding power self, which can result in selves jumping in and agreeing to new behaviors without the person checking with their whole internal system. This is where Voice Dialogue is invaluable.

Once a person has chosen the behavior change to gift to his/her partner, I ask him or her to check internally to get a sense of any resistance, fear, or unease about making this change. If the answer is yes (as it usually is), I ask the person to physically move over to where he or she senses that part to be. I then talk to this part to find out what is the concern or fear, and what would help that part feel better (if the person stays with the decision to give the gift). Next I speak to the part that wants to give the gift; to learn more about that self, its motivation, and what would help it if the person decides *not* to give the gift at this time.

After the person has connected with the resistant self and has experienced some separation from the gift-giver self, I ask the person to revisit the decision of which gift to give, and see if any changes are needed. Sometimes people make changes, and sometimes they don't. What is most important is that the person is making a more conscious choice; this is a tremendous gift to the relationship.

Imago for Singles

At the request of many singles seeking a fulfilling committed partnership, Dr. Hendrix wrote his second book, *Keeping The Love You Find, A Guide for Singles* (1992), and created a workshop with the same name. Although I think it a brilliant piece of work, it is largely overshadowed by the popularity of the books and workshops for couples.

Remember, Imago's basic underlying principle is that we are born, wounded, and healed in relationships. Therefore a single person's deepest healing must wait until he/she is in a committed love relationship. There *must* be that committed partner, fused with the parents by the unconscious, who finally meets enough of the unmet needs from childhood so that healing can occur. While this can be difficult for single people to accept, the good news is that Imago provides the tools for them to grow in the ways they need in order to have that kind of committed, healing partnership. This growth is ignited through powerful exercises to help singles reclaim their disowned parts, and learn to stretch out of the defensive behaviors that have prevented them from getting their needs met in relationships (and then keeping the love they've found).

All of the lectures, written exercises, and interactive processes in the book and workshop for singles are designed to provide them the data and tools they need to create a Personal Growth Plan that they then practice on a daily basis. With my understanding from Voice Dialogue of the power and value of primary selves, I knew that without consulting with their primary selves in some way, singles were likely to have a tougher time making the changes they were designing for themselves. I became committed to finding a way to bring in this understanding and these tools to support singles doing their Imago growth work, while in no way violating the integrity of Imago.

I had my first opportunity to address this issue when, as one of the four "Keepers" (Imago therapists collaborating to bring the *Keeping the Love You Find* material for singles into greater awareness in the Imago community), I helped create *Deepening the Conscious Self: An Advanced Toolbox for Working with Individuals, Couples and Groups*.

Later, when the Keepers were invited to redesign the *Keeping the Love You Find* workshop and manual, I focused on the sections "Working with Resistances" and "The Personal Growth Plan." While staying true to the Imago framework, I explained that defenses and resistances are parts of the psyche to be recognized and interacted with. Since most Imago therapists are not trained in the Voice Dialogue method, I created alternative exercises that they could use to enable singles to consciously experience the tension of these opposites (old behaviors and new behaviors) in order to draw on the wisdom generated from that process.

The Personal Behavior Change Request Dialogue for Singles

A pivotal exercise for promoting change and growth in singles is the Personal Behavior Change Request Dialogue. Since there is no committed partner of whom to make a behavior change request, the individual (the "sender") works on a frustration from a past relationship, and dialogues with a participant who stands in as the past partner. This process guides the sender to discover what she could have done differently to increase the possibility of getting her needs met. From this discovery, the sender comes up with several behavior changes requests of her- or himself to promote self-growth.

Originally, the exercise ended there. In the Keeper's *Toolbox*, I added the following steps to incorporate the Voice Dialogue concept of holding the tension of both sides:

The sender checks for any resistance to doing the new behavior, and if there is resistance, the facilitator encourages the sender to experience (as fully as possible) the tension of both wanting to change and not wanting to change. The sender then states his willingness to sit with the tension this creates within him (Fein Baker, et al., 2002).

This added step allows singles to create a blueprint of how to handle future relationships in a way that increases the likelihood of their following through with their Personal Growth Plan, and finally getting their needs met. (One of the aspects of Imago singles work I value most is that it enables people to use their past failures as building blocks for future success.)

For Imago therapists trained in Voice Dialogue, I actually combine both the Imago dialogue and Voice Dialogue facilitation. Once the sender has described her resistance, the facilitator invites her to physically move into that self, finds out who the self is and what its fears or concerns are, and — if the sender decides to do the new behavior — what might help the self to feel better about that decision.

After moving back to the ego position, the facilitator now asks the sender to physically move into the self that wants the new behavior in order to find out who the self is, why it values the change, and — if the person decides *not* to do the new behavior — what would help that self deal with that decision.

The facilitator instructs the sender to go back to the ego position, and from there to experience being in relationship with each self, sitting between the two selves, to see what each has to offer. Then, from a more Aware Ego, the sender revisits her personal behavior change request to see if any changes are needed. (Having experienced both selves, the sender often makes changes that create a more balanced, organic, and doable next step.)

To complete the exercise, the facilitator instructs the sender to resume the Imago process with her/his past-partner stand-in to either communicate the new behavior-change request or to restate her/his commitment to the original request. The past partner mirrors, validates, and empathizes with the sender.

Holding the Tension of the Old and the New – Visualization

Since the majority of Imago facilitators are not trained in the Voice Dialogue, I created a visualization called Holding the Tension of the Old and the New, designed to follow and deepen participants' understanding of the reality of the opposite selves they experienced in the Personal Behavioral Change Request Dialogue. They go through this visualization before they complete the list of behavior changes in their Personal Growth Plan Journal. This was incorporated into the Keeper's *Toolbox* (Fein Baker et al., 2002) and later into the *Keeping The Love You Find* workshop manual update (Hendrix, 2007).

In this exercise, participants visualize themselves experiencing the behavior change for a day, then a week, a year, and then for the rest of their lives. The exercise guides them to experience both the positive and the negative aspects of the change. They then visualize themselves doing the old behavior for a day, then a week, a year, and the rest of their lives — experiencing both the positive and negative. Participants repeat the process, moving back and forth from new to old behavior several times. They complete the visualization by imagining holding each experience in each hand, being aware of the tension of the opposites and what each side has to offer.

After returning to normal consciousness, participants make whatever changes are needed to the Personal Growth Plan Journal in their manuals, in order to be able to truly commit to it. In the *Toolbox* (Fein Baker et al., 2002), I also included a dialogue about the "Old" and the "New" in dyads, as well as a movement exercise to experience the physicality and energy of each.

Honoring Resistance

In collaboration with the other Keepers, I wove underlying Voice Dialogue concepts into the updated theory section of the Imago *Keeping The Love You Find* manual on honoring resistance (Hendrix, H., 2007). A summary of those key points:

- ◆ Wholeness is accepting all of who we are, not rejecting any of ourselves.

- ◆ The old parts have done their best to protect and take care of us and deserve to be respected and empathized with.

- ◆ Changing the status quo is likely to bring up fear in these parts. It is important to hear their concerns in designing a behavior change request that, working with both the old and the new, contributes to a richer, more doable Personal Growth Plan.

Mission Accomplished

I started exploring Voice Dialogue and Imago to learn how I needed to change to be in a fulfilling, committed relationship. Coming full circle, I now want to share what, to me, is the most important event that occurred when I combined my own Imago Personal Behavior Change Request with Voice Dialogue.

When I signed up to attend the *New Age Journal's* Millennium Celebration on Kauai at the end of December 1999, I was motivated to revisit my Personal Growth Plan from the *Keeping the Love You Find* workshop, where I found my written commitment to reclaim my disowned Aphrodite energy. I set up an appointment with a therapist, Steve, in order to use my Voice Dialogue tools and practice consciously pulling in Aphrodite with a male.

In the session I experimented with first moving into my primary "Prim and Proper" self, and then moving into Aphrodite. I could move into her energy, but as soon as I made eye contact with Steve, my primary self came back in and snuffed my budding Aphrodite as I felt my face become flat and wooden. I could channel Aphrodite energy only if I kept my eyes closed; otherwise my Prim and Proper self felt too embarrassed and threatened to allow Aphrodite out in front of a man.

Steve and I were both going to be in Austin the following weekend, so we set up an appointment for Saturday afternoon. That morning Steve called to cancel because he had the flu. Due to a number of synchronistic events, I was staying at a friend's house, as was Neil, the lovely man I referred to earlier. Because Steve had cancelled, Neil and I had a wonderful day getting to know each other.

As I was preparing to leave, I realized that life had given me a replacement for Steve with whom I could "practice." I suggested to Neil that we have a moment of silence in order to consciously say goodbye. As we stood there facing each other, I remembered that energy follows thought, so I began thinking, *Aphrodite, Aphrodite, Aphrodite.* At last I was able to turn my Prim and Proper self down, and with my eyes open, Aphrodite zapped Neil.

A few weeks later, Neil joined me in Kauai, and we brought in the new millennium together. We celebrated our ten-year anniversary in 2010. Over the years, we have used Voice Dialogue and Imago to help us over the rough spots and enrich our relationship.

That story illustrates the perfect confluence of Voice Dialogue and Imago that changed my life. I had been drawn to each approach, sensing it would provide the knowledge and tools to help me have the relationship I yearned for. As it turned out, I needed both. Bringing them into my practice with my clients, and teaching other professionals how to use both, became and remains my passion.

References

Dougherty Jr., J. H., L. Dougherty, M. de Leonni Stanonik, C. Licata. "The Neurobiology of the Aware Ego-Redefining the Self, Consciousness Reframed." 6th International Research Conference, Beijing, China, November 2004.

Fein Baker, J., M. D. Cartwright, C. Kramer Slepian, S. Slade. *Deepening The Conscious Self: An Advanced Toolbox for working with Individuals, Couples and Groups.* 1st ed., privately printed, 2002.

Hendrix, H. *Getting The Love You Want: A Guide for Couples.* 1st ed. New York: Henry Holt & Co., 1988.

Hendrix, H. *Keeping The Love You Find: A Guide for Singles.* 1st ed. New York: Pocket Books, 1992.

Hendrix, H. *Keeping The Love You Find: Workshop Manual.* 3rd ed. New York: Imago Relationships International, 2007.

Siegel, D. *The Mindful Brain: Reflection and Attunement in the Cultivation of Well-Being.* 1st ed. New York: W. W. Norton & Company, Inc., 2007.

CONTRIBUTORS

DASSIE HOFFMAN, PhD, LCAT, BC/DMT, has been a member of the Voice Dialogue community since the 1980s. Her original work, "Dancing With The Selves," was first presented at Summer Kamp in Philo, California. She is a senior staff member of Voice Dialogue International.

Dassie is co-founder of The New York Voice Dialogue Institute, where she maintains her private practice and teaches. She has taught at The Voice Dialogue Institute in Seattle and at Renfrew Center Conferences in Philadelphia. She co-leads Voice Dialogue Trainings and *Power Your Creativity* workshops in New York City. Dassie is the editor of this anthology, and has been editing *The Voice Dialogue Newsletter* since 2007.

Websites: <www.drdassiehoffman.com> and <www.newyorkvoicedialogueinstitute.org>

DR. PAUL ABELL holds a PhD in human behavior from Ryokan College. He has been a teacher and consultant in private practice using traditional Asian medicine, Voice Dialogue, and Western holistic methodologies for over thirty years in Los Angeles. While working as staff at Hal and Sidra's early "Summer Kamp" Voice Dialogue trainings, he discovered that combining the Psychology of Selves consciousness model and the Chinese Five Element theory created a practical tool for transforming illness and maintaining wellness. Using this integrated approach, he has observed significant breakthroughs and health-related behavioral shifts in his clients.

Website: <www.Dr-Paul-Abell.com>

◆

ANA BARNER was born in 1956 in northern Germany. After studying psychology and social work in the Netherlands, she trained in a variety of therapeutic modalities and meditation techniques. Moving to Australia in 1985, Ana helped organize Drs. Hal and Sidra Stone's first tour in Australia. Since then she has been training and working with them as a senior staff member in Australia and internationally. In the early '90s Ana started the Sydney Voice Dialogue Centre and took Voice Dialogue to New Zealand. Ana developed Voice Constellations, an interactive group technique, and Transpersonal Dialogue, a process that allows participants to access and ground spiritual energy in their daily lives. She works as a facilitator and trainer in Australia, New Zealand, and Germany.

Website: <www.voicedialogue.net>

◆

JASON BENNETT, BFA, is the founder of The Jason Bennett Actor's Workshop. In 2010 he was runner-up for Best Acting Coach in New York City, and is runner-up again in 2011, as well as for Best Scene Study Teacher. He has been featured in articles, interviewed on international radio programs, and has various articles published. Jason studied acting, voice, singing, and movement with thirty teachers, including Voice Dialogue for fifteen years. He studied Musical Theater at the University of Cincinnati College-Conservatory of Music, and then received a BFA in Acting from Florida State University.

Website: <www.JBActors.com>

◆

RUTH BERLIN, LCSW-C, a practicing psychotherapist for forty years, co-founded InnerSource, a center for psychotherapy and healing in Annapolis, Maryland, was an associate professor at the University of California Medical School, San Francisco, directed the Family Group

Institute, San Francisco, and has taught in the field of Transpersonal Psychology. Ruth has been a practitioner and teacher of Voice Dialogue and the Psychology of Selves since 1983. She also applies Voice Dialogue to her environmental-health advocacy work as executive director of the Maryland Pesticide Network, a coalition working to reduce pesticide impact on public health and the environment.

Website: <www.innersource-inc.com/_practitioners/pr_berlin.htm>

◆

GENEVIÈVE CAILLOUX, IDF, and Pierre Cauvin, IDF, are personal and organizational development consultants. After different professional careers, they created their own consulting company, Osiris Conseil, in 1989. In France, they have introduced and developed the Type Approach and Voice Dialogue, which they combined to create the "Intelligence of Self."

The authors of five fundamental books and several brochures and articles, they have given many presentations on radio and TV as well as in professional conferences. They are now primarily training consultants and coaches through their various workshops, including a three-year training in coaching.

Website: <www.osiris-conseil.com>

◆

M. DORSEY CARTWRIGHT, LPC, LMFT, advanced Imago clinician and workshop presenter, is the author of *Voice Dialogue and the Psychology of the Selves Teacher's Training Manual,* and, with Bill Crawford, PhD, *Healing Relationships through Voice Dialogue and Imago Relationship Therapy* CDs. She's writing *Who's Practicing Your Practice?* At The Texas Institute of Voice Dialogue Training, she and her partner, Neil Meili, offer professional trainings and personal retreats combining Voice Dialogue, expressive arts, and other modalities. They teach partners safe, fun-filled ways of integrating this work. The retreat-like stillness of their

land, in the heart of Austin, Texas, facilitates restoration and healing.
Website: <www.VoiceDialogueTrainings.com>

◆

CAROLYN CONGER, PhD, consultant and teacher, conducts seminars
internationally in psychological growth, healing, dreamwork, intuition,
creativity, and spirituality. She has lived with tribal societies throughout the world, studying their healing and metaphysical arts. From her
research in psycho-immunology and human energy fields, she also
teaches mind/body techniques for optimum health. Her doctorate is
in clinical psychology.
Website: <www.carolynconger.com>

◆

BRIDGIT DENGEL GASPARD, LCSW, DBT-certified, CBT-certified,
cofounder of New York Voice Dialogue Institute and psychotherapist
in private practice, has been engaged in Voice Dialogue since 1995. Her
focus has been on the healing and creative aspects of exploring Inner
Selves. She co-leads seminars teaching Voice Dialogue as well as "Power
Your Creativity" workshops. She writes in various forums on health, wellness, and humor, and has contributed to Renfrew's Perspectives, <More.
com>, The Passion Test Daily, and others. She is currently expanding
the concepts introduced in her anthology chapter into the book *The
Final Eighth: The Art of Finishing*.
Website: <www.newyorkvoicedialogueinstitute.org>

◆

MARY DISHAROON, MA, LMFT, is a warm and engaging woman
who is personally and professionally enlivened by the creative process of
Voice Dialogue. Mary is a licensed psychotherapist as well as an experienced Voice Dialogue facilitator and teacher. She practices in northern

California, working with individual adults and couples. Mary also offers case consultation by phone with new and experienced Voice Dialogue facilitators. She is the author of *Conscious Eating with an Aware Ego Process*.

Websites: <www.VoiceDialogueCalifornia.com> and <www.MaryDisharoon.com>

◆

LeAnne Dougherty, DSW, LCSW, began training with the Stones in 1994 and has returned yearly ever since. Her professional background is rich and varied; she was the founder of an adolescent day program, an inpatient supervisor, the Program Director of the Tennessee Wellness Community, and an adjunct professor of clinical social work at the University of Tennessee. She has presented at conferences on Voice Dialogue and neuroscience and taught Level One trainings in Knoxville. She has been a staff member at the Stone's trainings and at the New York Voice Dialogue Center. She is a psychotherapist in private practice; Voice Dialogue and the development of the Aware Ego Process are the center of her work.

Email: ConscJD@gmail.com

◆

Miriam Dyak, BA, is the author of *The Voice Dialogue Facilitator's Handbook* and co-founder of The Voice Dialogue Institute in Seattle. She has been facilitating and teaching Voice Dialogue since the mid-1980s, has served as a senior staff member at the Stones' trainings since 1994, and as staff for Voice Dialogue Conferences in Europe. Miriam offers Voice Dialogue sessions for individuals and couples, and Voice Dialogue Sandplay sessions in Seattle, and works with clients and students via tele-sessions worldwide. She has published three books of poetry and has trained extensively in Social Artistry with Dr. Jean Houston.

Website: <www.thevoicedialogueinstitute.org>

◆

JUDITH HENDIN, PhD, directs the Conscious Body & Voice Dialogue Institute. She is the author of the book *The Self behind the Symptom: How Shadow Voices Heal Us*. Hendin has taught extended Conscious Body trainings in Italy, Germany, Finland, Estonia, and the Netherlands. She served frequently on the Voice Dialogue staff of Shakti Gawain, has taught at Omega and Kripalu (preeminent US centers) and at the Association for Body Psychotherapy (in the US and Vienna). A former principal dancer with premier companies, her academic degrees specialized in cross-cultural movement, body perception, and the profound interplay of body and psyche.

Website: <www.ConsciousBody.com>

◆

CATHERINE KEIR, BA, CC, lives in Seattle, maintaining a professional counseling service for individuals and couples. As a teacher and facilitator of Voice Dialogue, she travels nationally and in Great Britain as an instructor for counselors, therapists, bodywork practitioners, actors, and those seeking to develop their own consciousness process. She offers her own Voice Dialogue trainings, and teaches on staff at Thera, the center for the Stones' intensives. Catherine has a degree in Theater Arts, is certified with the Academy of Intuitive Studies, and is on faculty with the Institute of Structural Medicine.

Email: catkeir@gmail.com

◆

YOLANDA KOUMIDOU-VLESMAS, LCSW, BCD, CHt, psychotherapist and poet, has been accompanying people on their voyages of self-exploration for more than thirty years. In 2000 Yolanda created the Koumidou Center, pioneering a series of programs that integrate cutting-edge theories and methodologies with age-old teachings. Yolanda travels throughout the USA, Europe, Asia, and Australia offering Retreats for Inner Life Exploration, Couples Retreats, Voice Dialogue facilitations, and her Dieting Know More program. The latter, a psycho-spiritual approach to physical transformation, is also being offered in New York in a weekend format or as a series of meetings.

Websites: <www.dietingknowmore.com>
<www.koumidoucenter.com>
For her poetry: <www.veiledsoul.com>

◆

J'AIME ONA PANGAIA, RN, a resident of Portland, Oregon, enjoys life by dancing, gardening, being in partnered relationship, teaching/learning, scholarship, writing, beekeeping, making good food (for body and soul) dreaming, community service, and bringing people together. She is the author of numerous articles, the book *The Benefit of People Who Bug You: a Voice Dialogue Introduction*, and the theatre production *Death is a Familiar Surprise*. She has been practicing and intertwining the Psychology of Selves and the Aware Ego with Depth and Buddhist psychologies for most of her adult life.

Website: <www.VoiceDialogueWork.com>

◆

GABRIELLE PINTO, BSc, RS Hom, is a classically trained homeopath and Voice Dialogue facilitator. Over the past twenty-five years she has worked in private practice in London as well as in the National Health Service. Gabrielle has taught homeopathy and supervision at the leading UK colleges, including the University of Westminster, and is the coauthor of *Homeopathy for Children*. Since 1981 she has arranged trainings for Hal and Sidra in the UK, as well as taking part in Summer Kamp in LA and courses at Thera. Her qualifications: BSc Hons (Zoology); Registered homeopath; RS Hom Licensed acupuncturist; Voice Dialogue facilitator.

Website: <www.gabriellepinto.co.uk>

◆

J. TAMAR STONE, MA, RPsy, was inspired by the revolutionary work of her father and stepmother, Drs. Hal and Sidra Stone. Tamar has been in private practice for over twenty years and offers in-depth teaching and training in the field of Voice Dialogue. She created an extension to Voice Dialogue called BodyDialogue — honoring the overall voice of the body and its numerous selves. In addition, she published "Selves in a Box" — an interactive card deck for working with the inner selves.

Websites: <www.voicedialogueconnection.com> and <www.selvesinabox.com>

HAL STONE, PhD, and SIDRA STONE, PhD, both licensed clinical psychologists, are the originators of Voice Dialogue, the Psychology of Selves, and the Aware Ego Process. They have written a total of eight books, including *Embracing Our Selves,* the groundbreaking classic introduction to Voice Dialogue and the Psychology of Selves. Their books have been translated into many languages and their work is taught all over the world. Their books, CDs, mp3s, videos, and a wealth of reading material are available on their website:

<www.voicedialogue.org>

MARTHA-LOU WOLFF, PhD, has studied with Hal and Sidra Stone since 1984, is on their senior staff, and in its beginning was responsible for responding to dreams on the their website Dream Room. From 1990 to 1995 she created and was director of the Mountain Oaks Voice Dialogue Center in Idyllwild, Calif. In 2000 she founded the Southern California Voice Dialogue Institute with Lawrence Novick and Marsha Sheldon in Los Angeles, Calif. Currently she lives in Berkeley, Calif. In 2010 she began an extensive training program for people learning to facilitate and for those teaching facilitators. Since 1997 she has been traveling throughout the US, Canada, Europe, and Israel, assisting in the creation of Voice Dialogue centers and networks where she offers training to the senior staff. Martha-Lou has a graduate degree in Anthropology from

University of California, Los Angeles, and a PhD in Clinical Psychology. She has experience surviving cancer, divorce, and the death of a brother and a son. Zen Buddhism, Alanon, and Aikido have made important contributions to her life. Native American spirituality is a source of sustenance for her, as is being a grandmother.

Website: <www.Martha-LouWolff.com>